FERENCZI AND BEYOND

FERENCZI AND BEYOND

Exile of the Budapest School and Solidarity in the Psychoanalytic Movement during the Nazi Years

Judit Mészáros

LONDON AND NEW YORK

First published in Hungarian in 2008 as *"Az Önök Bizottsága"* – *Ferenczi Sándor, a budapesti iskola és a pszichoanalitikus emigráció* by Akadémiai Kiadó, Budapest

First published 2014 by Karnac Books Ltd.

Published 2018 by Routledge
2 Park Square, Milton Park, Abingdon, Oxon OX14 4RN
711 Third Avenue, New York, NY 10017, USA

Routledge is an imprint of the Taylor & Francis Group, an informa business

Copyright © 2014 to Judit Mészáros

The right of Judit Mészáros to be identified as the author of this work has been asserted in accordance with §§ 77 and 78 of the Copyright Design and Patents Act 1988.

All rights reserved. No part of this book may be reprinted or reproduced or utilised in any form or by any electronic, mechanical, or other means, now known or hereafter invented, including photocopying and recording, or in any information storage or retrieval system, without permission in writing from the publishers.

Notice:
Product or corporate names may be trademarks or registered trademarks, and are used only for identification and explanation without intent to infringe.

British Library Cataloguing in Publication Data

A C.I.P. for this book is available from the British Library

ISBN 9781782200000 (pbk)

Translation by Thomas A. Williams

Edited, designed and produced by The Studio Publishing Services Ltd
www.publishingservicesuk.co.uk
e-mail: studio@publishingservicesuk.co.uk

CONTENTS

ACKNOWLEDGEMENTS vii

ABOUT THE AUTHOR xi

SERIES EDITOR'S FOREWORD by Peter L. Rudnytsky xiii

FOREWORD by André Haynal xvii

INTRODUCTION xxi

CHAPTER ONE
Towards psychoanalysis (1897–1908) 1

CHAPTER TWO
The forming of the Budapest School (1908–1918) 23

CHAPTER THREE
"Budapest will now become the headquarters 39
of our movement"

CHAPTER FOUR
The first wave of emigration in the early 1920s 51

CHAPTER FIVE
A period of consolidation 71

CHAPTER SIX
The USA's immigration policy: the sum of 89
conflicting vectors

CHAPTER SEVEN
"Your Committee": the Emergency Committee on Relief 105
and Immigration of the American Psychoanalytic
Association

CHAPTER EIGHT
The time has come (1938–1941): the second wave of 133
emigration

CHAPTER NINE
Emigration: losses and gains 183

Epilogue 219

NOTES 221

REFERENCES 239

INDEX 261

ACKNOWLEDGEMENTS

The research documents I used were drawn primarily from collections at European and American psychoanalytic societies and institutions as well as medical history archives: Archives of the British Psycho-Analytical Society; the Freud Museum, London; The Archives & Special Collections of the A. A. Brill Library, The New York Psychoanalytic Society and Institute; the Payne Whitney/Cornell Archives, New York Academy of Medicine; Archives of the Chicago Psychoanalytic Institute; Archives of the Menninger Clinic, Topeka, Kansas; the Archives of the Sándor Ferenczi Society & International Ferenczi Centre, Budapest.

I certainly owe a debt of gratitude to the staff at these and other institutions, especially: Nellie Thompson, curator at the Archives & Special Collections of the A. A. Brill Library, The New York Psychoanalytic Society and Institute; Michael Molnar, the former director of the Freud Museum in London; Connie Menninger, former librarian at the Menninger Foundation. I am grateful to Paul Bunten, previously with the Payne Whitney/Cornell Archives, New York Academy of Medicine, for providing me with access to documents on Hungarians. I am also thankful to the following for their assistance in my library and archive research: László András Magyar, Semmelweis Medical

History Library; Tibor Sándor, Budapest Collection, Szabó Ervin Central Library; the senior staff at the Petőfi Literary Museum, particularly Csilla Csorba, Ida Kovács, and Katalin Varga. I owe a debt of thanks for permission to publish documents to: Nellie Thompson, curator at the Archives & Special Collections of the A. A. Brill Library, The New York Psychoanalytic Society and Institute; Ken Robinson, Honorary Archivist of the British Psychoanalytical Society; Dr Rainer Funk, literary executor for the Erich Fromm estate; Aurelia Young, sculptor Oscar Nemon's daughter.

In researching the images, I received helpful support from Judith Dupont, Juca Magos, Anna Vincze, Cathy Michel-Székács, and István Hollós.

Thanks are certainly due to André Haynal for the support he has extended to me from the very beginning of the research and for the inspiring conversations. I am also grateful to my friends and colleagues Roberta J. Apfel, Bennett Simon, Axel Hoffer, and Anna and Paul Ornstein for being able to count on them in my work. Without the selfless support of John Lampe and attentive assistance of Herman Lebovics, the period I spent researching in the USA would certainly not have turned out to be as effective as it was. The humour and love of life exhibited by my friends Kathleen Kelley-Lainé, Bea Ehmann, George Sagi, and Bob Kramer have aided me through the difficult patches on numerous occasions. I am most thankful to all of them as I am to Valéria Csépe and Donna Culpepper for their many gestures of support. I was always able to rely on the attention of Anna Valachi in literary matters. Thank you to her as well as to Tibor Frank, Csaba Pléh, and István Czigler for their valuable comments on the manuscript.

I wish to take this opportunity to express my gratitude to the sponsors of my research: the Soros Foundation (Research Grant, 1995); the Woodrow Wilson International Centre for Scholars, Washington, DC (1995-96); the Research Support Scheme—Soros Foundation (1997–1998); the IPA Research Training Programme, London (1999); the IPA Research Committee (Research Grant, 2000–2001).

I also wish to thank the translator of the volume, Thomas A. Williams, for his dedicated, attentive work, István Balázs for finalising the manuscript, Peter Rudnytsky for his useful assistance in publishing the English-language volume, and Giselle Galdi for allowing me to turn to her so often with my questions. The English translation would not have been possible without funding from the Budapest Bank for Budapest Foundation. The book on which it is based was published in part through the support of the Hungarian Academy of Sciences and Donna Culpepper, Fogelsong Family Trust.

Finally, I am most grateful indeed to Sándor Ferenczi and the Budapest School for the legacy they have left us, to those who put their solidarity into action to come to the aid of their exiled peers, and to the colleagues and friends who have laboured to preserve and build on this legacy. It should be noted that this English-language version of the book is being published during the centenary of the Hungarian Psychoanalytical Society founded by Ferenczi in 1913, which—while this is actually a curious coincidence—expresses the continuity of the past realised in the present in spite of all the changes in between.

ABOUT THE AUTHOR

Judit Mészáros, PhD, is a training and supervising analyst with the Hungarian Psychoanalytical Society (IPA) and honorary associate professor at the Eötvös Loránd University, Budapest. As President of the Sándor Ferenczi Society and International Ferenczi Foundation, she has played a key role in raising awareness to the Ferenczi legacy. She has written and edited books on Ferenczi, the Budapest School, and their contribution to the theory and technique of modern psychoanalysis. She has also curated exhibitions at the Freud Museum, London, and the Gallery of the Open Society Archives, Budapest, and consulted on a documentary on Ferenczi's life.

For János, with gratitude
For Dani, on your journey ahead

SERIES EDITOR'S FOREWORD

It is, to paraphrase Jane Austen, a truth universally acknowledged that Sándor Ferenczi is a psychoanalyst of unsurpassed importance to contemporary theory and practice. It is, likewise, widely recognised that Ferenczi was the *fons et origo* of the "Budapest School" of psychoanalysis, which comprised an array of men and women extraordinarily gifted and inspiring in their own right. What has hitherto not been available to English-speaking readers is a comprehensive cultural history of the Budapest School, particularly as its destiny became intertwined with the tragic events of the twentieth century, which led to the exile and dispersion of almost all its members during the Second World War.

This is the panorama afforded to us by Judit Mészáros in *Ferenczi and Beyond*. As a leading Hungarian analyst of the post-war generation, who has spearheaded the establishment of the International Ferenczi Center in Budapest and whose research was supported by a grant from the Woodrow Wilson International Center for Scholars in Washington, DC, Mészáros is ideally positioned to tell the enthralling story contained in the pages of this book. Mészáros's scope is far-reaching, beginning as she does with an invaluable account of Ferenczi's pre-analytic period and ending with a judicious assessment of the distinctively Hungarian contribution to the psychoanalytic armamentarium. Lacking, as we still do, a Ferenczi biography, Mészáros fills in at least one conspicuous lacuna in his personal saga.

Although, like any history, Mészáros's story is, from one perspective, the sum total of a great many individual lives (and she does not fail to weave these unique threads into her tapestry), her main focus here is on the juggernaut of collective forces and mass phenomena to which individuals are forced to adapt as best they may, if, indeed, they are not crushed by its irresistible might. Thus, though she does not quite put it this way, Mészáros shows that the history of the Budapest School has the diphasic structure of a trauma in Freud's classic definition of this term. There were, that is, two waves of emigration, the first coming in the early 1920s, on the heels of Freud's 1918 prophecy that Budapest would "become the headquarters of our movement", which was almost immediately belied by the economic collapse and series of political upheavals in Hungary after the First World War, and the second from 1938 to 1941, when Nazism began to spread its deathly shadow over Europe. That these two peaks of crisis were separated by a "period of consolidation", in which, despite Ferenczi's death in 1933, the ideas and institutions of the Budapest School began to take root and to flourish in their native soil, made the second wave all the more calamitous, not least because its victims no longer had the possibility of returning to Hungary after living temporarily elsewhere in Europe, but were constrained to seek permanent refuge on transoceanic shores.

The vast majority made their way to America, either straightaway or by a prolonged and circuitous route. Only Michael and Alice Balint settled in England, and even they at first not in London but in Manchester (where Alice died prematurely), since Ernest Jones, smouldering with resentment of Ferenczi, his former analyst, "restricted his assistance", in Mészáros's words, "to the sort that would keep the Hungarian analysts far away from Britain". Two lucky ones, Sándor Radó and Franz Alexander, came to the USA by invitation as early as 1931, but when the situation became dire, beginning in 1933, those seeking to escape the peril found themselves facing obstacles not only to getting out, but also to getting into a country that by no means welcomed new arrivals with open arms.

Here, we encounter the second major strand of Mészáros's narrative, a remarkably detailed and informative account of the USA's immigration policies as these took shape in the early decades of the twentieth century, including the laws obtaining in the various states pertaining to medical practice by foreigners, and the "conflicting vectors" of politics that buffeted the Roosevelt administration. Ironically, the *numerus clausus* that had restricted the number of Jews in Hungarian universities since 1920 found a counterpart in the national quota system implemented concurrently in the USA that imposed particularly severe limitations on immigrants—Italians, Slavs, and Jews—whose ethnicity was deemed ill-suited to assimilation with the hegemonic Anglo-Saxon majority.

Embedded within this portion of her narrative, but possessing its own autonomy, is the heart of Mészáros's book: the story of the Emergency Committee on Relief and Immigration, whose key members included Lawrence Kubie, Bettina Warburg, and Bertram Lewin, which co-ordinated the efforts by American analysts to rescue their European colleagues by securing the necessary affidavits, including a guarantee of financial support, that would enable them to gain entrance to the promised land. In addition to contending with the larger political realities, the analytic community had to cope with its own internal tensions, which were exacerbated by the influx of refugees. These tensions centred on the ongoing power struggle between the International Psychoanalytic Association and the American Psychoanalytic Association, the latter of which staunchly opposed the practice of "lay" analysis, and were augmented by the economic threat posed to indigenous analysts by the arrival of so many competitors, who fled, of course, not only from Hungary, but also from many other European countries, above all Austria after the Anschluss in 1938. These considerations led the Emergency Committee "to direct the newly arrived analysts to less populated communities", thereby protecting the interests of its supporters while extending the reach of analysis throughout America. As Mészáros documents, although the original mandate of the Emergency Committee had been " 'to restrict and control immigration' ", after the Anschluss its actions were increasingly guided by humanitarian considerations and a "philanthropic outlook" became paramount.

With great dexterity, Mészáros integrates the distinctively Hungarian story of the "exile of the Budapest School" with an American perspective on "solidarity in the psychoanalytic movement during the Nazi years". And if, as she writes in the final paragraph of

Ferenczi and Beyond, "Europe's loss was indeed America's gain", it must not be forgotten that those refugees who so enriched the psychoanalytic culture of their adopted land also brought with them the scars of the history to which they were living witnesses, and that the legacy of this trauma has likewise been transmitted through the generations.

Professor Peter L. Rudnytsky
Series Co-Editor
Gainesville, Florida

FOREWORD

. . . To whet the reader's appetite

Judit Mészáros's studies represent an important contribution to writing on the history of psychoanalysis. Like all histories, this one has its exquisite pages and fascinating discoveries. At the same time, it is also a wonderful testament to human solidarity. It is the story of an intellectual movement, in which—as is frequently the case in scholarly life—passions are aroused by competition, rivalry, and the search for certainty. However, in spite of these passions, the difficult situations arising from war and persecution bring a sudden and marvellous loyalty to the surface. Neither the value of this solidarity nor the sheer scale of the assistance provided is diminished by the range of conflicts the émigrés experienced in their new homes, particularly with regard to earning a livelihood, and Judit Mészáros paints a clear picture of all those seemingly contradictory forces for the reader.

In addition to a description of the work undertaken by the American and British organisations that came to the aid of those in need, the reader will also learn more about the great figures of psychoanalysis from the period, names which are only otherwise familiar through the literature of the field. Here, the reader will witness those people demonstrating unusual nobility, generosity, determination, and selflessness.

Is it possible to attribute this to their being in the field of psychoanalysis, whose practitioners are thought to grow ever wiser through introspection? If we recall the human history of psychoanalysis and not merely its intellectual history, we tend to arrive at the opposite conclusion. Indeed, the author does not dismiss the more negative aspects of the story and paints the full picture. This is certainly in part because the fiery glow of debate is necessary to crystallise our thoughts, but also because not even the wisest among us are spared from experiencing the sympathies and antipathies between people—as we have known since Socrates. Indeed, there are those who would add that in the history of psychoanalysis there have been drinks passed round that are more harmful than a cup of hemlock.

It is to Judit Mészáros's great credit that, in contrast to the history writing so customary among various scholarly, political, and religious movements, she neither glorifies nor vilifies. The admiration of her peers, which characterised this project early on, has subsided, while their hypercriticism, born of envy, has left the author unfazed. As was thought particularly in the nineteenth century, most will agree that one should "tell it as it was". Since then, however, we have learnt that history writing proceeds from formulating questions rooted in the present day. Thus, it is no coincidence that the issue of solidarity arises in a world in which uncertainty is incomparably greater than it was in dear old Franz Joseph's seemingly stable world. The refugees from Budapest and Vienna, some of whom preceded the Berliners, others of whom followed them, were never able to find—as much as they wanted to—that breezy, operetta-like world they had left behind, free of the exertions forced on them by bureaucracy. Naturally, we must not forget the primary goal of their escape—to save their lives—and that it was goodwill and solidarity that contributed to this endeavour.

So far I have only discussed *one* of the topics in this book, though the book encompasses a thousand gems. One of these is the link between psychoanalysis in Budapest and the broader culture, which may shed light on the question so many outside of Central Europe so frequently ask: why and how was it that Vienna, Prague, and Budapest came to experience such a marvellous flowering in a hundred different areas of art and scholarship in the late nineteenth and early twentieth centuries? The Vienna School of Medicine and its offshoot in Budapest, painting, architecture, physics, and epistemology (the Vienna School of positivism and Karl Popper spring to mind)—not to mention other prominent scholars ranging from John (János) Neumann to Edward (Ede) Teller—all represent testaments to the interweaving of each of these areas and the culture at large.

Judit Mészáros sensitively demonstrates the link between Budapest psychoanalysis and the local culture—which represents an important expression of this Central European flowering. For example, certain writers of the period show the effect of psychoanalysis in their writings so convincingly that it is difficult to say where psychoanalysis begins and where we have entered the novel. If Freud marvelled that the descriptions of his cases became more readable when he wrote them as if they were works of literature (no doubt Freud's style contributed to this experience), then should Sándor Márai and Ignotus be considered writers first and foremost and Géza Csáth and Edit Gyömrői be seen primarily as psychoanalysts? Such attempts at pigeon-holing soon prove ridiculous. Many have argued that the culture of the time influenced psychoanalysis and this often serves to disparage it, but, if we accept the notion that psychoanalysis was somehow hanging in the cultural air, the opposite could probably be more accurate. Psychoanalysis opened up a world of free associations, and not just for poet Attila József. Indeed, it brought with it creativity and a kind of intellectual freedom. If Ferenczi published in the literary journal *Nyugat* (which means "West"), it was not only because he was a friend of its editor-in-chief, Ignotus, but also because psychoanalysis truly brought Budapest closer to Western modernity—to Vienna, London, and New York, to mention only a few of the centres. The thinkers of the Budapest School could be found in international journals, at international congresses, and in friendships as well. The most famous example of such a friendship was Freud and Ferenczi's, to which over 1200(!) letters bear witness and as part of which Freud even shared his precious holiday time with his friend for decades. Although the variously coloured upheavals that followed the collapse of Austria-Hungary ultimately saw the loss of both Ferenczi's professorship and his medical association membership, and although the uncertainty of postal and telephone links led to his resignation from the presidency of the International Psychoanalytical Association (IPA), his influence in the history of psychoanalytic thought remained powerful none the less.

Of the themes noted above, a key element of the book is an effective history of Hungarian scholarly thought, which the author carries off brilliantly. While Freud wrote little on these problems in the second half of his life, there is no question that present-day psychoanalytic practice (technique and mode of practice) is founded on Ferenczi's thinking and experience. It is primarily through the Freud–Ferenczi correspondence that it becomes clear how certain concepts were formed through the exchange of ideas between the two men. While a portion of Ferenczi's concepts became a topic of debate and, cast under the wheel of history, Hungarian psychoanalytic contributions were sometimes underestimated, the most recent history writing has certainly established their central influence. Mészáros follows up on this current thinking, and, based on her own research, she demonstrates how the seed planted by Ferenczi grew into an enormous oak with a great many branches that would stretch into the skies of psychoanalysis. Whether it is research on infants or children, developmental psychology, a psychoanalytic study of language or relationships, the theory of symbolism or the interpretation of dreams, the study of sexual problems or the treatment of neurosis, contributions by members of the Budapest School, which later became inestimable outside of Hungary as well, proved to be *fundamental*. The reader develops a full picture of this as well as of how indispensable the author's contribution is in shedding light on these facts of history.

As the writer of this preface, I wish to move beyond the confines of the task set before me and tie up the threads in the book further. However, I must limit myself to allowing the reader to enjoy the stimulation of her or his own thoughts, since reading the book will not merely be usefully thought-provoking, but also a source of pleasure and joy. *Historia docet*: history teaches, and perhaps good history even makes us better people—people who show greater solidarity, loyalty, and tolerance.

André Haynal
Professor, Université de Genève
Sigourney Prize-winning psychoanalyst (IPA)
Budapest and Geneva

Introduction

Simply put, the events described in this book tell an exceptional story of solidarity, and, thus, the volume the reader holds in his hands is indeed a book of solidarity—the notion fixed in the mounting of Ferenczi's work and offering a possible reading of the history and emigration of the Budapest School.

A "possible reading" suggests a certain point of view. Specifically, I have placed both the forming of the Budapest School and the later exile of a large portion of its members into the context of the cultural, social, and political events of early twentieth-century Hungary. I have highlighted processes that are central to the development of psychoanalysis and stressed the socio-political changes which led to two waves of emigration that arrested the development of psychoanalysis in Hungary. The exile of the Budapest analysts intersected with the destructive power of European Nazism and the exodus of members of the psychoanalytic societies in Berlin and Vienna. These processes brought about irreversible changes in the history of European psychoanalysis and caused serious losses. At the same time, the solidarity that emerged within the psychoanalytic movement and the exceptional realisation of this collaboration through the Emergency Committee on Relief and Immigration set up by America's analysts in the immediate wake of the Anschluss aided hundreds of analysts and, if necessary, their families in escaping and resettling. The assistance requested did not always match that which was received, but the Emergency Committee still offered aid even when there were a thousand reasons why a potential recipient could not make use of it.

Sándor Ferenczi played the same key role in the evolution of the Budapest School as he did in the growth of the international psychoanalytic movement, including the establishment of an organisational framework, the theoretical development of psychoanalysis, and the shifts in perspective within therapeutic practice. Owing to both domestic and international research over the past three decades, Ferenczi has come to occupy his rightful place not only in the history of psychoanalysis in Hungary and Europe in the twentieth century, but also in the scientific and intellectual history of the period. The concepts articulated in the 1930s by Ferenczi's peers and writer friends—among them Michael and Alice Balint and writers Dezső Kosztolányi and Sándor Márai—have re-entered the professional and cultural way of thinking of our day. As Kosztolányi put it, "Ferenczi was one of the true luminaries of psychoanalysis . . . of the intellectual revolution that today is still difficult for us to grasp fully" (Kosztolányi, 2000[1933], p. 55). To quote Márai, "Without the work of Freud and the refinements and contributions of Ferenczi, one could scarcely imagine the intellectual cross-section of this century" (Márai, 2000[1933], p. 48). In the 1930s, Balint believed that "with his new technique, Ferenczi managed to penetrate the human mind to a depth that no one had done before" (Balint, 2000[1933], p. 153). Ferenczi's openness, versatility, innovative power, and liberal-mindedness were coupled with his deep commitment to psychoanalysis. In the opening decades of the twentieth century, these features and abilities merged with the efforts of a Hungarian intelligentsia that was open to modernisation.

It is due to this very reciprocity, the personal characteristics, and the lucky satisfying of deep-seated needs in society that Hungary experienced the explosion of a new discipline that transcended the interests of a narrow profession—psychoanalysis. Beyond the innovations of various *avant-garde* groups with their scholarly and cultural aims, this rapid growth was significantly aided through Ferenczi's network of friends by constructive, open forums and by medical, literary, and sociological periodicals that then served the function of what today we would call the media. Thus, there were reasons beyond Budapest's hosting the International Psychoanalytical Congress in 1918 for Freud to declare that the city would "now become the headquarters of our movement" (Freud to Abraham, 27 August 1918, Freud, 1918, p. 382). It was also because all the forces were concentrated in Budapest that would be required for this central role: an energetic and dedicated *personality* (Ferenczi), who also enjoyed Freud's friendship; a society of individuals who had earned intellectually impeccable qualifications in a wide range of scholarly fields (including medicine, ethnography, literature, and education); an expressly receptive *city*; the *financial resources* necessary—even then— to operate on an international scale. The basis for the last element was made possible by a donation from Antal Freund of Tószeg, who was then travelling regularly from Budapest to see Freud for analysis and wished to express his gratitude and show his commitment to psychoanalysis. This created the possibility of establishing an international psychoanalytic publishing house for books and periodicals. Due to a series of stormy historical events, however, this was brought to fruition in Vienna instead, despite the plans made for Budapest. Since Ferenczi offered new chances to heal the enormous number of soldiers injured in the First World War by proposing psychoanalytic treatment for war neuroses, this area created an unexpected opportunity to win official state acceptance of psychoanalysis.

Psychoanalysis, therefore, stepped beyond the boundaries of the Budapest society during this period and found paths toward other scholarly fields and organisational forms. In Budapest in 1919, if only for a short time, psychoanalysis as a discipline was incorporated into the medical training at the university with its own department and clinic. However, the solidifying of Budapest as the centre of psychoanalysis was halted by a series of turbulent socio-political changes that had an impact on the whole of Europe in the aftermath of the First World War, by Hungary's economic and political restructuring, by the flames of anti-Semitism eagerly being fanned, and by the concurrent emigration of a significant portion of the intelligentsia.

A "possible reading" also suggests that one can imagine a multidirectional shift in emphasis in defining the Budapest School as a school/group. One may, for example, put the term *Budapest School* in inverted commas: there was never an actual school with walls, students, or a director. One might raise the question: if the name was not created as a geographic reference, then what does it refer to? What does it mean? In several earlier publications, I myself put the term in inverted commas in discussing it. However, I chose not to use them in this book. This is primarily because many of the analysts grouped around Ferenczi were bound by similar points of view in their approach, their theoretical way of thinking, and their work with patients, and these viewpoints remained demonstrable motifs in the work they did after they emigrated. At the same time, a question in further research might be answered as follows: who and in what context was the term *Budapest School* used and where are the limits of the legitimate use of the term?

In researching the exile of the Hungarian psychoanalysts, I also needed to answer the questions of who could be considered a *Hungarian* and who could be viewed as a *psychoanalyst*. Is a psychoanalyst considered Hungarian if that person completed her or his training in Berlin or Vienna and later lived in New York? In my research, I determined that analysts could be said to be originally from Hungary, or, simply put, to be Hungarian, either if they had received analytic training—or at least part of it—in Hungary, if they could be verified as having been influenced by the psychoanalytic thinking while in the country and been socialised there.

This process of socialisation is also significant in terms of the history of scholarship. After all, it is noteworthy that the majority of the Budapest analysts who had been forced to emigrate, like so many Hungarian exiles in other scholarly fields, later became internationally renowned experts. It is certainly true that the opportunities provided by UK or USA society after the Second World War far surpassed one's options in contemporary Hungary—a fact which favoured scholarly achievements. Add to this the ideological labelling under which psychoanalysis suffered in Hungary for a quarter of a century from the start of the Stalinist dictatorship there (1948) to the mid-1970s as well as the exclusion of analytic activity from the ranks of legitimate healing processes. Still, it can be said that, in education, the arts, and scientific development, even in the period leading up to the late 1930s, Hungary's cultural life demonstrated a system of interdependent values and resources, a richness, and a variety, in the soil of which a special sensitivity to problems and a creative way of thinking had grown. This is one of the important sources of the seemingly large number of "Hungarian" successes. It was in this soil that successful professionals began their development: individuals who would rise to prominence received their early education here, were socialised in this complex, multi-layered culture, and, under the effect of all this, achieved epoch-making results in other countries after their forced emigration. In the natural and social sciences and in the arts alike, such great figures include Leó Szilárd, Edward (Ede) Teller, John (János) Neumann, Albert Szent-Györgyi, and André (Andor) Kertész. The careers abroad of Hungarian psychoanalysts followed the same trend. Despite their small numbers, a very large percentage of them contributed fundamentally to enriching the theoretical system and therapeutic method of psychoanalysis and to deepening its interdisciplinary ties.

I have answered the question of whom I consider to be Hungarian in this research. However, I have also had to take a position on the not altogether simple question of who should be viewed as a psychoanalyst.

In this regard, I used the *contemporary qualifications of the field* as a basis. This is significant because the psychoanalytic way of thinking affected many, and because there were many who belonged to a variety of psychoanalytic groupings or were not tied to any groups or institutions at all but considered themselves analysts. In this research, I have determined that a psychoanalyst is anyone who was a member or candidate of a national society of the International Psychoanalytical Association (IPA), whether this be the Hungarian Psychoanalytical Society or the society in Vienna, Berlin, or, later, New York.

There was the further question of when the person had emigrated. The research covered those who had left Hungary before 1941 and had satisfied the criteria already noted. It is fascinating to observe the similarities and differences between the two great waves of emigration that swept the Hungarian analysts along (1919–1921 and 1938–1941). Both waves exercised a brain drain effect on the development of the Hungarian psychoanalytic movement to varying degrees. While, in principle, the émigrés were easily able to return to Hungary after the first period, if they wished, this would have been impossible after the second. During the first wave, the majority of the analysts remained within Europe (Vienna, Berlin, and Paris) and had the opportunity to contribute to the dialogue that enriched psychoanalysis on the European continent. Following the second wave, however, progress within the field came to a standstill in Europe. A serious situation also developed in Hungary, in which the discipline was seen as hostile by the dominant ideology after 1948. The tiny community that was left standing in that country after both the second wave of emigration and the Holocaust undertook to dissolve the society in early 1949, under political pressure. Its former members were then forced to operate underground for decades.

At the heart of the volume stands the history of the second exile. What happened to the European analysts and, specifically, the Hungarian analysts in the focus of the study, who were compelled to flee Hungary in a Europe under Nazi hegemony? What aid could they expect? And what forces impeded their escape and resettlement in peaceful lands?

A civil society organisation was established based on the psychoanalytic movement's own personal and professional network and the self-sacrificing efforts of its members, an organisation which—despite the restrictive tendencies in both British and US immigration policy—assumed an invaluable role in saving the European and, thus, the Hungarian analysts and in securing their future. This organisation was the Emergency Committee on Relief and Immigration, established by the American Psychoanalytic Association (APsaA) one day after the Anschluss. The representatives of this civil society initiative not only had to face developments in their country's own contemporary domestic and foreign policy power relations, but also conflicts within the field of psychoanalysis. After Hitler had seized power, the arrival of the analysts from Berlin and, after the Anschluss, from Vienna served to heighten the tensions that had emerged due to the divergent paths of development that had been taken by the European and American psychoanalysis. When I speak of a "book of solidarity", I am thinking of this very spirit that managed to rise above often passionate personal and professional clashes to save the lives of peers whose lives were now in jeopardy. While the conflicts that had raged previously were now subordinated to this effort, those who took in their peers did not deny that the difficulties and conflicts existed; however, they endeavoured to find common ground and arrive at a mutually satisfactory solution. This is illustrated exceptionally well by the New York Psychoanalytic Society and Institute, which received many of the analyst refugees, as well as by the Menninger Clinic, which played a key role in the process. Ernest Jones, the president of the International Psychoanalytical Association (IPA) and the British Psychoanalytical Society (BPS), applied a different strategy. He wished to keep far away from London any peers who, it was presumed, would present further difficulties for the psychoanalytic community there, which was already strained by the controversy between Anna Freud and Melanie Klein. Neither was Jones overly eager to see Ferenczi's students in London. At the same time, this did not prevent him from throwing himself into the effort of directing his refugee peers toward other potential receiving countries.

A study of the fates of the Hungarian analysts provides the contemporary context for a survey—if a brief one—of their work. The book also provides a framework within which to highlight motifs that link the innovations of the Budapest School with the professional efforts made by its members after their emigration and to outline trends within the field, which the émigré analysts from Hungary often played a pioneering role in identifying. Thus, we begin to see contours of the wide-ranging wealth of intellectual innovation, which the Hungarian analysts contributed to the renewal of the theory and technique of modern psychoanalysis and psychotherapies. Examples include the area of psychosomatics (Balint and Alexander), research on the personality-forming significance of the early mother–child relationship (Ferenczi, Balint, Spitz, Klein, and Mahler), the reinterpretation of the interpersonal dynamic in psychoanalytic therapies (Ferenczi, Balint, Benedek, and Alexander), clinical research (Rapaport and Benedek), and the spread of testing methods for use in psychiatric clinics (Rapaport). The Hungarian analysts had a great hand in developing training models, institutions, and educational structures. Consider the roles of Sándor Radó and Franz Alexander at their respective psychoanalytic institutes in New York and Chicago, as well as the work of Michael Balint within the British Psychoanalytical Society, all of which guaranteed a standard of professional training for the coming generations.

To paraphrase a contemporary in the USA, the psychoanalysts from Vienna, Berlin, and Budapest became our teachers and our friends, who had a great effect on our lives; Europe's loss represented an enormous gain for us. This gain not only enriched modern psychoanalysis and intellectual history, but made all of us that much richer from a humanitarian point of view.

Judit Mészáros
Budapest

CHAPTER ONE

Towards psychoanalysis (1897–1908)[2]

"Authoritarian arguments carry little weight"

(Ferenczi, 1999a[1899])

Sándor Ferenczi's early writings foreshadow not only Ferenczi's character and scholarly and therapeutic orientation as a psychoanalyst, but also the unique perspectives that would emerge in the Budapest School. These initial studies speak volumes about the thinking of a young professional in the process of finding his way. This was the process that virtually predestined him to stake out the fundamental questions of modern psychoanalysis and, at the same time, to become the "wise baby" and even the *enfant terrible*[3] of psychoanalytic history, although this was never his intention—indeed, it is safe to say this ran very much counter to his wishes.

A decade (1897–1908) of publications by Ferenczi—spanning both clinical topics and broader issues in healthcare—provide an insight into his early way of thinking and medical approach. Directions took shape that would become defining elements in his later writing on psychoanalysis. First and foremost, we see his constant need to experiment and to maintain a critical attitude of self-reflection—both in the interests of effective healing. The "maturity" grounded in the sensitivity of the "wise baby", on the one hand, and the unusual shifts in perspective and express resistance to being integrated into a senseless "order" represented by authority on the part of the "enfant terrible", on the other hand, constituted the basic features of Ferenczi's personality.

A critical attitude, self-reflection, and autonomous and creative thinking also left their mark on the work of the analysts that formed the Budapest School. For example, Ferenczi thought it perfectly natural that he should admit his own diagnostic errors—as an exercise in lessons learnt and with no sense of shame. In his view, it was hypocrisy that one should feel ashamed, because this throws up roadblocks to acknowledgement and creates distrust among people.

Ferenczi saw the most effective way to cure illness as being within a collaborative doctor–patient relationship. With this understanding, he broke away from the system of his day, which derived from an authoritarian way of thinking, subordinated the patient to the physician, and positioned the physician in a strict hierarchy. He proceeded gently, using his writings to revolt, and to incite revolt, against any form of subordination that stifled autonomous thinking. He sympathised with peers who advocated an independent way of thinking on behalf of the patient. For him, the illness could neither be separated from the patient nor from her or his personality, way of life, culture, or, indeed, sex. In his understanding, these two, the individual and her or his illness, formed a single system—and it was this complex structure that the physician encountered. Curing and being cured were, therefore, based on collaboration between doctor and patient.

However, the incongruity between Ferenczi's need for intellectual freedom and his desire for attachment to charismatic people represented a major source of tension that would accompany him to the end of his life. At times, maintaining his freedom meant that he lost favour with others. The fact that this incongruity was never overcome rendered Ferenczi's life often painful, even bitter towards the end, because of his inability to resolve emotional conflicts, and, indeed, fatal for his relationship with Freud—as attested by his last major study, *Clinical Diary*.[4]

It is important to take a closer look at this early pre-psychoanalytic, or pre-analytic, phase because it is in these writings that we uncover traces of the internal process that would eventually give shape to psychoanalytic thinking. The term *pre-analytic* is, therefore, descriptive, not evaluative; it designates a period which ended on 2 February 1908 with the meeting between Freud and Ferenczi. *Pre-analytic* is more accurate than more conventional descriptors such as *as a young man*, *his early work*, and *his beginnings*. Indeed, one would be hard-pressed to refer to an adult as being young throughout the course of a decade, to describe all the work that spans that period as early, or to speak, ten years into a person's career, of his beginnings.

An examination of this period enables us to link pre-analytic seeds of thought with the therapeutic and theoretical approaches initiated by Ferenczi, the mature psychoanalyst. This is particularly so because one can identify a consistent line that lent Ferenczi's *oeuvre* exceptional stability. At the same time, this line—as we will see—would have great significance in the Hungarian psychoanalytic community that formed around Ferenczi. Furthermore, the impact of the line was still being felt and could be observed in the approach among members of the Budapest School, once forced to emigrate.

The emotional and intellectual milieu of the relatively large Ferenczi family shaped the character of each member. Born to this liberal-minded, intellectual Jewish family in the north-eastern Hungarian city of Miskolc on 7 July 1873, Sándor Ferenczi was the eighth of eleven children. His father, Baruch Fraenkel/Fränkel[5] (1830–1889), had moved his family from Cracow in Poland to Hungary and fought in the country's Revolution and War of Independence of 1848–1849. He had trained to be a book merchant and became the proprietor of his own bookshop by 1856. His second wife, Róza Eibenschütz, had grown up in Vienna. The multilingual family thus knew Hungarian, German, Yiddish, and Polish. Sándor himself was bilingual, speaking Hungarian and German, and later learnt English and French. As an expression of assimilation into Hungarian society, his father Hungarianised the family name to Ferenczi in 1879. As Sándor had been born six years earlier, his family name was entered as Fränkel in the birth records of the Miskolc synagogue.

The family's bookshop played a key role in the cultural life of the city. Beyond selling and even lending books, it also dealt with publishing and planning cultural events, activities in which Ferenczi's mother played a key role (Kapusi, 2000). The bookshop saw a steady stream of famous writers, poets, and artists, who aroused Ferenczi's interest and had an impact on the range of friendships he would later nurture.

Ferenczi was often seen reading perched on the ladder used for the tall shelves, and we know from his own writing that he had an inquisitive mind that was given to experimentation: at sixteen, he attempted to hypnotise an assistant at the bookshop (Ferenczi, 1910). After completing secondary school, he studied medicine in Vienna, earning a degree in 1894. During the Vienna years, He was strongly influenced by the views of Professor Richard von Krafft-Ebing on sexual disorders, by Darwin's natural selection, and by the teachings of Jean-Baptiste Lamarck and Ernst Haeckel on phylogenesis and ontogenesis.

"Unconscious and semi-conscious": occultism, hypnosis, and the interpretation of dreams

Both occultism and unconscious or "semi-conscious" (Ferenczi, 1999b [1899], p. 47) manifestations of psychic processes aroused Ferenczi's interest in his twenties, and he was far from alone in this regard at the turn of the century. The major scientific discoveries of the nineteenth century—Darwin's theory of natural selection, Haeckel's theory on ontogenesis, and the law of conservation of energy—brought about revolutionary changes in the natural sciences and fundamental shifts in world view. This had a seesaw effect. In response to the ascendance of materialism, experiments were being conducted with renewed vigour to prove the immortality of the soul. At spiritist séances, mediums relayed signs from the beyond and communicated with spirits of the deceased.[6] The ancient desire for immortality reached a fever pitch in the late 1900s, with enthusiasts launching movements that spanned continents. This was when spiritism took root in Europe, having originated in North America. While Freud opened the door to a new era with his book *The Interpretation of Dreams* (Freud, 1900a), *Heavenly Light*, the journal of the Hungarian Association of Spiritists, was first published in Hungary in 1900. Thus, in an unconscious common pursuit at the *fin de siècle*, answers were being sought to phenomena that had slipped from the control of the human spirit—or human consciousness, in today's understanding—but emerged in hypnosis, dreams, and the occult, and even in the rich and varied symptoms of hysteria.

What was so unusual about a young man, having studied in Vienna and now embarking on his medical career in Budapest, showing an interest in all the phenomena that held the public in their mystical spell? It was not the object of his interest that was unusual; it was his approach. Ferenczi never joined the vocal ranks of either believers or doubters. He found another path: that of experimentation. As he put it, why not investigate disputed phenomena from the position of the unbiased experimenter? According to Ferenczi, "[t]he method of combat used by those opposed to spiritism should not be to reject it before, or without, investigating it" (Ferenczi, 1999a[1899], p. 29). He felt that one must rather set about conducting a critical study of the facts "with the objectivity of a true scholar" (1999a[1899], p. 29). Between 1897 and 1899, Ferenczi himself attended spiritist séances in the Budapest villa of noted professor of chemistry Emil Felletár (Hidas & Mészáros, 1988), and, based on his experience, encouraged his peers as follows: "Don't be reluctant to sit at the rapping table . . . Because I believe that there is truth to it even if it is *subjective* and not *objective truth*" (Ferenczi, 1999a[1899], p. 29, my italics). He went on to say,

> Psychology as a natural science is still in its childhood years, so to speak. . . . But what we know today proves without any doubt that the mental functioning includes a great deal of *unconscious* and *semiconscious* elements. And that we perform many logical actions and have thoughts of which our consciousness remains unaware. (pp. 29–30)

Ferenczi concluded that there are cracks in the functioning of the human psyche and that only a portion of one's experiences enters the "focus of the mirror of the conscious and the rest functions unconsciously" (Haynal, 1995, p. 20). Ferenczi contrasted contemporary discoveries in the natural sciences with the backward state of psychology in his day. According to him, "we have yet to see the Darwin and Haeckel of psychology. The ontogenesis and phylogenesis of the mind have still not been created" (Ferenczi 1999c[1900], p. 46).

In Ferenczi's argumentation, the elements of the development of the self-conscious mind were to be sought in the past. Here, Ferenczi was not referring to the personal past of the individual. He was, rather, expanding on Haeckel's theory of ontogenetic evolution to include the development of human consciousness. Thus, the development of the human mind carried the stages of the consciousness of various species. Ferenczi attempted to grasp the operation of living beings—including man—in generally understandable principles by applying knowledge gained through the most recent scientific discoveries. This effort is also characteristic of Freud's way of thinking in that his theory of the libido—his theory of the conversion of sexual energy into mental energy—shows clear signs of the general law of conservation of energy. A survey of the intersections of psychoanalysis and scientific discoveries motivated one of Ferenczi's essential later writings. In his bioanalysis within his book *Thalassa: A Theory of Genitality* (Ferenczi, 1989[1924]), he described the melding of the biological and psychological functioning of the human being. This work, which would become known simply as *Thalassa*,[7] discusses the concurrent emergence of the onto- and phylogenetic instinctive tendencies in the human sexual drive.

Ferenczi's writing is characterised by an implicitly monistic way of thinking. Body and mind create one unit, and the physical and psychological processes flow into each other (Pfitzner, 2005, pp. 38–48). If we add to this Haeckel's theory of onto- and phylogenesis and the symbolic expression of psychological problems in physical symptoms, we arrive at the approach through which Ferenczi considered the cooperation between body and mind, psychosomatic phenomena, and illness. According to this, the depth of psychological regression could be understood in or through symbols of physical manifestations. If regression was expanded from the level of ontogenesis—when earlier stages of the development of the ego appeared in the regressive state—to the phylogenetic level, we would arrive at the bioanalysis proposed by Ferenczi and one of its particular features, which came to be known as the "Thalassal regression": through intercourse one can reach not only to the beginning of individual life, the womb, but symbolically to the beginning of life itself, to the primordial sea of Thalassa.

Many of Ferenczi's earlier writings maintained the basic elements of his later thinking. In his first scholarly publication, an article entitled "Spiritism", he stressed the idea of subjective truth, separated psychic expressions of the unconscious and semi-conscious, and contrasted respect for facts arrived at through experimentation with a prejudicial way of thinking. These intellectual considerations can be found in all his later writing. The acceptance of subjective truth, for example, represented a conceptual departure in psychoanalysis and also plays a key role in the paradigm shift in Ferenczi's trauma theory (Mészáros, 2002; 2004b, 2010a).

Experiment and self-reflection in the service of recognition and healing

Experimentation, relations of reflective and self-reflective understandings, and the need for authentic expression are among the core values of Ferenczi's functioning, and they represent values that can be detected in the approach taken by the Budapest School.

For Ferenczi, the method for revealing truth was *experimentation*. By nature, Ferenczi was playful, creative, and drawn to experimentation. It characterised him in his early years as much as in his later years. At first, he attempted to capture the unconscious forces of the mind through automatic writing (Ferenczi, 1999a)[1899]. Like Freud, he also experimented with thought transference, with the *active technique* in the 1920s to enhance the effectiveness of psychoanalysis, and then later with *mutual analysis*. This is how mutual analysis with the patient became one of the most widely debated experiments in the history of psychoanalysis (Ferenczi, 1988[1932]). The idea of mutual analysis is not Ferenczi's. Freud and later all the first-generation psychoanalysts applied this method, and this is how they learnt from and trained one another.[8] However, Ferenczi was the only one to consider the patient to be equal when he sensed his own blockage in therapy, and, in order to raise the quality of psychoanalytic processes, he conducted experiments in mutual analysis with patients. He kept a clinical diary of his experiences in 1932 and even included the negative impact of his method. His purpose was to achieve the highest level of trust with the patient,

> a total immersion, right down 'to the mothers', impossible unless the analyst becomes an open book, that is to say, not only formally and professionally nice and polite but even harmless, by communicating his suppressed and repressed selfish, dangerous, brutal, and ruthless tendencies. (Ferenczi, 1988[1932], p. 74)

Truth is revealed through the careful examination of material obtained through experimentation and experience, but to glimpse facts it is indispensable to have an unbiased attitude, which also happens to be an essential condition for recognising mistakes. Ferenczi consciously represented these principles. As he put it,

> [o]ur memories carefully safeguard our successes, but our mistakes are covered by the veil of forgetting. How much could the medical

sciences gain if we were able to systematise our mistakes . . . or blunders! Or if at least our own mistakes could remain engraved in our memories! (Ferenczi, 1999k[1903], p. 175)

In the service of science, in addition to all this, one must have inner strength that enables the practitioner not only to record mistakes quietly, but also to share them with others. Ferenczi's unusual candour was not a manifestation of the rebellious youth, the "enfant terrible", pitting himself against the establishment, but, rather, an expression of the autonomy of the mature person capable of in-depth and self-reflective thinking. As he wrote in his 20s,

[i]t has long been known that we learn the most from our mistakes. However, we jealously guard the lessons we learn this way because we all consider it significant to appear in the eyes of our fellow man as being more clever and infallible. This is how it is in social life as well, especially in medical practice. (Ferenczi, 1999e[1900], p. 63)

After this introduction, Ferenczi gave an account of two of his mistaken diagnoses on the pages of *Gyógyászat* (Ferenczi, 1999e[1900], p. 63). Then, two years later, he enthusiastically wrote in one of his book reviews:

Finally, a book which unmasks the current state of the college of physicians and of medical science . . . whose practitioners are constantly compelled to conceal their own weaknesses so as to feign knowledge, when, in their depths, uncertainty and doubt reign. (Ferenczi, 1999i[1902], p. 118)

Over a quarter century later, as if picking up where he had left off, he declared that "[o]ne must never be ashamed unreservedly to confess one's own mistakes" (Ferenczi, 1980g[1928], p. 95) and that "[n]othing is more harmful to the analysis than a schoolmasterish, or even an authoritative, attitude on the physician's part" (p. 94).

In the 1920s, it was quite unusual to speak of the therapeutic effectiveness of the psychoanalyst's candour—that is, countertransference. Ferenczi, thus, introduced a new paradigm within the healing process. During therapy, the analyst must forsake the ideal of sterile neutrality and the position of the strict outside observer that was represented by Freud. Ferenczi did this in order to avoid professional hypocrisy, manifestations of authority, and the appearance of infallibility, mistakes that are so common in relationships between adults. Ferenczi's entire career as a psychoanalyst was characterised by the conviction that the almighty conscious of the adults and moral education based on the repression of thought (Ferenczi, 1980j[1908]) must be replaced by a learning process based on insight and mutual co-operation. Adults build a myth of unapproachability and infallibility around themselves and, thus, trigger a series of painful and even traumatic experiences in the child. There is no room for any kind of falseness in the analyst's surgery. Trustworthy behaviour is the cornerstone of safety in the relationship. The extent to which the cure is successful depends on the load-bearing qualities of the therapeutic relationship, which rests on a foundation of honesty.

Before delving into the characteristic topics of Ferenczi's preanalytic writings, many of which bear witness to internal processes that point towards psychoanalysis, we must ask: what factors prompted Ferenczi in publishing by the age of thirty-five—as far as we know today—fifty-four articles, twenty-four book reviews, and eight translations? This was unusually prolific for a young physician. The majority of his writing was published in the weekly medical journal *Gyógyászat*, but Ferenczi's writings also appeared in a wide range of other publications.[9] Who supported him? Who were his first adult playmates? And what impact did these early relationships and forums have—besides Ferenczi's own professional development—on the evolution of psychoanalysis in Hungary?

Miksa Schächter, Gyógyászat, *and the others*

It was probably the charismatic personality of Miksa Schächter that influenced Ferenczi the most at the beginning of his career (Mészáros, 1993a). Ferenczi met the owner and editor-in-chief of *Gyógyászat* at the age of twenty-five under unusual circumstances. In his first job at Rókus Hospital between 1898 and 1900, Ferenczi worked as an intern at the ward that dealt with prostitutes and patients suffering from venereal diseases. He was disappointed at being placed there by the hard-headed director of the hospital, since he was interested in neurology and psychic disorders. He found solace in his free time in attending spiritist séances and conducting psychological experiments on himself. One late night, he experimented with automatic writing. This might have been his first psychological experiment. He recounted it as follows:

> So, I picked up a pencil and, holding it loosely in my hand, I pressed it against a piece of blank paper. I decided to let the pencil move 'on its own', letting it write whatever it wished. Senseless scribbles came first, then letters, words (some of them strange to me), and finally whole sentences. Soon I was having a real dialogue with my pencil—I asked questions and got quite unexpected answers. Being young, first of all I demanded answers to big theoretical problems, but later more practical questions occurred to me. Finally the pencil suggested the following: 'Write an article on [spiritism] for *Gyógyászat*, the editor will be interested'.
>
> I did not know that, while *Orvosi Hetilap* [Medical Weekly] was the journal of the influential university circles, *Gyógyászat* [Therapy] was the forum of a single powerful man—Miksa Schächter. His voluntarily undertaken crusade was to protect medical justice and ethics from threatening attacks by any antagonists.
>
> The next day I wrote my first medical paper entitled 'On [spiritism]' (Ferenczi, 1993[1917], p. 430)

This is how the friendship between Ferenczi and Schächter began. Miksa Schächter (1859–1917) was an outstanding figure in Hungary's medical profession. He was a surgeon, a member of the country's Forensic Medical Board,[10] and an editor-in-chief, who spoke English, German, and French and was particularly knowledgeable about Anglophone culture. He had originally studied to become a rabbi and felt as much at home with Judaic Studies and the Hebrew language as he did with English literature. He edited his journal based on a British model. He possessed exceptional character and wisdom, which surely would have made him as successful a rabbi as it did a physician and public figure—as well as Ferenczi's first fatherly benefactor. He aimed at locating points of intersection in a variety of views and at creating opportunities to nurture talent. He was legendary in establishing professional balance and upholding strict ethics. These two features of his became characteristic of his journal, *Gyógyászat*, and served as a model for Ferenczi. Schächter provided a space for dissenting opinions and critical writing, stood against rigid conservatism, and regularly enabled ambitious young people to try their wings. It is, therefore, very likely that he entrusted Ferenczi with an editorship in recognition of his young colleague's talent. This is how the twenty-nine-year-old Ferenczi took on a senior position at *Honvédorvos* (Army Doctor),[11] which was a supplement to *Gyógyászat* (Mészáros, 1993a).

Since his university years in Vienna, Ferenczi had lived away from his extended family. As a young doctor in Budapest, he lived for years in bleak rooms for junior physicians in various hospitals. It is understandable, therefore, how much he longed for intimate family gatherings. The Friday evening dinners with the Schächter family represented an emotional boost. Schächter took the place of Ferenczi's father—whom he had lost as a teenager, leaving him with very ambivalent feelings[12]—and embodied the idealised father figure he had longed for. Ferenczi remembered him as follows, even a decade and a half later: "I felt that his personality could be compared to a single piece of perfect marble free of fractures or faults. . . . It was truly a period which shaped my character" (Ferenczi, 1993[1917], p. 431).

Certainly, many of Ferenczi's pre-analytic publications were written as a result of the encouragement he received from Schächter, including works that dealt with issues of medical ethics. Schächter's human greatness is perhaps best signified by the liberality with which he related to Ferenczi even as the younger man was beginning to think differently from him. As Ferenczi put it, "[t]here were two issues, however, about which he never joked: religion and morals. And I was fated to take a stand against him in both" (Ferenczi, 1993[1917], p. 431). The intensity of their friendship waned after Ferenczi met Freud, but it never ended entirely. Although Schächter disagreed with the psychoanalytic approach to sexual matters, he evinced the greatness of the most consistent of liberal thinkers. In Ferenczi's words, "seeing my insistence on these principles, he did not prevent me from publishing them in *Gyógyászat*. This again demonstrates Schächter's character: though conservative himself, he has never obstructed liberal progress" (Ferenczi, 1993[1917], p. 432). So much so that Schächter introduced Ferenczi's study "Psychoneuroses" (1909) in the journal's editorial entitled "How psychoanalysis can be used in treatment" (Schächter, 1909).

Hungarian psychoanalysis owes a debt of gratitude to the surgeon Miksa Schächter because he made writing on psychoanalysis accessible to the medical profession from the very outset. *Gyógyászat* immediately published every lecture Ferenczi held both in Hungary and abroad, and Ferenczi compiled two volumes of these studies on psychoanalysis in 1910 and 1912.[13] The journal soon emerged as a sort of news source on psychoanalysis and supplied information on the activities of psychoanalysts and the development of their international organisations; for example, Ferenczi announced the formation of the International Psychoanalytical Association (IPA) on the pages of the journal: "The period of guerrilla warfare has come to an end. Its benefits would now have turned into drawbacks. We must therefore continue to work together within an institutional framework" (Ferenczi, 1980a, p. 301).[14]

Gyógyászat regularly reported on the professional gatherings of psychoanalysts after the Hungarian Psychoanalytical Society (1913) had been established, as it did on many other scholarly meetings held by the associations of other medical specialities. This meant that psychoanalysis had also become a healthcare speciality like the rest. In addition to Ferenczi, other writers also published on psychoanalysis in the journal later: in an editorial, internist Lajos Lévy reported on the advances psychoanalysis had brought about in the field of war neuroses (Lévy, 1918), and, in another piece, he supported the instruction of psychoanalysis in higher education (Lévy, 2004[1919]). At the turn of the century, István Hollós also published frequently on psychiatric topics. As of the 1920s, newer generations of analysts also contributed to *Gyógyászat*, including Zsigmond Pfeifer, Michael Balint, and Lilly Hajdu.

At the beginning of his career, Ferenczi had established a lifelong relationship with internist Lajos Lévy (1875–1961) and psychiatrist István Hollós (1872–1957), both of whom played a central role in the psychoanalytic movement, not only in Hungary, but also internationally.

Ferenczi met Lévy through Schächter. Lévy was already on the staff of *Gyógyászat* at the time and worked as a junior doctor at the Tenth Ward for Internal Medicine at Rókus Hospital, as did Ferenczi. Lévy became a legendary internist of twentieth-century Hungary and author of editorials for *Gyógyászat* for many years, signing his review articles on the journal's weekly topic on the first page each week with the Greek letter lambda (λ). After Schächter's death in 1917, Lévy edited the journal, along with Sándor Szénásy and Mihály Mohl. Who would have thought in those early years that Lévy would come to be a founding member of the Hungarian Psychoanalytical Society formed by Ferenczi, become the family physician to the Freud family in Vienna and Ferenczi's physician in Budapest, and, later, after he had emigrated to Britain, treat Anna Freud (1895–1982) in London? In addition to these outstanding biographical elements that signify the appreciation of Lévy's work as an internist, Lévy was also one of the most influential representatives of the field of psychoanalytic psychosomatics, which was emerging in Hungary. Approaches to illnesses involving the doctor–patient relationship and psychoanalysis itself, which were tied to the names Sándor Ferenczi, Lajos Lévy, and Michael Balint, began to develop significantly after the turn of the century as a result of the early friendship between Lévy and Ferenczi.

It was during this period that Ferenczi met psychiatrists Fülöp Stein (1867–1917) and István Hollós, who were intensely active in the international temperance movement in the early 1900s. Under the leadership of Stein, who was a king's counsel, the Hungarian branch of an anti-alcohol Freemason lodge, part of the Good Templar order, was formed under the name *Egészség* (Health) in 1901. The Hungarian lodge considered its top priority to fight against alcohol. The Tenth International Congress Against Alcohol held in Budapest between 11 and 16 September 1905 was probably the biggest gathering of the age, with 1,000 registered participants. Among those attending were Ferenczi and Eugen Bleuler, the world-famous professor at the Burghölz Clinic, with whom Jung (1875–1961) worked as a young instructor. Through Bleuler, Stein established a working relationship with Jung regarding the examination of word associations. Stein included his young colleague from Budapest in his study of associations, and Ferenczi, with the intense curiosity and devotion that were so typical of him, attempted to find participants for these experiments wherever possible. He purchased a stopwatch, and from then on he sought participants everywhere. He enthusiastically conducted examinations in Budapest's cafés with writers, poets, painters, waiters, and cloakroom attendants (Harmat, 1994). Through his experiments with word associations, Ferenczi moved one step closer to psychoanalysis by bypassing the defensive bastions of psychological resistance through free association and, thus, rendered approachable those memories that had been expelled from the conscious mind.

He was likely to have met István Hollós for the first time during meetings of the Budapest Royal Medical Society.[15] They both lectured frequently during these meetings and sessions of the society's neurology and psychiatry section.[16] Hollós joined the temperance movement and fought tirelessly for the liberation of patients suffering from psychosis or mental illness—or, in today's parlance, for the recognition of their rights.[17] In 1906, Hollós established a group under the name *Új Élet* (New Life), part of the Hungarian branch of the Good Templar Freemasons lodge. The group operated within the framework of the Budapest-Lipótmező Hungarian Royal State Mental Institution, which would later be called the National Institute for Psychiatry and Neurology and was known as the Yellow House for its bright exterior (Kárpáti, cited in Takács, 2002). Hollós was considered to be a pioneer internationally both in applying psychoanalysis in psychiatry and in developing the "open-door system" in Hungary that provided humane conditions and opportunities for healing psychiatric patients.

In addition to his professional relationships, Ferenczi also was active in the *fin de siècle* literary and artistic world. He had been surrounded by the atmosphere of liberalism since his childhood years since his father's bookshop in Miskolc had formed the hub of the city's intellectual life, providing a meeting place for the local intelligentsia and artists travelling through. From the first decade of the century, Ferenczi was on friendly terms with Sándor Bródy,[18] Ignotus,[19] and Róbert Berény.[20]

In 1903, Bródy began *Jövendő* (Future), which was a weekly devoted to literature and politics and considered to be one of the forerunners to *Nyugat* (West). Ferenczi exposed a larger audience to current research and the history of the sciences through his articles in the natural science section (Zsoldos, 1996). Some of these writings had been published earlier in *Gyógyászat*, but it was felt that various articles called for a second printing for a lay readership. Bródy's suicide attempt in 1905 most probably contributed to the short life of the journal, but Ferenczi's devotion and inspiration—which was a source of strength in the recovery of the depressed writer—deepened their friendship for decades.

Lifelong friendships and working relationships evolved out of Ferenczi's many acquaintanceships in his youth. In conjunction with Lajos Lévy, István Hollós, Ignotus, and Sándor Radó, Ferenczi established the Hungarian Psychoanalytical Society in 1913 before the First World War, and it became the cradle of the Budapest School.[21] After his death two decades later, these peers were there to pay their final respects to Ferenczi. Lévy and Hollós were there from Budapest, Ignotus from Vienna, and Radó from New York (Mészáros, 2000a).

The main themes of Ferenczi's pre-analytic writing, much like his friendships, accompanied him throughout his career. The way he expressed himself, which captured his personality, interest, and world view—his openness, receptiveness, thirst for knowledge, sensitivity to social problems, rejection of authoritarian arguments, and guiding principle as a physician on the optimal collaboration between doctor and patient—makes one recognise the young physician in the internationally renowned analyst. It becomes clear, then, that these early features favoured the development of the psychoanalytic way of thinking that would characterise Ferenczi later.

Topics in Ferenczi's pre-analytic writings

Attempts at explaining the genesis of *dreams* are as old as humanity itself. In the early twentieth century, when efforts were made to grasp internal and external realities simultaneously and to interpret unconscious experiences, interest in dreams—which had already been a preoccupation within Romanticism—grew in both the arts and the sciences. Those interested were able to find a multiplicity of approaches in the contemporary European book market as well as in medical journals. Ferenczi expressed his keen interest in dreams for the first time in 1902, by reviewing a book by a psychiatrist in Rome named Sante de Sanctis:

> In the main, dream theory to date has only appeared in literature as an interesting subject of novels. But it could not avoid its fate. Scientific psychology has taken possession of it, as it has the other psychic processes, and has attempted to create a system out of the chaos of our knowledge of dreams using all the methods at its disposal: self-observation, the distribution of thousands of questionnaires, and experimentation. Of those who take on this tiring work, Professor de Sanctis occupies an outstanding place for the results of the diligent efforts he has made for over eight years ... [however] he deals little with the theory of dream formation. (Ferenczi, 1999j[1902], p. 134)

By then, Ferenczi must surely have heard of Freud's *The Interpretation of Dreams*. If he had not read the review of Freud's work published in *Orvosi Hetilap* at the beginning of 1901, he must have known of the book, since he had received a copy from Fülöp Stein earlier, which he returned unread. This can be explained by his personal confession, which was published with the honesty so characteristic of him after Ferenczi had met Freud: "why did the assumption of a purely sexual pathogenesis of the neuroses rouse such a strong aversion in me . . .?" (Ferenczi, 1980b[1908], p. 31). He felt such strong antipathy towards these ideas that he simply took no notice of Freud. It is safe to say that he not only ignored Freud's new approach regarding the pathogenesis of hysteria, but he also repressed everything tied to Freud (Lorin, 1983) and pushed Freud's work aside. The reviewer for *Orvosi Hetilap* (Anon, 1901) listed in vain all the revolutionary ideas in *The Interpretation of Dreams*, from the method of free association to the manifest and latent content of dreams to the essential concept of the interpretation of dreams, according to which dreams are nothing but desire or thought excluded from one's conscious mind, yet Ferenczi brushed all of this aside.

Ferenczi dealt with the Freudian approach to hysteria in the same way. He had also reached the point where he felt that treating hysteria with electricity was no different than "all the other procedures used to affect mood and imagination" (Ferenczi, 1999l[1904], p. 197), yet he ignored the works of Freud and Breuer, the unprecedented new approach to the phenomenon of hysteria (Freud, 1895d), and other studies by Freud published later on the same topic.

I am not suggesting that Freud's method of therapy met with a unanimously favourable reception in Hungarian medical circles at the beginning of the century, or that this was conveyed by journalists in *Orvosi Hetilap*. Opposing voices, on the other hand, who wanted nothing of Freud's therapy, could also be heard and, when push came to shove, they openly declared that it posed no problem at all for them if they did not reveal the real cause of hysteria but limited their medical efforts to mitigating the symptoms. The debate, however, had started—and without Ferenczi for the time being.

During this period, Ferenczi wrote a number of times about the possibilities of using hypnosis, but he did not even mention Freud's name in connection with this topic. He made references, however, to Möbius[22] since this German physician had had a great impact on Ferenczi's thinking on dreams, hypnosis, and characteristics of the female gender. Ferenczi's interest in hypnosis can be traced back to his teenage years, which he remembered years later with his usual self-deprecation:

> My first experiments with hypnosis, which I conducted while still in secondary school on the apprentices in my father's bookshop, proved successful without exception. I can hardly say the same for my later results: true, I lacked by then the absolute self-confidence that only ignorance could produce. (Ferenczi, 1910, p. 776)

Ferenczi was very circumspect in judging hypnosis. He himself used it with good results in connection with physical changes of psychological origin, various cases of hysteria, sleeping disorders, impotence of psychic origin, and states of anxiety. On the other hand, he found that this form of treatment was unsuccessful in treating obsession and traumatic neurosis. Ferenczi also discussed the responsibility of post-hypnotic suggestion and fought against a ministerial order that required the presence of a third party during hypnosis. His argument had a certain sarcastic simplicity: if a physician's integrity cannot be trusted with this particular consciousness-altering medical intervention, then it cannot be trusted with any. He pointed out that it was impossible to implement the order: "the fault is not in us but in the order" (Ferenczi, 1999n[1906], p. 265).

The few years he spent in Rókus Hospital were followed by his work at the neurology ward of the Erzsébet Poorhouse[23] from 1900, where he was finally able to deal with what he had always longed for. He enthusiastically jumped into the pathology and treatment of neurological and psychiatric diseases. Whatever case he encountered, he never separated the patient from the illness, and his talent as a clinical doctor, besides his intuitive skills noted so often, can be captured in this holistic way of thinking, among other things. Ferenczi was an excellent clinician, an outstanding diagnostician, and a physician with great intuitive skills, able to weigh numerous aspects of a case at the same time, but also quite a practical man. We might be surprised today to learn that it was Ferenczi who observed that it is a matter of life and death to pull forward the tongue when it slides backwards into the trachea in the case of a stroke patient who has lost consciousness, as a result of which the physician saves the patient from death by asphyxiation. Choking, therefore, as he pointed out, is far from being a primary consequence of a stroke (Ferenczi, 1999g[1901]). The way Ferenczi considered the patient and his or her illness as well as the future interests of the patient beyond recovery is a model for a careful and circumspect patient-centred approach. This is illustrated by his discussion of treating boils: the surgical approach to the infected area deals with the illness elegantly and immediately, but the scar that is thus created leaves the poor patient disfigured for life. Ferenczi's suggestion, therefore, was that instead of a scalpel the treatment should return to the ancient compress, especially in the case of women, where the aesthetic consequences of medical intervention should be taken into particular account.

His clinical strengths were also often demonstrated during psychoanalysis. Ferenczi's primary aim was to heal patients. He readily diverged from theory if it was unfruitful during therapy. This was the opposite of Freud's attitude. When curing patients, Freud always placed theoretical considerations first. He was not interested in healing itself; for him, practising psychoanalysis provided for his living expenses and represented an unlimited source for developing theory.

Ferenczi's tolerance, liberalism, and social sensitivity were most obvious in his attitude to sexual disorders and healing people who lived in poverty. In his writings, his circumspect consideration and tolerance of what was then considered sexual disorders are first expressed in connection with a transgendered patient. Ferenczi, in certain cases of sexual disorders—transsexuality and homosexuality—offered Darwin's theory of the survival of the fittest in order to mitigate feelings of antipathy and expressions of hostility and discrimination. He argued that these people, as a result of their illness, were unable to produce offspring and, therefore, did not create further social problems. Ferenczi clearly emphasised the lack of social harm in these conditions. We need not agree with the content of his argumentation to recognise the attempts of the humane and tolerant physician in his innovations. "Every sexual disorder is only a disorder in so far as and because it deviates from the order of sexual intercourse suited to the propagation of the species" (Ferenczi, 1999h[1902], p. 114). Outcasts wandered between "poorhouse, jail, vagrants' prison, and mental institution" (1999h[1902], p. 114) Those who were both mentally handicapped and suffered from sexual disorders had to find places and ways of life in which "they can enjoy a tolerable freedom, perhaps they can even work, and they are more or less protected from people's ill will and abuse" (1999h[1902], p. 114).

This represented a point of agreement for Ferenczi and Hollós, the Hungarian representative of humanist psychiatry of the age.

Ferenczi considered homosexuality a transitory sexual stage, a kind of developmental disorder that posed no danger to society. Therefore, as a representative of the Physicians' Circle (*Orvosi Kör*), he called on his peers to join the Memorandum of the Wissenschaftlich-Humanitäres Komitee[24] signed by 2,800 German physicians in 1905. Ferenczi agreed with many of them that, aside from qualified cases, acts of homosexuality between adults were neutral for society and that punishing them was unfair and unnecessary (Ferenczi, 1999m [1906]).

As a specialist at the neurology outpatient ward of the General Workers' Sick-Benefits Society[25] and later as its head, Ferenczi gained a great deal of experience in the myriad illnesses that do harm to the poor. Printers, textile workers, and others living under miserable circumstances sought treatment from him whenever he was on duty. Ferenczi believed that numerous illnesses arose from poor living conditions. For example, he stressed the primary role of lead, alcohol, and syphilis in early arteriosclerosis. He pointed out that it is a "social utopia" to think of prevention until machines replace human physical labour and as long as financial troubles overburden certain social strata. He considered resting the vascular system to be the only treatment for arteriosclerosis. Through the Workers' Sick-Benefits Society, he created an opportunity for patients to go on holiday in order to treat not only vascular but other traumatic neurotic cases that developed, for instance, as a result of accidents.

His personal feelings filter through his scholarly writings as well. This is the case in his article entitled "A szerelem a tudományban" (Love in science). No doubt an unusual collocation of words. He asked the question: What is love, actually? Love is a "borderland", he answered, between the healthy and ill states of the human mind. He reminded the reader of the depressed and manic states that "favour the imagination at the expense of the intellect", the greatest passion of mankind and inexhaustible source of the arts. Only poets and novelists had provided psychological approaches up to that time. Scholarly analysis with the strict procedure of a scientist was still to come. "The general pathology" of love had not been described. In forensic medicine, for example, when considering the extent to which a person was responsible for her or his actions, one should not only take into account mental constraints due to alcohol but also those due to love. As Ferenczi put it, "[i]n terms of being responsible for one's actions, it is all the same whether alcohol has clouded one's judgement or that far more powerful poison which we call love" (Ferenczi, 1999f[1901], p. 78).

Ferenczi could not have known that seventy years later a member of the Budapest School, Robert Bak, would look at love in a similar vein: "Self-love is completely absorbed by the object; the object replaces the ego-ideal, leaving the self unprotected, humble and sacrificial. The self is thus left open to injury" (Bak, 1973, p. 3).

Neither is it any coincidence that both of them suffered a great deal as a result of their not very harmonious relationships and neither of them had a child from these "poisoned states". Ferenczi mentioned the need for the exact psychological study of love while he was driven by the unveiled ironic doubt regarding the scientific approach to passion. Despite this, or perhaps along with it, Ferenczi described the special state of the merging of the ego—later the self—and the object in 1901, with which he placed within a dynamic field the experience of love and numerous psychopathological phenomena.

At this point, we are reminded of all the internal brakes whose restraining power eventually caused Ferenczi to forsake real love, a development foreshadowed by this early piece. These internal brakes can be regarded as an expression of the strict superego that regained their strength through Freud's prohibition and the bitter feeling of guilt after the flow of passion—but the outcome in the end was self-surrender.[26]

Ferenczi was ambivalent towards women. During this period, he enthusiastically shared Möbius's negative views about the female gender, according to which women, given their excessive instincts, were "confident and joyful creatures with no initiative. . . . Morality based on insight is inaccessible as far as they are concerned, and thinking simply ruins them" (Ferenczi, 1999d[1900], pp. 55–56). He went on to note: "longing from a distance, the power of imagination, and the desire for knowledge merely make a woman uneasy and distracts her from her motherly vocation" (p. 56).

Behind his ambivalence lies his relationship with his mother, from whom he received too little love and too much strictness. An attempt to analyse Ferenczi's need to be gentle toward women and his repressed aggression, however, would take us far from his pre-analytic writings. His childhood experiences had a fruitful impact on his psychoanalytic activities, as when, for example, he turned his attention to the significance of the early mother–child relationship. Nevertheless, the lack of this caused him a great deal of pain in his own private life. It is interesting that the liberal-minded Ferenczi agreed with Möbius's view on the female gender. This completely contradicted his firmly grounded liberalism, but offers an interesting example of the intrapsychic conflict that existed in him between his accepted values and repressed experiences. It was perhaps through the works of Möbius that the especially tolerant and enlightened Ferenczi expressed the unconscious pain that he experienced by the side of a very active, dominant mother as the eighth—emotionally much neglected—child when "the woman" failed to live up to the expectation of "being primarily a mother" (Ferenczi, 1999d[1900], p. 56). With regard to his mother, who he felt was "troubled in her vocation as a mother", Ferenczi wrote thirty years later in his *Clinical Diary*: "[My mother] wounded me most by claiming that I was killing her; that was the turning point at which, against my own inner conviction, I forced myself to be good, and obedient" (Ferenczi, 1988[1932], p. 99).

Ferenczi's softening towards Freud might have been influenced—although we do not know this with certainty—by his meeting with Jung, who, by that time, enjoyed a close relationship with Freud. It is a fact, however, that his opposition had relaxed so much by 1907 that he finally read *The Interpretation of Dreams*. Afterwards, he immediately shared Fülöp Stein's wish to meet the Viennese physician. Jung mediated between Stein and Freud in a letter dated 28 June 1907:

> Dr. Stein of Budapest and another mental specialist, Dr. Ferenczi, want to visit you sometime in Vienna and have asked me to inquire when it would be most convenient to you. Dr. Stein is a very decent fellow with a good intelligence, who has done some experimental work with me. He is still something of a beginner in the art, but has grasped the essentials surprisingly quickly and put them into practice. (Jung to Freud, Jung [1907] 1994, pp. 65–66).

Ferenczi put pen to paper on 18 January 1908 and very happily thanked Freud for receiving him in Stein's company without having met him before (Brabant, Falzeder, & Giampieri-Deutsch, 1993, p. 1). After this, in a few lines to Ferenczi on 30 January 1908, Freud invited both of them to Vienna to his home in Berggasse 19 at 3 o'clock in the afternoon on 2 February 1908 (Brabant, Falzeder, & Giampieri-Deutsch, 1993, pp. 2–3).

This Sunday visit brought about a turn in the history of psychoanalysis. Freud might have expected a fairly pleasant meeting with two unknown but interested peers from Budapest. Prior to the meeting, Freud might have imagined that Stein was the more promising of the two, since Stein had been following his work for years and had long been preparing to meet him. In Budapest, Ferenczi also could not have thought that then and there, during an afternoon discussion, he would find the missing link that would aid him in understanding a whole series of neurotic diseases. The new organising principle: the various ways of indirectly acting on sexual desires as forms of expression with compromises of unconscious conflicts immediately shed light on symptoms that were chaotic and did not fit the pathology of mental or organic diseases. Freud was amazed by the flexibility and creativity of Ferenczi's thinking. They became friends for decades and—despite all their later differences—inseparable from the point of view of the development of psychoanalysis. Ferenczi joined the discourse developed by Freud which "represented not only ... the discovery of the unconscious and the development of a new method in therapy, but also the grounding of a new mode of discourse" (Erős, 2004, p. 11, translated for this edition). Ferenczi shaped this special discourse and, with a number of innovations, became the precursor to modern psychoanalytic theory and practice.

After Ferenczi and Stein's visit, events speeded up both in Budapest and Vienna. On 28 March 1908 at the Budapest Royal Medical Society, Ferenczi held his first lecture on psychoanalysis entitled "Neuroses in the light of Freud's investigations and psycho-analysis" and Freud, in the spring, responding to Ferenczi and Stein's proposal, mounted the first international meeting of psychoanalysts in Salzburg.

CHAPTER TWO

The forming of the Budapest School (1908–1918)

> "[Ferenczi,] who is a close acquaintance of mine, and who is familiar, to an extent that few others arc [sic, are], with all the difficulties of psycho-analytic problems, is the first in Hungary to undertake the task of creating an interest in psycho-analysis among doctors and men of education in his own country through writings composed in their mother tongue. It is our cordial wish that this attempt of his may succeed and may result in gaining for this new field of work new workers from the body of his compatriots"
>
> (Freud, 1910b)

How did Budapest become suited to serve as the potential hub of psychoanalysis in Europe in the space of a decade? What happy congruence of motives spurred on this explosive growth?

In addition to Ferenczi's own considerable efforts, we can identify a number of forces of modernisation that not only encouraged the growth of the Budapest School, but also shaped the economic, scholarly, and cultural development of Hungary in the first two decades of the twentieth century. A young avant-garde intelligentsia was ready for the changes offered by modernisation, and many would later become leading figures of the scholarly and cultural legacy of the last century.

Already a seasoned professional in terms of his experience and achievements in psychiatry, neurology, and general medicine, Ferenczi met Freud at the age of thirty-five. An expert in forensic medicine, Ferenczi headed the neurology polyclinic that was part of Hungary's Occupational Health Care Benefit Fund. He was fascinated by unconscious phenomena and psychic disorders. He sought organising principles to explain the psychological mechanisms that lie behind symptoms of non-organic neurological illnesses and even searched for phenomena that were beyond the ken of contemporary science.

Freud's system of ideas represented a compelling response to a number of unanswered questions. It also provided organising principles to grasp such myriad observable facts of everyday life as dream activity, forgetting, parapraxis, and the phenomena of "semi-conscious elements" (Ferenczi, 1999a[1899]), by which experiences are blocked out of the individual's consciousness. Just as these phenomena were becoming better understood, so, too, were various forms of sexual deviance and neurosis being seen in a new light. Clearly, Ferenczi was considering this notion of seeing things in a different light as he was formulating the title for his first article on psycho-analysis, "Actual and psycho-neuroses in the light of Freud's investigations and psycho-analysis" (Ferenczi, 1980b[1908])—though this is certainly more striking in the original Hungarian.[27] This study is noteworthy in a number of respects. First, it is a textbook example of Ferenczi's self-reflection mentioned earlier. In a later recognition of his earlier self, he confessed that he had rejected Freud's theories "so rashly at that time" (p. 31). He went on to ponder: "why did the assumption of a purely sexual pathogenesis of the neuroses rouse such a strong aversion in me?" (p. 31). Second, through this study, Ferenczi demonstrated a new way of presenting psychoanalysis: reach the widest possible audience. A paper he gave at the Royal Medical Society of Budapest was published that spring in the medical journal *Gyógyászat* (Therapy). It was from that point on that the journal was prepared to communicate developments in psychoanalysis to its physician readership.

Like Freud, Ferenczi viewed psychoanalysis as a theory, a therapeutic tool, a way of thinking, and a framework for understanding the diverse manifestations of human nature. Freud stressed the relationship between psychoanalysis and culture, while Ferenczi created an opportunity to spread the new discipline through various forums into the culture of Budapest's *avant-garde* intelligentsia. For a time, these channels made the new science available to various social strata with some degree of regularity. Importantly, this was entirely unique in Europe at the time.

At the turn of the century, a receptive Hungarian intelligentsia was open to the changes offered by modernisation, while both the sciences and the fine arts were embracing new directions and understandings.[28] With the unification of Budapest out of the once separate cities of Buda, Pest, and Óbuda in 1873, it became possible to set up institutions that represented the sort of development that inspired hope in young intellectuals returning home from their studies in Vienna or Paris—in some cases living away from home long enough to fully grasp what changes were needed in their homeland and how they might be put in place. Budapest now had a Music Academy, Opera House, and Folk Theatre, and, in addition to all this, an intelligentsia hungry for modernisation was establishing journals, groups, and other forums that served to inspire intellectuals open to new ideas that moved beyond the previous traditions of their still semi-feudal country.

A new perspective was introduced to literature primarily through generations of contributors to the literary journal *Nyugat* (literally "West")—including, first, writers and poets such as Endre Ady, Zsigmond Móricz, and Dezső Kosztolányi and, later, Gyula Illyés, Attila József, and Sándor Márai. In music, the groundwork was laid for a young generation that would set a new course for that art form in the twentieth century, including composers Béla Bartók, Zoltán Kodály, and Leó Weiner. In the fine arts, around 1909, a group of painters known as the Eight,[29] with figures like Károly Kernstok, Róbert Berény, Ödön Márffy, Béla Czóbel, and Lajos Tihanyi, introduced Hungary to such revolutionary modes of expression as Art Nouveau and the artistic trend of the Wild Ones, shook up Vienna's conservative academism, and took the artists' quarters of Paris by storm.

Ferenczi as catalyst

Freud saw great hope in the chance for further development. In the foreword to Ferenczi's first volume on psychoanalysis, published in 1910, he described Ferenczi as

> the first in Hungary to undertake the task of creating an interest in psycho-analysis among doctors and men of education in his own country through writings composed in their mother tongue. It is our cordial wish that this attempt of his may succeed and may result in gaining for this new field of work new workers from the body of his compatriots. (Freud, 1910b)

Ferenczi became a key figure in the evolving psychoanalytic movement, both domestically and internationally. It was at his recommendation that the International Psychoanalytical Association was formed in 1910. He was Freud's friend and a member of his inner circle of close colleagues, the Wednesday Society. Freud was a person who thought in methodically built structures and systems, and he saw in Ferenczi a partner in his efforts to bring the movement to completion. Freud knew that their work would need exposure among their peers internationally but still preferred "secret circles", while Ferenczi was much more a man of plenaries. Indeed, Ferenczi made use of every available contemporary forum to spread the message of psychoanalysis. These forums—or, in today's parlance, these media—ran the gamut from print journals and public lectures to the popular press.

Psychoanalysis in the media

Through Ferenczi's network, four forums were ready at very short notice to spread the ideas of psychoanalysis: the medical journal *Gyógyászat* (Therapy) and the literary journal *Nyugat* (West) (both mentioned above), the Free University for the Social Sciences, and the Galileo Circle. These were rounded out by the social sciences journal *Huszadik Század* (Twentieth Century) and the Society for the Social Sciences. The instantaneous effect of these forums cannot be overstated. The first decade of the twentieth century witnessed not only the first Freud–Ferenczi meeting, but also saw, in that very same year of 1908, the writer Ignotus's co-founding of *Nyugat* with fellow writer

Miksa Fenyő and critic and writer Ernő Osvát. It was also in that year that the Galileo Circle was formed, and one year later, the Free University for the Social Sciences was established. It was also around that time that the Eight set out to renew Hungarian painting. Among its members, Róbert Berény was a friend of Ferenczi's and an early adherent of psychoanalysis.

Gyógyászat was of invaluable use in communicating the message of psychoanalysis. So, too, was *Nyugat* under editor-in-chief Ignotus (Hugó Veigelsberg, 1869–1949), in so far as, beyond the world of literature, it filled its pages with the variety of other intellectual endeavours, including psychoanalysis, that also characterised that age. Many among the generations of *Nyugat* established personal ties to psychoanalysis, and many of these writers developed friendships with Ferenczi. Aside from Ignotus, these included Dezső Kosztolányi, Frigyes Karinthy, and Sándor Márai.

Psychoanalysis pointed beyond the healing of illnesses of the psyche. It represented a new approach that placed the functioning of the human psyche, personality development, social relations, and the complex system of relations tied to culture in a new light. Ferenczi shared this new approach with his receptive writer and artist friends. Ignotus described the cultural and scholarly complexity of the day and the transformative atmosphere inhabited by the avant-garde intelligentsia as follows:

> After Ferenczi's first writings came out, he, the Freudian, and I, the "*West*erner", got together day in day out at the Eight's exhibition in Róbert Berény's studio and garden in Városmajor [in Budapest]. Berény had also just emerged, and joining us . . . was the young Doctor Radó, who was a lawyer at the time . . . . We would discuss Ferenczi's amazing observations and conclusions throughout the afternoon and evening and into the next morning, along with Einstein's [theory of] relativity, which had taken the world by storm around the same time—and the next day we were already thinking differently than we had been before. (Ignotus, 2000[1933], p. 38, translated for this edition)

As György Kassai points out, "[i]t would be difficult to identify any other literary journals that have played a role in the history of psychoanalysis—*Nyugat* would appear to be the only example" (Kassai, 1990, p. 171). Indeed, *Nyugat* was publishing studies tied to psychoanalysis as of 1912. Ferenczi opened what would become a series with a piece entitled "A letter from Goethe to Schopenhauer in psychoanalytic terms" (Ferenczi, 2000a[1912]). This was followed by an article by István Hollós, "About a patient who recites poems" (Hollós, 1990a[1914]), in which he used a psychoanalytic approach to examine the poet's creativity. Then, in his study "Psychoanalysis and the spirit of a nation", Hollós explored the use of Hungarian words and expressions associated with dreams (Hollós, 1929).[30] His intention was to demonstrate to scholars in Hungary who had rejected psychoanalysis that the spirit of the Hungarian people reveals itself through its language usage and, thus, to vindicate Freud's dream theory (Takács, 2002). For example, he pointed out that, in exploring dreams, Hungarian uses the word *álomfejtés*, which suggests the solving of a puzzle or the decoding of a message, whereas it could just as well have coined the term *álomértelmezés*, which would approximate to the German *Traumdeutung* and the English *interpretation of dreams* (Hollós, 1929). The interpretation of dreams is, in fact, a method of *decoding* the condensed images to discover their symbolic meanings, which leads to an understanding of the unconscious processes of the dreamer. *Nyugat* proudly put out a study written by Freud and published *first* in Hungarian. Submitted with Freud's compliments to the journal, it was entitled "A difficulty in the path of psycho-analysis" (Freud, 1917a). One of Freud's notions, so often cited even to this day, first appeared in this study. According to Freud, "[t]he universal narcissism of men, their self-love, has up to the present suffered three severe blows from the researches of science": when Copernicus discovered that the Earth does not exercise control over the universe; when Darwin recognised that "[m]an is not a being different from animals or superior to them"; and when psychoanalysis pointed out that "[t]he ego feels uneasy; it comes up against limits to its power in its own house, the mind" (pp. 138–140).

Freud saw this study published as the First World War dragged on into its third year. As for so many others in Europe, this was a time of deprivation for Freud and his family. Groceries meant a great deal more than money in the middle of the war with the starving citizens of Vienna hard-pressed to get hold of any foodstuffs whatsoever. So it was that in 1916 Freud asked Ignotus to pay him his honorarium in the form of potatoes, given the shortages of the war.

Prof Dr Freud
Berggasse 19
Vienna

26/4/16

Dear Doctor,

I enclose the article as promised. I am not entirely certain if it is suitable in its present form, perhaps I will hear at some point that translating it was more than you had bargained for. In these troubled times, nothing merrier than this springs to mind.

I was entirely serious about being happy to accept my honorarium in groceries, particularly potatoes, if it can be arranged. Just today, I gave my paper the apt title "the potato casserole study".

My warmest regards to you and your lovely wife, who was prevented from accompanying you.

Most faithfully yours,

Freud

(See reproduction of original letter on the following page.)

Ferenczi was convinced that the insights provided by psychoanalysis were not merely suitable to changing social relations, but also to improving society, provided it was possible to optimise the restrictions, the excessive regulation, and the unnecessary constraints—be they in educating children (Ferenczi, 1980j[1908]), in coexisting as a society, or even in criminal psychology. As Ferenczi put it, "[i]t is senseless to sacrifice to the community a greater share of personal happiness than is absolutely necessary" (Ferenczi, 1980c[1913], p. 432). In a pithy contrast, he observed that "[d]octor and judge busy themselves with the Sisyphus [sic] task of curing and patching past and recurring evils; we could only begin to speak of a real advance if there were a social prophylaxis for these evils" (p. 432).

After all, he pointed out, "society's method of repressing emotions contributes a great deal to the ills of society"[31] (Ferenczi, 1982[1914], p. 172, translated for this edition). He concluded,

> The paroxysms of revolutions and wars are like hysterical discharges of pent-up primitive instincts ... Between anarchy and communism ... there must be somewhere a reasonable individual–socialistic juste

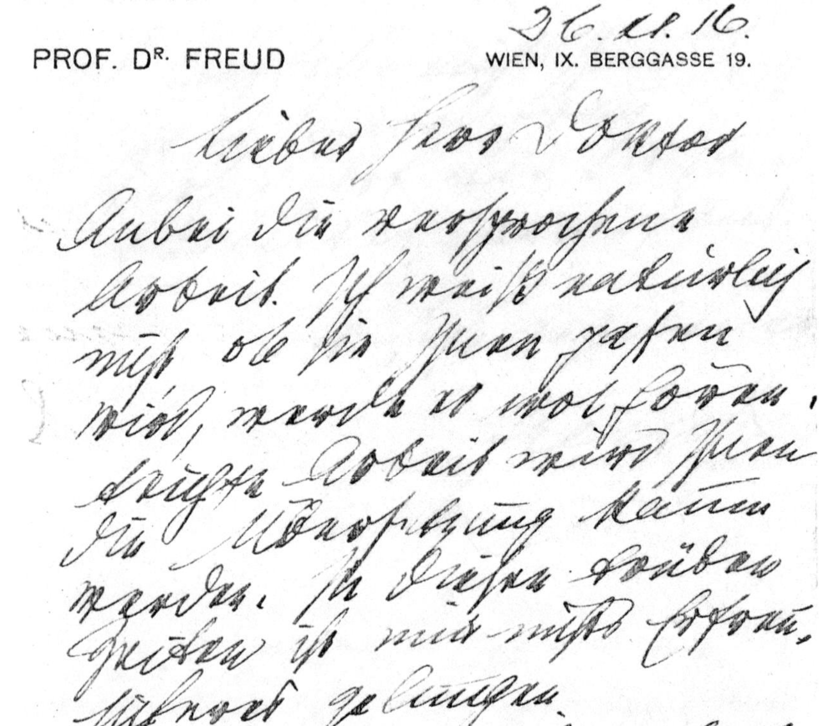
PROF. Dr. FREUD
WIEN, IX. BERGGASSE 19.

Letter from Freud to Ignotus, 26 April 1916.
Courtesy of the Petőfi Literary Museum, Budapest.

milieu that cares also for individual welfare as well as for the interests of society, that cultivates the sublimation instead of the repression of instincts. (1980c[1913], p. 433)

The intellectual firmament of the early twentieth century produced a number of societies and so-called free, or open, universities. The Society for the Social Sciences was formed in 1901 and became the most significant progressive workshop in Hungary. It was closely associated with the journal *Huszadik Század* (Twentieth Century), which had been established by social scientist (and future politician and professor) Oszkár Jászi and which also published pieces on psychoanalysis. This society set up the Free University for the Social Sciences, at which Ferenczi delivered lectures as of 1909. He gave a talk entitled "Psychic problems" several times that year.

Ferenczi reported to Freud on his efforts to educate the public: "The local Society for the Social Sciences has asked me to give four lectures on psychological subjects next semester" (Brabant, Falzeder, & Giampieri, 1993, p. 54). Those topics were as follows: the psychopathology of everyday life, the interpretation of dreams, sexual theory, and the psychological and pathological roles of sexuality. In 1910, Ferenczi told Freud of a new invitation: "In twelve days I am giving a lecture about 'Jokes' in the sociological 'Free School'" (Brabant, Falzeder, & Giampieri, 1993, p. 225). The first sociology workshops in Hungary, the Society for the Social Sciences and the Twentieth Century Circle, were highly responsive to ideas offered by psychoanalysis, which, "far from being a psychology of speculation and idealism ... proved perfectly suited to providing the foundation for a radical social critique" (Erős, 2000, pp. 18–19, translated for this edition).

Psychoanalysis came into contact with medical students through members of the Galileo Circle. Through them, Ferenczi's efforts would bear fruit within a decade. These students soon launched a process that would succeed in making psychoanalysis part of the curriculum for all future physicians at the university in Budapest. The Galileo Circle had actually been formed by students of medicine and engineering with an expressly bourgeois radical approach for the purpose of putting an end to the anti-culturalism of their semi-feudal country. They saw their efforts as a wake-up call for humanity, efforts that aimed at changing dimension rather than direction. Károly Polányi, Mihály Polányi's brother, was its founding president. It was

Mihály Polányi[32] who would emigrate and eventually assist Michael Balint (1896–1970) and his wife Alice Balint (1899–1939) in resettling in the United Kingdom in the late 1930s.

Ferenczi held his first lecture for the Circle in October 1909. Many later psychoanalysts joined the group: Imre Hermann, Jenő Hárnik, Lilli Hajdu, who was its president for a time, and her husband, Miklós Gimes, who would become a paediatrician and eventually an analyst candidate in the 1930s. The Galileo Circle did not merely set up lectures by key thinkers in Hungary and Europe, it also published pamphlets with the latest findings from both the social and natural sciences. Members shared a strong bond as well as clear ethical norms. For example, everyone—even the poorest student—made certain to pay her or his membership dues (Kende, 1974).

Many of the group of friends that later developed into the Sunday Circle with its own philosophical identity also became psychoanalysts, including Géza Révész, René Árpád Spitz, and Edit Rényi, who was later well known professionally as Edit Gyömrői.[33]

Five years after Ferenczi met Freud, he established the Hungarian Psychoanalytical Society (the Freud Society) on 19 May 1913. The names of the four other founding members have already been mentioned, but their areas of training might well be of interest here: Lajos Lévy was an internist, István Hollós a psychiatrist, Ignotus a writer, and Sándor Radó a lawyer, who was also studying medicine at the time. The founders represented a variety of disciplines, therefore, and this was emblematic of the interdisciplinary openness of the Budapest School.

A year after the Hungarian Psychoanalytical Society was founded, the First World War broke out. Despite this additional hardship, the Hungarian movement had, by war's end, developed a thriving psychoanalytic society consisting of members from a range of scholarly areas. These included physicians Lajos Lévy, István Hollós, Jenő Hárnik, and Zsigmond Pfeifer (1889–1945), an ethnographer, Géza Róheim (1891–1953), an economist, Jenő Varga (1879–1964), a poet, journalist, and attorney, Géza Szilágyi (1875–1958), a writer, Ignotus, a publisher, Dick Manó, and a chemist and brewery owner, Antal Freund of Tószeg. Curiously, Ernest Jones (1879–1958), the president of the British Psychoanalytical Society and later the International Psychoanalytical Association, was a member of the Hungarian Psychoanalytical Society in 1918. It is important to note that not everyone who joined the society was a practising analyst. Many felt a certain commitment to psychoanalysis and backed the movement with whatever means were available to them. For instance, Dick Manó was responsible for the early success of psychoanalytic book publishing and, several years later, Antal Freund of Tószeg made a substantial donation that would represent an enormous boost to the growth of psychoanalysis as a whole. In 1918, this small team of nineteen—the society's entire membership—constituted the first-generation core of the Budapest School.

Certain characteristics of the Budapest School began to gel, in particular its interdisciplinary organisation and openness and the presence of what were called lay analysts, thus resulting in its members each approaching psychoanalysis from a different perspective and, at the same time, each applying ideas from psychoanalysis to her or his own scholarly field. For example, this enabled psychoanalytic anthropology to develop, its first practitioner being Géza Róheim. It also made it possible for psychoanalysis to be incorporated into early childhood education in Budapest, including certain kindergarten programmes, where psychoanalytic aspects of dealing with children figured prominently. A two-sided internal relationship was established between psychoanalysis, which had now formed part of the culture, on the one hand, and literature and the writers associated with *Nyugat*, on the other. This fruitful collaboration became almost imperceptibly engrained in the culture of the city's intelligentsia. Among the educated of Budapest, an understanding of expressions of the unconscious trickled into their way of thinking and speaking. It surfaced in everyday jokes and banter. Psychoanalysis was woven into the conversations in the cafés of Budapest and even appeared in a folk song parody:

> With my pretty little instinct
> Nesting in the trees,
> I scrub my inhibition
> Clean at Ferenczi's.[34]

Compared to other large European cities, such as Vienna, Zurich, and Moscow, where psychoanalytic societies were also being formed in the late 1910s, Budapest was truly unique in the degree to which psychoanalysis had become embedded in the culture.

Ferenczi laboured tirelessly, publishing his new theoretical and therapeutic approaches, chiefly in Hungarian and German. His writings would become the building blocks of psychoanalysis. His studies appeared not only in scholarly journals, but also in books, thus becoming accessible to a broader Hungarian public as well. By 1918, his writings could be found in three volumes: Psychoanalysis (1910); Psychic Problems in the Light of Psychoanalysis (1912); and The Appearance and Disappearance of Nervous Symptoms and Other Studies in Psychoanalysis (1914).[35]

At the same time, Freud's writings gradually became available in Hungarian. It is in this period that the first Hungarian translation of Freud's work was published in 1912, his "Five lectures on psychoanalysis", originally delivered at Clark University in Worcester, Massachusetts, in 1909, and a primer, "On dreams"[36] (Freud, 1901a), in which he aimed to make findings from dream research publicly accessible. Work was proceeding apace on the Hungarian translation of Freud's original *The Interpretation of Dreams* (Freud, 1900a), to which István Hollós also contributed. For lack of funds, however, the Hungarian version of the book would not find its way on to Budapest's shelves until 1935.

Despite all the stumbling blocks thrown up by four years of war, Ferenczi carried on his work in psychoanalysis as an army physician. If psychoanalysis was a "new human view", as Ignotus called it, then, come what may, this would be the view to take. This was certainly always the view Ferenczi took. This is how both his theoretical approach to neuroses born of war trauma and his therapeutic experiments in that area developed as of 1916. Ferenczi described a host of neurotic processes that had arisen under the effect of traumatic experiences that can be categorised among the pathomechanisms of conversion hysteria (Ferenczi, 1980d[1916/1917]). He recognised that war trauma can bring about changes in an individual's personality, that symptoms of trauma occur in a number of organic diseases without any organic changes taking place, and that trauma suffered even by someone physically sound might, in fact, bring on long-term anxiety accompanied by irrational fears. Military hospitals, therefore, needed to learn to deal with trauma caused by war and with post traumatic stress disorder (PTSD), to use the current nomenclature. Ferenczi's experience with war neuroses would soon draw the attention of various Austro-Hungarian imperial military offices, which was

A medical officer's plaquette in commemoration of the military honour Ferenczi received, 1916. Archives of the Sándor Ferenczi Society & International Ferenczi Centre, Budapest.

further intensified by Ferenczi's active role at the Fifth International Psychoanalytical Congress, held in Budapest in the autumn of 1918.

By 1918, psychoanalysis had clearly moved beyond the confines of the analyst's office; it had become an integral part of the thinking among intellectuals. In the last year of the war, Dezső Kosztolányi published an interview that he had conducted with Ferenczi.[37] Through Ferenczi, the writer was seeking answers from psychoanalysis on the causes of the war. He wanted to know whether there was hope that "we could somehow avoid war" (Kosztolányi, 2000[1918],

p. 193). Ferenczi took the position that "if war can be defeated anywhere, it can certainly be defeated in the nursery" (p. 192). While this may reflect an idealistic view of society, from the point of view of psychoanalysis, long-term progress leads to a shift within the analyst towards an educator's perspective. Ferenczi was convinced that remedying society's problems lay in reforming the way children are brought up. He felt that future generations should not be raised to repress their instincts and that the banner of the idealised adult should stop being waved high as young people are forced to curb instincts already subjected to what today would be called a sort of strict and false superego.

In addition to engaging in his own theoretical and therapeutic work, Ferenczi acted as a sort of manager of Hungary's psychoanalytic movement. He either seized or created opportunities to spread the psychoanalytic way of thinking as widely as possible, and, with his liberal make-up, reinforced during the Schächter period, he naturally threw open the doors to people from a variety of disciplines and included them in the world of psychoanalysis, never standing in the way of their efforts to cultivate their talents in their own fields. This led to a number of interdisciplinary links that helped to shape the character of the Budapest School. A chief characteristic of the School was the diverse network tied primarily to the person of Ferenczi.

Ferenczi's role as catalyst was as necessary for a rapid and efficient development that went beyond the bounds of the field of psychoanalysis, as indeed was the close co-operation of the newly initiated. Typical of Freud's assessment of his Hungarian colleague—originally written in 1914 in "On the history of the psychoanalytic movement"— was that "Hungary, so near geographically to Austria, and so far from it scientifically, has produced only one collaborator, S. Ferenczi, but one that indeed outweighs a whole society" (Freud, 1914d, p. 32).

After four years, Freud would completely change his view on the situation in Budapest. During a holiday on Lake Štrba among the High Tatra Mountains in what is today Slovakia, Freud wrote a letter to Karl Abraham dated 27 August 1918, in which he saw Budapest becoming the hub of psychoanalysis (Falzeder, 2002, p. 381). In his book on Freud, Ernest Jones placed great emphasis on this idea; Jones (1955, p. 197) even reported that "Freud declared" that Budapest would "be the 'centre of the psychoanalytic movement'". During the period in which this "declaration" was made, Freud would not have been aware of numerous unseen events that would eventually justify his instincts, and neither could anyone have known of developments to come that eventually stood in the way of, and indeed prevented, the realisation of the ideas of Freud, Ferenczi, and the Budapest analysts, and, beyond that, launched an irreversible process that would have a far-reaching effect on the future of the movement.

CHAPTER THREE

"Budapest will now become the headquarters of our movement"[38]

"Ferenczi has become the first official university teacher [in] ΨA, (o.ö. Professor),[39] a success not dreamt before!"

(Freud, 1919j)

The Fifth International Psychoanalytical Congress

Originally, the site selected for the Fifth International Psychoanalytical Congress was Breslau (now Wrocław, Poland), but this plan had to be changed because of the difficulties of transport during the war. Thus, it fell to Budapest to host the international gathering, which was held on 28–29 September 1918. Conference preparations were painstaking, with news of the event being reported in mid-May in *Gyógyászat* (Therapy): Ferenczi points to the main theme of the conference in the title of his paper "The psychoanalysis of war neuroses" (Anon, 1918a, p. 488).

The ten-month period following the conference between late September 1918 and mid-July 1919 saw outstanding achievements in the Hungarian psychoanalytic movement that represented the culmination of a decade's work. This era is perhaps the most widely

40 FERENCZI AND BEYOND

V. Internationaler Psychoanalytischer Kongress in Budapest 1918.

Allgemeines:

Der für den 21. und 22. September nach Breslau einberufene psychoanalytische Kongress kann wegen Verkehrs- und Verpflegungsschwierigkeiten nicht in Deutschland stattfinden. Infolgedessen hat sich das unterzeichnete vorbereitende Komité dahin geeignet, dass

der V. internationale psychoanalytische Kongress in Budapest abgehalten wird.

Als Kongresstage sind der **28. und 29. September 1918** bestimmt worden. Anmeldungen wollen **sofort** an Dr. S. *Ferenczi*, in Budapest, Hotel Royal, woselbst der Kongress auch abgehalten wird, gerichtet werden.

Auswärtige Teilnehmer werden insbesondere aufmerksam gemacht, sich im Interesse rechtzeitiger Wohnungsbeschaffung umgehend bei Dr. Ferenczi an obiger Adresse anzumelden.

Programm:

Der Kongress wird Fragen der **Vereins-Organisation,** der wissenschaftlichen **Propaganda** und des Ausbaues der **Vereinszeitschrift** beraten.

Für die **wissenschaftlichen Sitzungen** wurden folgende **Vorträge** angemeldet:

Dr. Karl *Abraham*, Militärarzt (dzt. Allenstein, Ostpreussen):
Titel noch nicht feststehend.

Dr. van *Emden* (Haag, Holland):
Analyse einer Sensation am Kopfe im Traum

K. u. Regimentsarzt Dr. S. *Ferenczi* (Budapest):
Die Kriegsneurosen u. ihre Psychoanalyse.
(Referat mit anschliessender Diskussion).

Univ. Prof. Dr. S. *Freud* (Wien):
Zur Analyse der Homosexualität.

Dr. Marton *Jellinek* (Budapest):
Über die Freundschaft.
Ethnologische Studie.

Dr. van *Ophuysen* (Haag, Holland):
Die Frigidität des Weibes.

Pfarrer Dr. Oskar *Pfister* (Zürich):
Die primitiven Grundlagen der höchsten Gefühle.

Dr. Otto *Rank*:
Mythus und Märchen.

Dr. Theodor *Reik* (dzt. im Felde):
Psychoanalytische Studien zur Bibelexegese III.

Dr. Géza *Roheim* (Budapest):
Das Selbst. Eine völkerpsychologische Studie.

Dr. I. *Sadger* (Wien):
Neue Forschungen zum Kastrationskomplex.

K. u. k. Oberarzt Dr. Victor *Jausk* (dzt. Belgrad):
Psychoanalyse der Urteilsfunktion.

Das vorbereitende Komité.

Poster for the 5th International Psychoanalytic Congress, 28–29 September 1918, Budapest. Archives of the Sándor Ferenczi Society & International Ferenczi Centre, Budapest.

studied in the history of psychoanalysis in Hungary (Erős, 2004; Erős, Kapás, Kiss, & Giampieri Spanghero, 1987; Harmat, 1994; Kapronczay & Kiss, 1986). In this chapter, therefore, I wish to focus on certain aspects of the period in order to demonstrate that the process through which psychoanalysis grew into an academic discipline taught at university level in Budapest was, beyond doubt, the outcome of a systematic evolution and did not happen by accident. Neither was it elevated to that level merely out of the fervour of the revolutions of the day. Psychoanalysis in Hungary had reached a point in its development at which this was inevitable. Freud's observation about the central role of Budapest was not merely a reference to the situation offered by a congress. It pointed to real prospects.

In the closing months of the war, the question naturally arose: can psychoanalysis contribute to the healing of the numerous diseases and mental disorders that stem from war trauma? As a number of analysts—including Ferenczi, István Hollós, Max Eitingon (1881–1943), and Karl Abraham (1877–1925)—had been pressed into service during the conflict, they managed to acquire a great deal of personal experience. Ferenczi and Abraham were active in experimenting with new methods of treatment for war trauma. This is how the central theme of the conference came to be the psychoanalytic treatment of war neuroses. As we have seen before, Ferenczi had been working on this problem since 1916 and raised the issue of the institutionalisation of the treatment of the war injured, in particular the rehabilitation of patients who had undergone organic changes. The idea of institutional psychotherapy was first voiced in connection with this in 1915 in a letter from Ferenczi to Freud dated 24 July: "The therapy in such institutes is partly exercise therapy . . . partly psychotherapy" (Brabant, Falzeder, & Giampieri-Deutsch, p. 71). The Austro-Hungarian Imperial High Command showed interest in this new method of healing, since they saw the enormous need to find proper treatment for veterans. They even designated sites where the psychoanalytic method was to be made available to treat war trauma (Erős, 2007).

The congress was held in the bastion of Hungarian scholarship, the headquarters of the Hungarian Academy of Sciences. This fact, in and of itself, signified a recognition of psychoanalysis. István Bárczy, Mayor of Budapest, also lent the field his support by opening this international gathering. The presence of the members of Hungary's Ethnographic Society also highlighted the interdisciplinary interest in psychoanalysis. In Hungary, both *Gyógyászat* and *Világ* (World),[40] a middle-class radical daily, reported on the congress.

In his paper, Ferenczi clearly argued that traumatic neuroses were not caused by *organic* neurological changes. They were, in fact, functional illnesses; that is, neurotic symptoms that had come about through states of anxiety or through the formation of conversion symptoms. His earlier findings, through which he concluded that traumatic neuroses progressed along the pathomechanisms of hysteria, were supplemented by another concept: the development of symptoms through narcissistic regression. Ferenczi believed that the psyche manifested itself in the body generally, that the body was a sort of surface filled with symbols, the hidden messages of which could be revealed through psychoanalysis. Traumatic neuroses—pains, paralysis, inhibitions, and unjustified fears and anxieties—showed the dynamism of narcissistic regression and/or conversion hysteria, according to Ferenczi. In his approach, patients reached a phase in the development of the ego through a regression, which was supposed to service a lost sense of security. As a consequence of negative experiences, the

> sexual hunger (libido) of the patients is withdrawn from the object into the ego. There thus comes about a damming-up of the sexual hunger (libido) in the ego, which is expressed in those abnormal hypochondriacal organic sensations and over-sensitiveness. (Ferenczi, 1921[1918], p. 18)

Ferenczi's theory of regression recognisably integrated Haeckel's theoretical model of ontogeny and phylogeny, according to which the development of the individual repeated the evolution of species, as expressed in the catchphrase "Ontogeny recapitulates phylogeny". Ferenczi believed that this process was flexibly bidirectional for the operation of the psyche: during regression, the development of the individual became reversed and the individual fell back to former stages of her or his own ego development. Moreover, as Ferenczi developed in his bioanalysis, which became very popular as *Thalassa: A Theory of Genitality* (Ferenczi, 1989[1924]), the experience that accompanied regression symbolically led one to the beginning of individual and ontogenetic existence. Regression, thus, took the individual to a former, still peaceful state, and some of the traumatic neuroses used this very regressive mode of functioning to protect the individual through the dysfunction of a particular part of the body from exposing herself or himself to a traumatic situation again, one which could threaten the individual's life. Naturally, the individual was unaware of this process, felt desperate, and suffered because of these dysfunctions.

The success of the Budapest congress strengthened the community of Hungarian psychoanalysts and gained even more widespread support for psychoanalysis itself. Personal and professional recognition of Ferenczi was expressed in a vote of the members of the International Psychoanalytical Association (IPA) to elect him as their next president. While the military leadership of the Central Powers could not put their planned military healthcare programme into practice, they integrated the experiences of the conference and, within days, they developed and published a directive entitled "The expansion of neurology stations and the treatment of veterans with neurological conditions". It was due in large part to Ferenczi's efforts that the army integrated psychoanalysis as a method in its operations. Another idea also took shape at the conference: collect the papers on war neuroses in an edited volume. Its publication was linked to an impressive, long-term publishing programme based on the concepts of the first significant patron of the psychoanalytic movement.

Towards new structures: a university department, clinic, and publishing house

Antal Freund of Tószeg[41] donated a huge fortune, two million Austro-Hungarian crowns—nearly half a million dollars at the exchange rate of the day—to back psychoanalysis, to found a psychoanalytic publishing house and library, and to establish a psychoanalytic outpatient clinic in Budapest that would also treat modest-income patients. He also planned to support the training of analysts and the teaching of psychoanalysis at university.[42]

Inspired by Ferenczi's lectures, students of the Galileo Circle called for psychoanalysis to be incorporated into higher education as part of a regular course of study. The success of the congress and the joy over the end of the war accelerated the implementation of these plans. General changes in university education paved the way for the integration of psychoanalysis into the curriculum.

Medical students played a major role in the efforts to integrate psychoanalysis into higher learning by collecting signatures: first, in October 1918, they submitted a petition to the university's rector in support of hiring Ferenczi as a lecturer, but this first attempt was unsuccessful. At the beginning of 1919, therefore, they made a second attempt. On 28 January, they submitted 243 signatures along with a letter of explanation to Zsigmond Kunfi, minister of education.

Portrait of Antal Freund of Tószeg. Archives of the Sándor Ferenczi Society & International Ferenczi Centre, Budapest.

Concurrently, experts in psychoanalysis publicly voiced the necessity to integrate psychoanalysis into university training, and Freud, Ferenczi, and Lajos Lévy lent support to the students' initiative in their writings (Ferenczi, 1919; Freud, 1919j; Lévy, 2004[1919]; Schröter, 2011).

The dean of medicine at the university in Budapest asked internist and neurologist Professor Ernő Jendrassik to provide an opinion on this proposal for a meeting of the faculty council. By then, Jendrassik must have had access to a copy of Ferenczi's recommendations "Comments on educational reform at the university level", in which Ferenczi emphasised that

> *the current curriculum is lacking in attention to psychotherapy (psychoanalysis).* ... It is in the primary practical interests of humanity that physicians should also be in possession of methods with which they

can assist the mentally ill, not the physically ill—indeed, physically ill patients as well, because there is no disease for which it would not be in our primary *interests* to attend to the psychic condition. *The knowledge of those entering practical medicine must not be lacking in the science of psychic healing.* (Ferenczi, 1919, cited in Erős, Kapás, Kiss, & Giampieri Spanghero, 1987, p. 588, translated for this edition, original italics)

Nevertheless, Jendrassik sarcastically dismissed psychoanalysis, describing it as "pornography and interpretation of dreams", and, at its meeting on 25 March 1919, the faculty council unanimously rejected the proposal to introduce the study of psychoanalysis at the university.

Naturally, there had to be a new power that would finally throw open the doors to a field that was ready to enter the halls of higher education as a fully fledged scholarly discipline. This new power was the commune. Ferenczi's proposal was finally approved by the commissars of Hungary's new Soviet government, as they were now instituting a structure based on central power to replace university autonomy. Erős captured the events of the day well when he said "it was the irony of fate that the first department of psychoanalysis was established and . . . that Ferenczi was appointed a university professor through undemocratic means" (2004, p. 139, translated for this edition). It should also be noted that it was an individual and a body in authority (the dean and faculty council) that had rejected the original grass-roots initiative, while it was another authority (the commissariat)—amid the struggle between conservative and reform-minded forces—that now gave a green light to the proposal, which had culminated from many years of work.

The Commissariat for Education of the Soviet Republic of Hungary appointed Ferenczi as full professor on 25 April 1919 and ordered the establishment of the Department of Psychoanalysis at the university in Budapest. At the same time, Ferenczi was also charged with running a planned psychoanalytic clinic tied to the university. The site designated for the facility was the former Batizfalvy sanatorium (at No. 82 Aréna Road in Budapest's working-class 8th district), whose equipment would also be made available. Ferenczi would be assisted there by one research fellow, two assistant lecturers, and three paid interns. A person named Jenő Hárlik is known to have worked there, and Radó's name also appeared a number of times as a staff member, but

Ferenczi's request for scholarly books for the psychoanalytic clinic, 1919 (excerpt).

we do not have a clear record of this and Radó made no mention of it in a biographical interview (Roazen & Swerdloff, 1995).

Ferenczi's appointment to a professorship and the establishment of the department of psychoanalysis at the medical university as well as the clinic linked to it comprised a construction which—had it enjoyed sufficient time to develop—could have determined the further development of European psychoanalysis as a key component of a Budapest hub. Although he disliked the Soviet-type government, Freud was pleased about this development and shared the news with Jones in a letter dated 19 June 1919: "Ferenczi has become the first official university teacher [in] ΨA, (o.ö. Professor), a success not dreamt before!" (Paskauskas, 1993, p. 349).

At the same time, Ferenczi became a member of the country's leading body on healthcare, the National Medical Board, headed by József Madzsar. The twenty-one members of the Board at the time included such notables as Janós Bókay and Sándor Korányi—now prominent figures in medical history.

These two positions meant that, as a department head, Ferenczi had the opportunity to introduce psychoanalysis to regular medical studies as well as to create an institutional structure by planning curricula for physicians' education, practice, and in-service training. As a member of the National Medical Board, he was in a position to make psychoanalysis even more acceptable for specialists of other, classical areas of medicine.

Under the Soviet Republic of Hungary, not only were a department and clinic for psychoanalysis established, but also an institute, where a number of staff members would eventually become involved in psychoanalysis.

The institute for psychology

A laboratory for experimental psychology was in operation under Géza Révész (1878–1969) within the faculty of humanities at the university in Budapest.[43] This was the second workshop for experimental psychology in Hungary after another such laboratory headed by Pál Ranschburg (1870–1945). Révész dealt with general psychological topics: the psychology of seeing, hearing, and touching; the psychology of thinking, creativity, and talent; child psychology;

and the psychology of music. On 14 April 1919, Tódor Kármán, who was responsible for university affairs, approved the plan to establish a university institute of psychology. It was, thus, under the Soviet Republic that the laboratory was developed into an institute, which became part of the faculty of humanities.[44] In June 1919, Révész requested 100 thousand crowns for equipment for the laboratory, an amount that was registered by the commissar for finance as a projected expense—because of the lack of a central budget at the time. Some of the development programme, however, ended up being implemented the very same month.

On 21 April 1919, Révész submitted a request to the commissar for education to ask Dr Imre Hermann to take the position of assistant lecturer at the institute for psychology and for Alice Cziner and Júlia Láng to be hired as interns.[45] Imre Hermann (1889–1984) had begun working in Révész's laboratory as a second-year medical student (Harmat, 1994), and, if we add that he had received his medical degree in 1913, his sheer commitment to experimental psychology becomes clear. As an assistant lecturer, Hermann conducted scientific studies and was also responsible for overseeing the work of doctoral candidates. This is where he met the woman he would marry, Alice Cziner (Hermann) (1895–1975), who also became a psychoanalyst later. Hermann had encountered the works of Freud and Ferenczi during the First World War. He had even attended one of Ferenczi's seminars earlier, but, as an experimental psychologist, he initially felt a certain resistance to psychoanalysis. Soon, however, he linked the two fields. Ferenczi noticed Hermann after a lecture he had given and reported this to Freud in a letter dated 3 March 1918:

> Frau G. was so kind as to listen to the lecture in my place. . . . Herr Herrmann [sic, Hermann] is supposed to have spoken full of enthusiasm about $\Psi\alpha$, about you, and also about me. The explanations did not go deep, but they were skilfully presented. Herr Herrmann [sic, Hermann] places himself frankly on the $\Psi\alpha$ side. (Brabant, Falzeder, & Giampieri-Deutsch, 1996, pp. 270–271)

In 1919, Hermann became a member of the Hungarian society and began his training analysis with Erzsébet Révész, Géza's sister. Révész's institute ceased to exist after the fall of the Soviet Republic. He then immigrated to Germany and resettled in the Netherlands.

Later, in a ceremony on 25 October 1933, he was named a professor of psychology at the University of Amsterdam (Róbert-Kelen, 1933).

A grim portent

The initiatives that had been put in place and were to be implemented were significantly overshadowed by the historical events that followed the war. All the foundations of the promising ideas put forth in so many areas by Antal Freund of Tószeg now grew fragile from the economic destabilisation that followed the collapse of the Austro-Hungarian monarchy (1867–1918), which had formed the linchpin between the two countries. The donation Freund had deposited in Hungary began to melt away due to runaway inflation. It was, thus, essential to safeguard the remaining amount by transferring it out of the country. Economically, Austria was more stable, and so the independent psychoanalytic publishing house was established in Vienna, not in Budapest. The volume that included a selection of lectures from the Budapest congress—the first publication planned for the psychoanalytic publishing house, entitled *Zur Psychoanalyse der Kriegsneurosen* (The Psychoanalysis of War Neuroses)[46]—thus did not come out in Hungary either. This case is emblematic of an important feature of psychoanalysis in Hungary: important Hungarian ideas and plans on both the institutional and theoretical levels were realised somewhere else, in another country or on another continent. The psychoanalytic polyclinic, the idea for which had been conceived in Budapest in 1918, was sooner brought into being in Berlin (in 1920) and in Vienna (in 1922) than it finally was in Budapest (in 1931).

Political persecutions effectively shortened the lifespan of psychoanalysis at Budapest's medical university to that of the ephemeral mayfly on the Danube, and they similarly destroyed the university's institute for experimental psychology headed by Révész, as well as all the prospects that had made Budapest a focal point of European psychoanalysis not long before.

CHAPTER FOUR

The first wave of emigration in the early 1920s

"I don't see the possibility of a peaceful life here in the future"

(Lóránd, 1925)[47]

The end of the First World War did not simply mark the end of a war. Empires crumbled—and so, too, Austria-Hungary. The monarchy disappeared as a form of government in the region, and new borders were drawn where none had existed before. Hungary saw dramatic changes between 1918 and 1920: in October 1918, the Aster Revolution (led by liberal, radical opponents of the First World War) formed the catalyst for the country's first republic (the Republic of Hungary), which was unstable and short-lived due to domestic and international political power relations. This was followed in 1919 by the Soviet Republic, which "was largely imported from Soviet Russia by former Hungarian prisoners of war" (Frank, 2009, p. 80) and lasted only a few months. Then came a right-wing White Terror under Admiral Miklós Horthy.[48] As a consequence of such powerful unrest and changes of such seismic proportions, the potential for Budapest to remain a hub for the psychoanalytic movement disappeared.

After the signing of the Treaty of Trianon, which established the peace between the Entente and Hungary in 1920, Hungary lost two-thirds of its territory and, thus, most of its sources of raw materials as well as over half of its population. In the wake of these changes, agricultural output plunged, the entire industrial supply chain capsized, and both markets and transport fell into chaos. As a destructive reaction to these processes—and to the social convulsion whose effects are still felt to this day—the first anti-Semitic law of twentieth-century Hungary and Central Europe, the Numerus Clausus Act, was passed in 1920. Its aim was to restrict the percentage of Jews at universities to 6%, a figure that represented their portion of the entire Hungarian

Anti-Semitic poster from the early 1920s.
"Down with the Parasite Press! Christian National Press!!"
Original in the Budapest Collection of the Szabó Ervin Central Library.

population at the time, while the share of Jewish students at the universities in Budapest and in some bigger cities in Hungary stood between 24% and 40% (Kovács, 1994). If one adds the fact that university students in general had come from urban middle-class families in Budapest and other cities—not from the countryside—the political manipulation of an "overrepresented" Jewish population at the universities becomes clearer.

Action taken during the White Terror concerned everyone who had played a social role during the Soviet Republic. The most lenient punishment was the loss of one's job, which was achieved by revoking appointments made under the previous regime; this was followed by expulsion from professional associations. The strictest punishment was meted out for active political involvement: this often involved the death penalty. The lives of many who were members of the Hungarian Psychoanalytical Society at the time were strongly affected by the retaliatory measures taken by the right-wing government at the time. From a historical perspective, it can be concluded unquestionably that the psychoanalytic movement was dealt its first heavy blow during this period.

Losses suffered by the Hungarian psychoanalytic movement (1919–1921)

Ferenczi's appointment as a university professor was revoked on 8 August 1919, and, thus, almost automatically, teaching psychoanalysis ceased to exist as part of Hungarian medical training. It was not only a teaching post and a department that Ferenczi, and, indeed, the entire psychoanalytic movement, were forced to forsake. With the stroke of a pen, forces pushing through a political restructuring lost for psychoanalysis for long decades both the status it had just barely attained in medical training and its academic standing in higher education generally. Now psychoanalysis was pushed back again and confined within the walls of private practice and of professional societies for quite some time—not only in Hungary, but also throughout Europe.

Plans that had been made for a university clinic in the former Batizfalvy sanatorium, both to treat patients and to train future professionals, now simply evaporated. In addition, the possibility of developing the institute of psychoanalysis which was to integrate treatment with pre- and in-service training also vanished. Another quarter century was to pass before a similar structure was put in place, when psychoanalysis emerged again as part of medical training and as an independent institution. It is no coincidence that this new formation appeared in 1944 at Columbia University in New York, since it was a Hungarian émigré analyst, Sándor Radó, a founding member and former secretary of the Hungarian Psychoanalytical Society, who laid the groundwork there. However, before we leap forward in time to discuss this otherwise significant parallel, let us return to our discussion of the events during the period of political restrictions.

Ferenczi was deprived of his university post as well as of his membership of the Budapest Royal Medical Society, which he had joined in 1900 (Mészáros, 1999a). The procedure was conducted by the Board of Governors of the Royal Medical Society on the order of the Hungarian National Medical Society and affected everyone who had a played a public role in either the Aster Revolution or the Soviet Republic. Ferenczi fell victim to this process of expulsion along with twenty-two of his peers at an extraordinary meeting of the Royal Society held under stormy circumstances on 28 May 1920 (Kapronczay & Kiss, 1986, p. 144).

The list of losses for Budapest includes the transfer—to Vienna and the eventual use there—of the generous donation made by Antal Freund of Tószeg. Further losses can be seen in the first issue of the newly established English-language periodical, *The International Journal of Psycho-Analysis*. On the page following the table of contents, Ferenczi's open letter greeted the reader and reported on the process that led to the establishment of the journal. Ferenczi stated that, having consulted with his peers in the psychoanalytic leadership, he decided he would meet the growing demand in Anglophone countries not by publishing a version of the German-language *Zeitschrift für ärztliche Psychoanalyse* in English, but by putting out an English-language journal with a new format. Ferenczi said, "*I have decided* (my italics) that the most satisfactory method would be to found a distinct Journal in the English language, in close contact with the Zeitschrift, and if possible under a similar editorship" (Ferenczi, 1920a[1919], p. 1).

In the letter, Ferenczi passed on his duties in the IPA to Ernest Jones, explaining that this was necessitated by delayed communication and the slow process for implementing decisions:[49]

one of our present editors, Dr Ernest Jones, who from his central geographical position and knowledge of the conditions in different directions seemed the most suitable person to undertake this task, and he has consented to do so and also to act for me as President of the 'International Psycho-Analytical Association' until the next Congress. (Ferenczi, 1920a[1919], p. 2)

Ferenczi wrote the open letter in October 1919 and signed it as president of the IPA (Ferenczi, 1920a[1919]). We do not know exactly what transpired during a conversation in Vienna on 24 September 1919 when Jones visited Freud, but it is certain that Jones urged Ferenczi's resignation. On 12 October 1919, he wrote the following to Freud:

as regards the Vereinigung, Ferenczi has only the right to transfer the duties, not however the office—which he could only lay down to either the congress or to the Obmänner. In English this would be expressed by the words '*Acting* President', and perhaps you will be good enough to ask him to write to the Obmänner in this sense. (Paskauskas, 1993, p. 357)

Freud clearly made the request of Ferenczi during the latter's next visit to Vienna, although we can see from the above extract that the actual suggestion was not originally his. This, however, does not change the fact: "On Freud's recommendation Ferenczi transferred the presidency of the IPA to Jones" (see footnotes for Freud to Ferenczi, 5 September 1919, Brabant, Falzeder, & Giampieri-Deutsch, 1996, p. 368).

Thus, Ferenczi was knocked off his throne not only in Hungary, but also internationally. These are tiny signs, but clearly reflect Jones' powerful ambitions and the rivalry he felt even early on with Ferenczi.

From then on, Ferenczi—who had realised the great dream of winning university-level recognition for psychoanalysis and who could well have developed the first psychoanalytic institute and clinic—was forced to endure a series of losses and no little humiliation. It beggars belief that Jones, who was an important member of the inner circle, did not know all about this. Neither can we presume that Ferenczi—who was never otherwise attracted to power and position—was untouched by these events despite all of his self-discipline.

He made a subtle reference to this in a letter to Freud (20 November 1919) after a visit to Vienna in October 1919: "After the beautiful days in Vienna—despite all the calamities I had to learn of there, they were still the most beautiful of the year gone by" (Brabant, Falzeder, & Giampieri-Deutsch, 1996, p. 368).

According to Braham (1988), one major effect of the *numerus clausus* was to radicalise institutions of higher education so that they became hotbeds of anti-Semitism. Ferenczi wrote about this to Freud on 28 August 1919 as follows: "The blackest reaction prevails at the university. All Jewish assistants were fired, the Jewish students were thrown out and beaten. From these few data you may get a picture of the situation that prevails here!" (Brabant, Falzeder, & Giampieri-Deutsch, 1996, p. 366).

Historian Tibor Frank provides a clear explanation of the spark that set alight a smouldering anti-Semitism in Hungarian society:

> It seemed that the 'Soviet' Republic of Hungary tried to realise the dreams of the Bolsheviks. . . . Many of the leaders in both revolutions, but particularly of the 1919 Republic of Councils, came from a Jewish background. About two-thirds of the 'people's commissars' (as ministers of the government were then called) and their deputies were Jews. (Frank, 2009, pp. 80–81)

As noted above, this government lasted only a few months and was followed by a backlash of rightist White Terror. As Frank points out,

> [a]fter the takeover by Admiral Miklós Horthy's White Army in August 1919 and a succession of extremely right-wing governments, 'Jew' and 'Communist' became almost synonymous. . . . Bolshevism was considered 'a purely Jewish product', as sociologist Oscar Jászi described in his reminiscences. (Frank, 2009, p. 82)

Anti-Semitic assaults were endured by medical students in Budapest on a daily basis. István Székács, who later became a psychoanalyst, wrote that "on 5 August 1919, that is on the fourth day of the White Terror, Jews were now being beaten at the medical university" (Székács, 1981–1982, p. 450, translated for this edition). This was not merely a report of a short-lived burst of hatred. Indeed, he even had to suffer experiences of exclusion as a medical student in 1926:

the percentage of Jews at the institutions attached to the Faculty of Medicine—the institutes and clinics—was 'numerus nullus'. In other words, Jews were excluded from medical research and postgraduate training at the Budapest Faculty of Medicine. (Mészáros, 2012, p. 85)

Another part from an earlier letter by Ferenczi, written to Freud on 28 August 1919, also communicated that firings could be considered a direct consequence of a wave of hatred that had reached enormous proportions:

> After the unbearable 'Red Terror', which lay heavy on one's spirit like a nightmare, we now have the White one. . . . [T]he ruthless clerical anti-Semitic spirit seems to have eked out a victory. If everything does not deceive, we Hungarian Jews are now facing a period of brutal persecution of Jews. They will, I think, have cured us in a very short time of the illusion with which we were brought up, namely, that we are 'Hungarians of Jewish faith'. I picture Hungarian anti-Semitism— commensurate with the national character—to be more brutal than the pretty hateful type of the Austrians. . . . It will very soon become evident how one can live and work here. It is naturally the best thing for Ψα. to continue working in complete withdrawal and without noise. Personally, one will have to take this trauma as an occasion to abandon certain prejudices brought along from the nursery and to come to terms with the bitter truth of being, as a Jew, *really* without a country. (Brabant, Falzeder, & Giampieri-Deutsch, 1996, pp. 365–366)

The retaliation primarily punished leftist, Jewish, anti-dictatorship intellectuals. Many assimilated Jews, especially young ones, now longed to leave their homes: these were people who had been deprived by the *numerus clausus* of a university degree, of an intellectual lifestyle, and of the career they had hoped for. Most of them were forced to leave the country and apply their talents elsewhere.

The first wave of emigration in general

In 1919–1920, the country saw the departure of outstanding scientists, philosophers, and artists. Many of them belonged to social groups that had contributed significantly to Hungary's modernisation. Neither could the emigration of the psychoanalysts be considered a life choice that was characteristic of only a tiny professional group. In 1919, it was primarily intellectuals who left, a portion of whom were those who had extensive ties to members of leftist and liberal radical circles—including the analysts of Budapest. A general discussion of the first wave of émigrés, therefore, points to interesting aspects of the future of the psychoanalytic movement. Most émigrés at the time headed for other European countries and not the USA. The émigrés' destination was influenced by the attractions of Berlin as well as by the restrictive USA immigration policy, which imposed a quota system on both individual European countries and occupational categories, which, as we shall see, would lead to a dramatic situation two decades later.

In the early 1920s, people leaving the country included not only those who were fleeing retaliation after the Soviet Republic, the groundswell of anti-Semitism, and the *numerus clausus*, but also those who simply did not wish to live under the White Terror, endure the dismantling of liberal values, or experience the chaos of economic collapse and general disorder. Based on the model of push and pull factors (Palló, 2004, p. 34), which captures the dynamic of migration, it is clear that the wave of emigration was triggered by a series of social and economic crises in 1918–1919 as the push factor. A 1920 entry from a diary kept by writer and film critic Béla Balázs is an emblematic description of great intellectuals in exile:

> [w]e set off with walking sticks in hand and sleep with our satchels on our backs. Come autumn, we will likely have to move on. . . . We are truly everywhere. Edith stuck in Milan . . . [Béla] Fogarasi in Prague . . . [Károly/Karl] Mannheim and Juliska Láng in Bavaria, [Arnold] Hauser in Italy . . . Gyuri [György Lukács] in Vienna. But the ties do not break. And they cast a strong net over Europe. (Balázs, 1982[1920], p. 407, translated for this edition)

The majority of the people who had created this "strong net" were outstanding scholars, artists, writers, and creative intellectuals, who were all hoping to be able to adapt to the way of life in another country. Among the first to leave the country were the mathematician Tódor (Theodore) Kármán, the distinguished physical chemist Mihály (Michael) Polányi, and the theoretical physicists Leó Szilárd and Ede (Edward) Teller, who would both later take part in the Manhattan Project, as well as art historian Arnold Hauser, philosopher György Lukács, and sociologist Karl Mannheim. Among people in the cinema who would earn world fame later were directors Sir Alexander Korda and Michael Curtiz and the poet and film theorist Béla Balázs. Poet Lajos Kassák, writer and journalist Sándor Márai, and Ignotus were also forced to emigrate, as were numerous artists such as Aurél Bernáth and Károly Kernstok, as well as the composer Béla Bartók. Although many of them thought of emigration as transitory, most of them never returned to Hungary.[50]

For émigrés, German-speaking countries seemed to be an obvious choice as they represented numerous pull factors. Culture and education in Hungary had long been influenced by Germanophone culture, including the education system, science, literature, and art. Under the Austro-Hungarian monarchy, it was natural for Hungarian intellectuals to be bilingual. Many of the émigrés had even spoken German as children. Ferenczi himself grew up in a multilingual family, and, if we wish to be very precise, his mother's native language was Viennese German, his father's mother tongue was Polish, and the family spoke Yiddish and Hungarian. Psychoanalyst István Székács-Schönberger (1907–1999) wrote about his own childhood years in the following way:

> The natural way in which a well-to-do intellectual family took on a German governess for their child and bound the child's future to German culture was a characteristic feature of Hungarian—and, more specifically, Jewish Hungarian—society at the time. (Székács-Schönberger, 2007, p. 47, translated for this edition)

German-medium instruction had formed an integral part of the Hungarian education system, and it had been considered prestigious to study at the universities in Berlin, Göttingen, and Heidelberg even beforehand. Borrowing Frank's words, "[t]he average middle-class 'Hungarian' was generally of German (Swabian) or Jewish descent, and for him it was German culture and civilisation that linked Hungary and Austria-Hungary to Europe and the rest of the world" (Frank, 1999, p. 11, translated for this edition).

Why Berlin?

Berlin was considered the cultural capital of Europe in the 1920s with an effervescent musical and literary scene, regular cinematic and

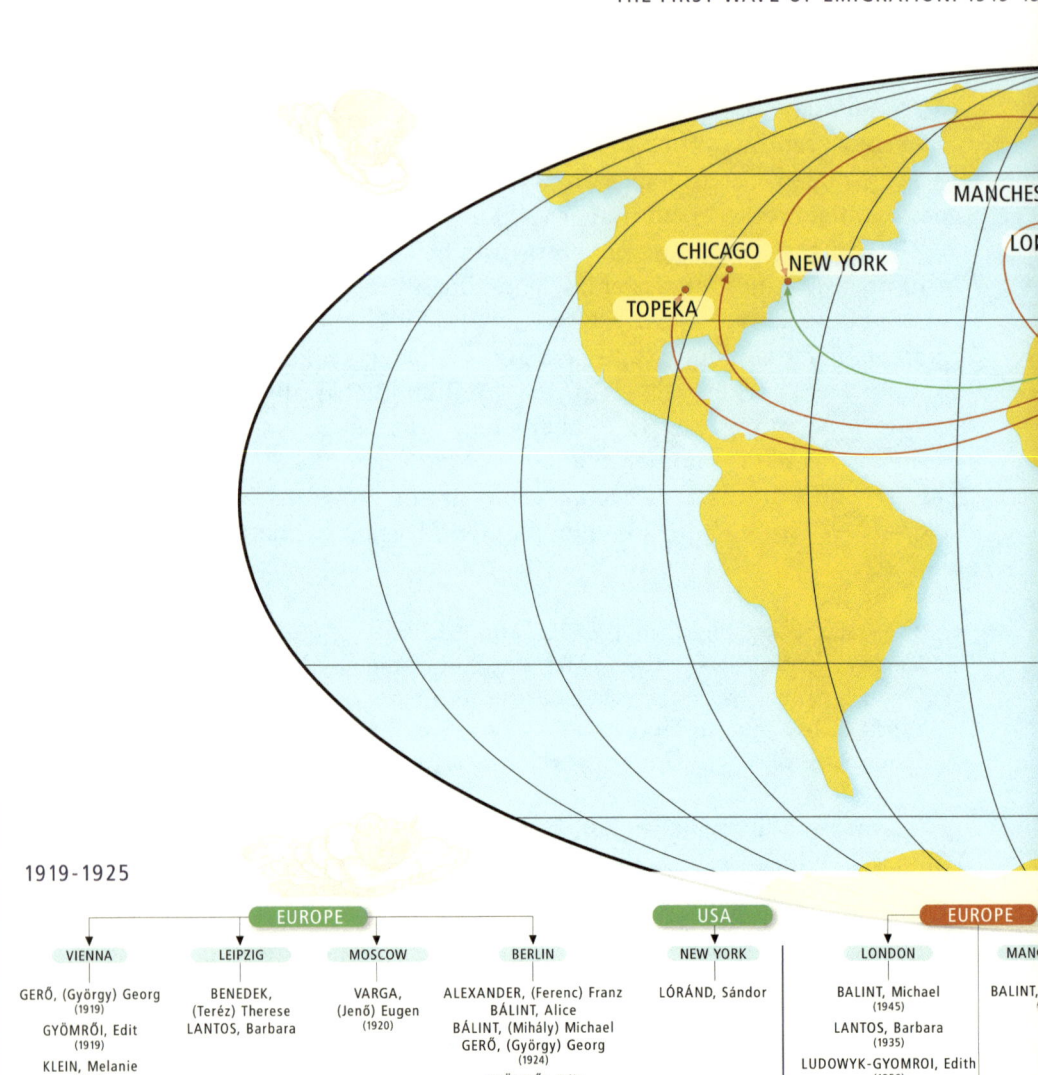

Emigration of Hu...

THE FIRST WAVE OF EMIGRATION: 1919-19

1919-1925

EUROPE

VIENNA
- GERŐ, (György) Georg (1919)
- GYÖMRŐI, Edit (1919)
- KLEIN, Melanie (1921)
- MAHLER, (Margit) Margaret
- SPITZ, A. René (later Berlin, Paris & New York)
- VARGA, Jenő (1919)

LEIPZIG
- BENEDEK, (Teréz) Therese
- LANTOS, Barbara

MOSCOW
- VARGA, (Jenő) Eugen (1920)

BERLIN
- ALEXANDER, (Ferenc) Franz
- BÁLINT, Alice
- BÁLINT, (Mihály) Michael (1924)
- GERŐ, (György) Georg
- GYÖMRŐI, Edit (1923)
- HÁRNIK, Jenő
- KLEIN, Melanie (1922)
- LANTOS, Barbara
- RADÓ, Sándor
- SPITZ, A. René

USA

NEW YORK
- LÓRÁND, Sándor

EUROPE

LONDON
- BALINT, Michael (1945)
- LANTOS, Barbara (1935)
- LUDOWYK-GYOMROI, Edith (1956)
- KLEIN, Melanie (1926)

MAN...
- BALINT,

PARIS
- DOBÓ, György (DEVEREUX, George)
- LANTOS, Barbara
- SPITZ, A. René

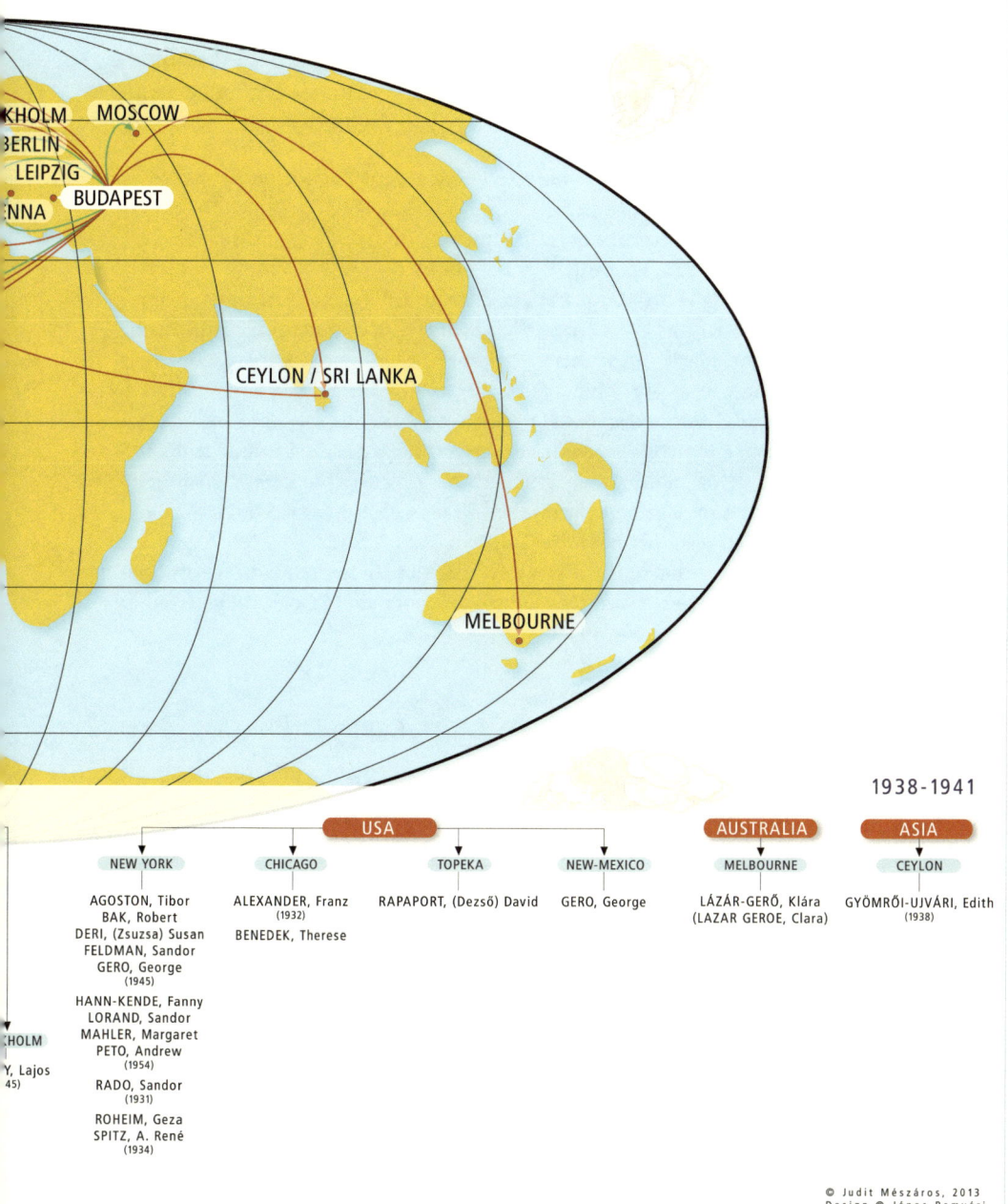

ian Psychoanalysts
SECOND WAVE OF EMIGRATION: 1938-1941

1938-1941

USA				AUSTRALIA	ASIA
NEW YORK	CHICAGO	TOPEKA	NEW-MEXICO	MELBOURNE	CEYLON
AGOSTON, Tibor BAK, Robert DERI, (Zsuzsa) Susan FELDMAN, Sandor GERO, George (1945) HANN-KENDE, Fanny LORAND, Sandor MAHLER, Margaret PETO, Andrew (1954) RADO, Sandor (1931) ROHEIM, Geza SPITZ, A. René (1934)	ALEXANDER, Franz (1932) BENEDEK, Therese	RAPAPORT, (Dezső) David	GERO, George	LÁZÁR-GERŐ, Klára (LAZAR GEROE, Clara)	GYÖMRŐI-UJVÁRI, Edith (1938)

© Judit Mészáros, 2013
Design © János Romvári

theatrical events, and arts and scholarship purveyed by outstanding creative and intellectual figures in their myriad workshops. After the First World War, with nearly 120 newspapers and magazines being published, forty theatres in operation, and around 200 chamber orchestras and more than 600 choirs giving concerts in concert halls and churches, Berlin, a thoroughly cosmopolitan city, even came to rival Paris (Frank, 2009). In fact, as István Deák describes it,

> Berlin harboured those who elsewhere might have been subjected to ridicule or prosecution. . . . Comintern agents, Dadaist poets, expressionist painters, anarchist philosophers, *Sexualwissenschaftler*, vegetarian and Esperantist prophets of a new humanity, *Schnorrer* ('freeloaders'—artists of coffeehouse indolence), courtesans, homosexuals, drug addicts, naked dancers and apostles of nudist self-liberation, black marketeers, embezzlers, and professional criminals flourished in a city which was hungry for the new, the sensational, and the extreme. Moreover, Berlin was the cultural centre of Central and Eastern Europe as well. Those who now dictated public taste and morals, who enlightened, entertained, or corrupted their customers were not only Germans, but [also] Russian refugees from the Red and Hungarian refugees from the White terror, voluntary exiles from what was now a withering and poverty-stricken Vienna, Balkan revolutionaries, and Jewish victims of Ukrainian pogroms. (Deák, 1968, cited in Frank, 2009, pp. 148–149)

Vienna, Berlin, Leipzig, and Paris

Of the members of the Hungarian Society, those who left the country in the first wave of emigration include Jenő (Eugen) Varga, Sándor Radó, Sándor Lóránd, Melanie Klein, and Jenő Hárnik—and most of them chose the Weimar Republic. Let us examine more closely what prompted them to leave.

As the Commissar for Finance, Social Affairs, and Production in Hungary's Soviet Republic as well as the chairman of the People's Economic Council, Jenő Varga was in mortal danger when he escaped to Austria, since he had been sentenced to death after the fall of the regime. While imprisoned in Karlstein Castle (in Karlstein an der Thaya) in Austria, he wrote *Economic Problems of the Proletarian Dictatorship*. After his release, he journeyed to Vienna and visited Freud. During his short stay in Vienna between February and June of

1920, he attended meetings of the Vienna Psychoanalytic Society. Afterwards, he travelled to Moscow for the Second Congress of the Communist International, after which he resettled in Soviet Russia and soon became a colleague of Lenin's (Tögel, 2000).[49]

Sándor Radó also played an active role in Hungary's Soviet government and had a hand in Ferenczi's university appointment. According to Ferenczi, it was Radó "who whipped the matter through the education section" (letter from Ferenczi to Freud dated 29 April 1919, Brabant, Falzeder, & Giampieri-Deutsch, p. 353). Interestingly, Radó never made any mention in writing or in interviews later that he had left Budapest because of his role in the Soviet government there. Perhaps he had never suffered any consequences because of it, and he simply felt that the psychoanalytic circle of Budapest was too small for him. Who knows?

We do know that Radó wanted to undergo analysis, but was on too close terms with Ferenczi—though it should be noted that this should not have ruled out analysis given the practice of the day. Radó, however, was a strictly rational thinker and soon recognised the drawbacks to personal analysis between close colleagues. As he recalled,

> I told him about everything I knew; and he reciprocated with his own observations. I discussed with him dreams and symptoms. It was a kind of supervisory situation, and our sessions were conducted in the most informal and casual manner. . . . It was impossible for me to be analysed by Ferenczi; by that time we were bosom friends except for the years we were separated during the war. (Roazen & Swerdloff, 1995, p. 69)

Then he decided to seek out Karl Abraham in Berlin. Soon after his arrival, he was asked to join the work at the Psychoanalytic Institute established in 1920 from a donation by Max Eitingon. Radó began his teaching career in January 1923.

Berlin took on a new significance in the psychoanalytic movement between 1930 and 1933. The Psychoanalytic Institute there was the first to establish a system for psychoanalytic training with which it set down the basic structure for the training requirements. In this endeavour, the institute relied on the experience and knowledge of Budapest analysts such as Radó. Unlike the approach in Budapest and Vienna, the Berlin Institute departed from previous tradition in training, in which the practice of psychoanalysis was not considered a medical activity exclusively. The institute in Berlin, however, only allowed those with a medical degree to participate in psychoanalytic training. The Berlin model was eventually borrowed by the American training system, a process that began with an invitation to Radó in 1931 to join the Psychoanalytic Institute in New York to adapt the training model from the Berlin Institute. This model stood in opposition to that espoused by Freud and Ferenczi, since they opposed the medicalisation of psychoanalysis and supported professionals from a variety of disciplines being involved in psychoanalytic practice.

The first analyst from Budapest who, in 1925, left not only his homeland, but also Europe, and was the first of the Hungarian psychoanalysts to resettle in New York, was Ferenczi's student, Sándor Lóránd. He saw Ferenczi for training analysis between 1923 and 1924, five times a week for nine months and even twice a day towards the end, in the mornings and afternoons.[47] Lóránd otherwise went to Vilma Kovács (1880–1940) for supervision and attended a seminar by Imre Hermann.[51]

Sándor Lóránd (1893–1987) was born in Kassa (Košice in present-day Slovakia) and was conscripted into the Czechoslovak army for only three days in 1924, as he later recalled, on the heels of an attempted royal coup in Hungary by Charles IV, the last Austrian emperor and Hungarian king. However, the Battle of Budaörs that quashed the coup had actually taken place in October 1921. Lóránd, therefore, must have been a few years off in his recollection. Being drafted, however, must have represented a change of fortune for him as well as a confirmation of the ongoing unpredictability and uncertainty around him. This might have been the reason why he stated a bit later—to Ferenczi's greatest surprise—that he was considering emigrating: in his own words, "I don't see the possibility of a peaceful life here in the future".[47]

As it turned out, Ferenczi would have liked Lóránd to be the ambassador of Budapest psychoanalysis in Czechoslovakia, but, having learnt of Lóránd's decision, he asked his American colleague, A. A. Brill, a founding member of the New York Psychoanalytic Society,[52,53] to support his immigration. As a result of Ferenczi's mediation, Brill contacted Professor Kirby, head of the New York State Psychiatric Hospital, who sent Lóránd an invitation a few weeks later and gave him a job at the hospital.[47]

Jenő Hárnik enjoyed a close relationship with the leaders of the Soviet Republic and participated in developing the plan for psychiatric reform in state hospitals. Although Ferenczi had an expressly poor opinion of him—"a terribly ambitious, but untalented person; psychosexually impotent, which he would like to overcompensate for" (letter from Ferenczi to Freud, 3 March 1912, Brabant, Falzeder, & Giampieri-Deutsch, 1993, p. 354)—he employed him at the psychoanalytical society for college students in 1919. Despite his unfavourable view of him, Ferenczi knew that Hárnik was diligent and could always be trusted with the teaching of students. Hárnik emigrated in 1922, became a member of the Berlin Psychoanalytic Society and taught at the Institute in Berlin. At the beginning of the 1930s, however, he developed a serious case of paranoid psychosis,[54] and Jones made mention of this to Freud on 9 September 1932 in his little report on the congress in Wiesbaden (Paskauskas, 1993, p. 708).

Melanie Klein (1882–1960) started her career in Budapest, although she moved to Budapest in 1910 after growing up and marrying in Vienna. She saw Ferenczi for depression in his office in 1912. A great deal of tension and animosity developed in her through her unhappy marriage, and, thus, occasional meetings for therapy led, as of 1914, to regular analysis, which would last for years. Ferenczi recommended that she deal with children. As he mentioned to Freud in a letter dated 29 June 1919, "Frau Dr [Melanie] Klein . . . recently made some very good observations on children, after she had several years of instruction with me" (Brabant, Falzeder, & Giampieri-Deutsch, 1996, p. 361).

Klein became a member of the Hungarian Psychoanalytical Society in July 1919 with a paper entitled "The development of the child". After her emigration to Berlin in 1921, she completed her second analysis with Karl Abraham. In 1923, she joined the Berlin Psychoanalytic Society. The German capital, however, was, in many ways, unsuited to her. She divorced her husband, but could not escape the hostile atmosphere that surrounded her in Berlin from the beginning and which she herself most probably had a hand in creating. She developed a number of relationships steeped in tension with Radó, Franz Alexander, and Otto Fenichel, among others. She felt that these people were particularly hostile to her. Finally, after Abraham had passed away and, thus, her obvious supporter had disappeared, she moved to London with Jones' help in 1926. The new situation was mutually advantageous to both of them, since Klein analysed Jones' children, while Klein herself became a member of the British Psychoanalytical Society a year later in 1927. She was now able to breathe for a few years, but, after the emigration of Anna Freud to London (in 1938), the professional conflict between them reached a nearly religious fervour by the early 1940s, which stood in contradiction to the sober thinking of the sciences (James Strachey to Edward Glover, 23 April 1940, cited in King & Steiner, 1991, p. 33).[55]

Young people who received their training somewhere other than Budapest represented further losses for Hungarian psychoanalysis. Many of the Hungarian experts who found themselves in big cities in Central and Western Europe during the first wave of emigration—but still before the second—returned to their homeland. Michael Balint and his wife Alice, for example, started analysis with Hanns Sachs in Berlin, and, although they became well known in the Society there, they came back to Budapest in 1924. A similar road was taken by Edit Gyömrői (1896–1987), who, after a long period away from home, was yet again forced to escape Berlin in 1933—when Hitler seized power— and ended up back in Budapest as well.

Gyömrői was among a number of analysts who held very powerful political convictions. As a communist, she immigrated to Vienna after the fall of Hungary's commune. Her multi-faceted talents as a writer and graduate of Budapest's college for applied arts enabled her to provide for herself even under difficult circumstances:

> Among her friends were Hermann Broch, who translated some of her poems into German, as well as composer Hanns Eisler, Czech writer Egon Erwin Kisch, and a Hungarian writer, Béla Balázs. After brief sojourns in several Hungarian-speaking towns in both the former Czechoslovakia (Užhorod/Ungvár) and Romania (Timişoara/ Temesvár and Cluj/Kolozsvár), she was expelled from Romania for her Communist involvement and moved to Berlin with her second husband László (Glück) Tölgy, living there between 1923–1933. In the early years, she was a costume designer at the Neumann Produktion film studio. She was also involved in translating, interpreting and photography, and she worked on the staff of the *Rote Hilfe* Communist party newspaper for a time. Her training analyst was Otto Fenichel between 1925 and 1929, and then she opened her own practice. Gyömrői's immediate circle of friends included young Marxist and other leftist peers, such as Annie and Wilhelm Reich, Otto Fenichel, Edith

Jacobson and Siegfried Bernfeld. She was part of the legendary "child seminar" organised by Fenichel. (Borgos, 2006)

These last examples—the Balints and Gyömrői—illustrate that it was possible to return home between 1924 and 1938, but very few people availed themselves of the opportunity. Most of the émigrés did not resume—or restart—their professional lives in Hungary; for instance, Melanie Klein, Margaret Mahler (1897–1985), René Árpád Spitz, Franz Alexander, Therese Benedek, Georg Gerő, and György Dobó (later George Devereux)[56]—who left for Paris at the age of eighteen—never returned back to Hungary.

There were two Hungarian émigrés in Berlin who resettled in the USA in response to an invitation from America under circumstances that were still peaceful in the early 1930s—before Hitler snatched the reins of power: these were Franz Alexander and Sándor Radó.

Franz Alexander (1891–1964), who would gain his reputation by that name in Berlin, was born Ferenc Alexander in Budapest. His father was Bernát Alexander, a renowned professor of philosophy at the university in Budapest, and as Alexander "recounts in his partly autobiographical work (Alexander, 1960), he was influenced by the intensive academic and non-academic networks around his father and around turn-of-the-century Budapest at large" (Pléh, 2008, p. 156). Like other young intellectuals of the age, Franz Alexander received his medical training both in Budapest and at many prominent centres of learning, such as Göttingen in Germany, and graduated in 1912. Through the mediation of Sándor Ferenczi, he met Freud before the First World War, and their relationship deepened during his years in Berlin. Alexander devoted himself to psychoanalysis. He would later recall, "To turn to psychoanalysis meant to give up every idea of an academic career, for which I had prepared myself since my early school years and to which I was predestined by family tradition" (Alexander, 1960, p. 55). The first important stage of his career was in Berlin. He practically exploded on to the scene within the psychoanalytic movement in that city as the first trained analyst of the Institute there and as someone who would immediately win the Freud Prize for his first psychoanalytic study "The castration complex in the formation of character" (Alexander, 1923). He completed his personal analysis with Hanns Sachs. Freud paid particular attention to him, they met often, and, thus, Alexander had the opportunity to discuss his patients with him. In 1926, he was already working as a training analyst at the Berlin Psychoanalytic Institute. In 1930, he received an invitation from the University of Chicago to teach psychoanalysis as a guest lecturer. He soon became a central figure in modern psychoanalysis, primarily in the area of psychoanalytic approaches to psychosomatic medicine.

Similarly, Radó also spent a decade at the Institute in Berlin, and they both became defining figures of the training there. Sándor Radó (1890–1972) was born in Kisvárda, a small town in southern Hungary. He studied in Berlin, Bonn, and Vienna. In 1911, he earned a degree in politics and enrolled at the faculty of medicine in Budapest afterwards. As was described earlier, he came into contact with Ferenczi quite early and, through him, with the psychoanalytic movement when he became one of the founding members and the secretary of the Hungarian Psychoanalytical Society. In 1924, Freud appointed Radó to replace Otto Rank as editor-in-chief of the *Internationale Zeitschrift für Psychoanalyse*. Radó also worked as an editor for the journal *Imago*. He was an outstanding theorist within the movement and an analyst to Wilhelm Reich (1897–1957), Heinz Hartmann (1894–1970), and Otto Fenichel (1897–1946), among other luminaries of psychoanalysis. He engaged in lively discussions with Freud as well as maintaining regular contact with him through correspondence on business matters related to the *Zeitschrift*. In 1926, he edited two volumes in honour of Freud on his seventieth birthday (Roazen, 2005). They were still in personal contact for a time after Radó had resettled in the USA. Freud, however, took umbrage with him—as he did with everyone who not only had left him and Europe, but also actively aided other European psychoanalysts in emigrating.

One of the most promising young doctors from Hungary also chose the Weimar Republic in the first wave of emigration. Teréz (Therese) Benedek (1892–1977) was born in the historic northern Hungarian town of Eger as Teréz Friedmann. While still in grammar school, she heard a lecture on psychoanalysis by Jenő Hárnik and this experience determined her later career: she attended the medical faculty at the Budapest University (1911–1916). As a first year student, she joined the Galileo Circle and heard Ferenczi's lectures. As a result of his influence, her attention turned toward the early mother–child relationship. As she wrote in a letter then, "I heard a series of lectures by Dr Ferenczi. It was during that time that an interest in paediatrics was awakened in me, and so that became my speciality" (Benedek to

Abraham, 31 August 1921, cited in May, 2000, p. 86). Benedek then worked as a resident at the children's clinic of St Elizabeth University in Pozsony (Bratislava in present-day Slovakia) from 1916 to 1919, but the school was moved to Budapest during the war in 1918. Then she met Ferenczi for her analyst training for five months. She made the first observations of children that are significant from the perspective of psychoanalysis. As a young specialist with a good eye, she noticed that babies demonstrate certain symptoms of their mothers; later, she analysed this phenomenon as a symbolic relationship in her study "Psychosomatic implications of the primary unit: mother–child" (Benedek, 1949). In 1919, she married internist Tibor Benedek, with whom she immigrated to Leipzig due to the political situation in Hungary. Her husband found a job there, and she was soon able to join the work of the Berlin Institute.

Peers who were interested in psychoanalysis in Leipzig developed into a professional group through Benedek's efforts. Indeed, she was the only trained analyst in Leipzig to undertake the task of training. The news of Benedek's activities reached Freud as well. When they met for the first time in 1922 at the psychoanalytic congress in Berlin, Freud expressed surprise: "What a tiny woman you are! I thought you were big and strong" (Pollock, 1973, cited in May, 2000, p. 60). Benedek needed to work a great deal to be accepted as a full member of the society in Berlin, but this came to pass in 1924 after she had given an excellent lecture. It was at this point that Abraham expressed his strong admiration for her to Freud: "This woman deserves enormous credit for involving young people and for her own invaluable practical work" (Abraham to Freud (3 December 1924), 1964, cited in May, 2000, p. 63). Benedek was the head of the group in Leipzig until 1933, and many analysts and other specialists who would later earn great fame started their analysis with her, including Barbara Lantos, Gerhard Scheunert (later president of the German Psychoanalytic Society), and Ehrig Wartegg (the creator of the Wartegg Drawing Completion Test (WDCT). Hitler's rise to power, however, drove Benedek further on—and away from Europe.

The Hungarian Psychoanalytical Society had nineteen members, including the writer Ignotus. Six of them, that is, about one-third of this small group, left the country during the first wave of emigration, as well as eight young people who later became well-known analysts in other countries and on other continents (Table 1).

Table 1. First wave of emigration (1919–1925).

Vienna	Berlin	Leipzig	Paris	New York
Members of the Hungarian Psychoanalytical Society				
Ignotus, Hugó	Hárnik, Jenő			
Varga, Jenő	Klein, Melanie			
	Radó, Sándor			Lóránd, Sándor
Future analysts				
Gerő, György (Georg) (1919–1920?)	Alexander, (Ferenc) Franz	Benedek, Teréz (Therese)	Dobó, György (Devereux, George)	
Gyömrői, Edit (1919)	Bálint, Alice		Spitz,	
Mahler, Margaret	Bálint, Mihály (Michael)		René A.	
Spitz, René Árpád (1920)	Gerő, Georg (1924)		(1932)	
	Gyömrői, Edit (1923)			
	Spitz, René A.			

In spite of these losses, Ferenczi's optimism and clarity of vision with regard to politics remained undiminished:

[R]evolutions are favourable to viewpoints which are either new or neglected by officialdom. Psychoanalysis belongs to that category . . . this branch of psychology has never aspired to anything other than to scientific accuracy; in any case, it has never accepted to ignore the truth, to turn away from it, in one direction or the other, in order to appease the powers that be. . . . Far from following this or that political or philosophical dogma, it has considered philosophical conceptions as well as political tendencies as expressions of human psychology. . . . Naturally, this particular position has not prevented psychoanalysis from expressing its viewpoint whenever it had the possibility to do so. (Ferenczi, 1999o[1922], p. 211)

CHAPTER FIVE

A period of consolidation

> "The teachings of psychoanalysis are in the air, they are part of the public domain"
>
> (Kosztolányi, 2001[1931], translated for this edition)

After an era of crisis and chaos, in a hopeful age of political and economic consolidation between 1925 and 1937, the tiny Hungarian Society managed to find itself again. By that time, the particular perspective of the Budapest School—that is, the analysts that belonged to it—had taken shape (Haynal & Mészáros, 2004).

Psychoanalytic methodology saw a fundamental shift in viewpoint, and new points of crystallisation emerged in theory as well. A review of the dynamism of the relationship between analyst and analysand was initiated with experiments in technique that Ferenczi had begun as early as the late 1910s (Ferenczi, 1980e[1919]) and completed in 1932 not only with conclusions he had drawn from mutual analysis with the patient (Ferenczi, 1988[1932]), but also with the paradigm shift in trauma theory (Ferenczi, 1980k[1933]; Mészáros, 2010a). This series of experiments and observations on the operation of psychoanalysis led to recognitions and discoveries that are still in

Dinner party for Ferenczi's fiftieth birthday, 1923. *Back, left to right*: Lillian Rotter Kertész, Michael Bálint, Alice Hermann; *long outer side, left to right*: Tivadar Kertész, Alice Bálint, Imre Hermann, Margit Dubovicz, István Hollós, Mrs Hollós, Sándor Ferenczi, Gizella Ferenczi, Frigyes Kovács, unknown; *bottom, left to right*: Klára Lázár-Gerő, Lilli Bródy, unknown; *short table at the back, heads turned towards camera*: István Schönberger, Vilma Kovács; *closer short table, facing camera, left to right*: Lajos Lévy, unknown; *opposite them with backs to photographer*: Mrs Róheim, unknown; *opposite long side*: Lilly Hajdu Gimes; Endre Almásy. Archives of the Sándor Ferenczi Society & International Ferenczi Centre, Budapest.

effect today. For example, it was found that to make therapy truly effective, a mutual dialogue must be developed between analysand and analyst, both intellectually and emotionally. Therefore, the topic of the analysis covers everything that the patient's transference reactions unconsciously trigger in the analyst—including the intellectual and emotional factors in the manifestations of countertransference. This represented an important change over Freud's previous ideas. Freud thought that from the point of view of therapy it was more effective for the analyst to remain outside the process emotionally in all situations (Freud, 1910d). This attitude, however, impairs the emotional authenticity of the communication between patient and therapist, and the factual knowledge often multiplies the strength of resistance in spite of the intellectual insight gained. Ferenczi realised that lack of authenticity limited the depth of trust felt by the patient, which is an indispensable condition for discovering and working through the traumatic experiences and memories that have been pushed out of the conscious mind. Most members of the Hungarian Society agreed with this attitude. Indeed, it was based on this function of the therapist as authentic, accepting, and emotionally involved that Michael Balint introduced one of the key elements of the psychotherapeutic process: the corrective phenomenon known as a new beginning (M. Balint, 1936), where, in the safety of psychotherapy, the patient himself can regulate the tension of his formerly repressed traumatic experiences and, thus, move beyond them.

The Budapest analysts also paid special attention to the significance of the early mother–child relationship characteristic of the preverbal period with their recognition of the character-shaping power of the earliest object relations.

The theme of early object relations plays a central role in later writings by Ferenczi, Michael Balint, Alice Balint, Imre Hermann, Therese Benedek, Melanie Klein, Margaret Mahler, and René Spitz—even if they represented different viewpoints on the interpretation of the quality and genesis of this relationship. These differences were clearly expressed in arguments over whether objects should be viewed as a component or a source of instinct, or, in contrast, whether objects originate in relations, not in instinct—that is, whether they form part of a pattern created through interpersonal communication during the earliest developmental period. By the mid-1930s, the ideas of the Budapest analysts differed from those of the London group organised around Melanie Klein (Grosskurth, 1986) with regard to early object-love, or, as they called it then, "primary archaic object relations" (A. Balint, 1949[1939], p. 258). In the words of Alice Balint,

> there are object relations with respect to the libido [at birth], but our ability to distinguish between the ego and the outside world, that is our sense of reality, has not reached the stage where we can grasp the existence of external objects. In other words, if we use the term narcissism, we describe phenomena around us with respect to our own sense of reality. (A. Balint, 1993[1933], p. 33, translated for this edition)

With the exception of Imre Hermann, who emphasised the clinging instinct in the early mother–child relationship, the Budapest School argued for the dynamic of object relations developing through primary object-love, while the Klein group in London supported the concept of inborn primary narcissism (M. Balint, 1949a).

Many of the members of the Budapest School pioneered the use of the psychoanalytic approach to psychoses, the first among them being István Hollós. Hollós located the essence of psychosis in the unregulatable nature of regression, which is considered to be a special capacity in humans. Unlike the poet, who can find expression for a state of regression, a psychotic returns to the past, that unprocessed world of the unconscious region (Hollós, 1990b[1927], p. 66). Regression played a central role in Ferenczi's bioanalysis and in Michael and Alice Balint's work in psychotherapy. An invaluable contribution of Hollós's was his open-door system, the humanistic psychiatric attitude

István Hollós and Paul Federn, ca. 1924. Archives of the Sándor Ferenczi Society & International Ferenczi Centre, Budapest.

in Hungary that he introduced at the National Institute for Psychiatry and Neurology in Budapest, the erstwhile "Yellow House". Soon, a young analyst, Lilly Hajdu, would also take an interest in the extent to which the theory and therapeutic method of psychoanalysis could be used to understand and cure psychosis (Hajdu, 1993[1933]).

Characteristics of the Budapest School included a flexible application of the science of psychoanalysis and an interplay with other disciplines, which led to a shared approach to various phenomena, specialised fields, and a psychoanalytic framework. It will come as no surprise that a move toward this interdisciplinarity first appeared in Budapest, illustrated by the emergence of psychoanalytic anthropology, which is associated with Géza Róheim.

Representing a unique mix of folklorist, ethnographer, anthropologist, and psychoanalyst, Géza Róheim (1891–1953) was the founder of psychoanalytic anthropology. He was engaged in mythological research within Hungarian folklore studies, which had started in the nineteenth century. His findings on historical layers of Hungarian folk beliefs and folk customs retain their value and influence even today. He was interested in ethnological topics, magic, and totemism. In keeping with the general thinking of the age, he believed that pre-literate tribal cultures and European folk customs and beliefs, as well as their social institutions, directly correspond to, and, in fact, capture, the stages of development of psychic processes (Róheim, 1918). He also maintained that, like their counterparts elsewhere, European folk customs bear out the understanding that humanity and its psychic world represent a unified whole (Róheim, 1918).

Róheim started his analytic training with Ferenczi, and his writings were published as of the late 1910s in international psychoanalytic journals.[57] He was celebrated as a pioneer in the psychoanalytic community as he was the first to apply the theory of psychoanalysis in ethnography. His work was acknowledged by the Freud Prize in 1921. Since it was important for the psychoanalytic community to ensure that their theory should be universally applicable beyond the area of treatment, Róheim was presented with an exciting research opportunity. Financial backing by Greek princess and French psychoanalyst Marie Bonaparte made it possible for him to conduct studies in technique and psychoanalysis between 1928 and 1931 in Central Australia, Somalia, New Guinea, and among the Yuma people in Central America.

Géza Róheim (in front, wearing glasses) and his wife Ilona, late 1920s.
Sándor Ferenczi and his wife Gizella are in the background.
Courtesy of Cathy Michel-Székács.

In line with analytic practice, Róheim's attention focused on the elements of daily life: dreams, sexual practices, childhood games, rites of initiation, myths, and narratives, as well as characteristic cultic objects, such as the tjurunga.[58] The desert of Central Australia became an analyst's office for Róheim (Verebélyi, 2005). By uniting his knowledge of folklore and psychoanalysis, Róheim developed the ontogenetic theory of culture (Verebélyi, 1990). During his research, he demonstrated that both the psychodynamism of dreams and the Oedipal complex represent general human phenomena, independent of particular cultures. He observed mother–child relations in indigenous cultures and found that this positive relationship increases the power of unity within a community later. He published the findings from his Central Australian research in his book *A csurunga népe* (The People of the Tjurunga) (Róheim 1992[1932]) and contributed an invaluable array of objects to the Oceania collection at the Ethnographic Museum in Budapest.

Róheim found collaborators among the Budapest analysts for his research in both analysis and ethnography. This fact in itself represents an addendum to the interdisciplinary openness that characterised the Budapest analysts. In 1928, Alice Balint praised Róheim's book *Magyar néphit és népszokások* (Hungarian Folk Belief and Folk Customs) on the pages of the journal *Századunk* (Our Century) (A. Balint, 1928), which was edited by Rustem Vámbéry, who would go on to teach at The New School for Social Research in New York.

In discussing the activity of the Budapest School during this period, we cannot ignore the further deepening relationship between literature and psychoanalysis. Volumes have been devoted to analysing and evaluating this connection.[59] Thus, the examples mentioned here merely serve as illustrative elements of analysts' use of literature and linguistics in the context of psychoanalysis and of the way psychoanalysis appeared in a revitalised literature. It is not merely that studies by psychoanalysts, such as Freud, Ferenczi, Hollós, Róheim, and others, were published in the country's leading cultural journals—these were primarily *Nyugat* (West), *Szép Szó* (Beautiful Word), and *Századunk*—but also that works of literature clearly reflected psychoanalytic perspectives in the authors' choice of topics and in their representation of the characters' internal conflicts.

For instance, novelist Dezső Kosztolányi created a new kind of hero by the end of the 1920s. In his short stories about a man named Kornél Esti, he was depicting his own alter ego through the psychic dichotomy of the id and superego which his character represents—a reflection of the influence of Freudian teaching. In the early 1930s, in an interview for the journal *Literatura*, Kosztolányi observed that

> the teachings of psychoanalysis are in the air, they are part of the public domain, people cannot talk about matters of the psyche the way they once did. We must accept the findings in this discipline the way we accept other findings in the natural sciences. (Kosztolányi, 2001[1931], p. 126, translated for this edition)

The multitude of connections between psychoanalysis, culture, and scholarly endeavour influenced and shaped the relationships of the people tied to these areas. Many of them were not only acquaintances, friends, or rivals, but also often related by blood or marriage. These family ties noticeably permeated their network. Just to mention some of the more familiar ones, among the psychoanalysts, for example, Vilma Kovács, Alice Balint, and Michael Balint were related as mother, daughter, and husband, respectively. István Hollós and Edit Gyömrői were linked as uncle and niece. Ferenczi and Gizella Pálos were husband and wife, while Zsófia Dénes was Gizella's niece. Likewise, Antal Freund's sister Kata married Lajos Lévy and became known as Kata Lévy (1883–1969).

A number of writers also reinforced the network of relationships through family ties: Frigyes Karinthy, for instance, encountered psychoanalysis in the 1910s through physician and fellow novelist Géza Csáth, who in turn was a cousin of Kosztolányi's. The impact of psychoanalysis can be detected through Karinthy's early humoresques and short stories, which, as time passed, unfortunately became two-faced and contradictory. Initially, he had been an enthusiastic devotee of psychoanalysis. However, in 1924, in his article "The psychology and morality of the Macbeth prophecy", published in the journal *Világ* (World), he compared psychoanalysis to the operation of a self-fulfilling prophecy: a prophecy is only fulfilled because it is repeated again and again. Ferenczi responded to this in *Nyugat* with "The discipline as sedative or wake-up call", in which he reminded a disillusioned Karinthy of earlier categories in the field which the author himself had created.[60]

Writer Milán Füst's interest in psychoanalysis is obvious even for those who did not know about his psychotherapeutic relationship with Georg Groddeck (1866–1934) and later with Imre Hermann. His novel The Story of My Wife—nominated for the Nobel Prize in Literature—is the most outstanding psychological analysis of envy.[61] At the recommendation of both Ferenczi and his primary physician István Hollós, Füst spent a number of months at Groddeck's sanatorium in Baden-Baden (Germany). Groddeck was a German physician and a great figure in psychosomatic medicine, which applied the psychoanalytic approach. Groddeck's character and teaching had a seminal effect on Füst, and he later confessed to being a student of Groddeck's in psychoanalysis (Hárs, 2004).

In the early 1920s, young radicals joined the debates on psychoanalysis. The journal *Korunk* (Our Age) offered a platform for left-wing, liberal, radical, and social democratic intellectuals. During its existence (1924–1940), it published some 300 studies and reviews on psychoanalysis. Ferenczi contributed, as did Sándor Feldman and so

Imre Hermann with his wife Alice Hermann, late 1930s. Archives of the
Sándor Ferenczi Society & International Ferenczi Centre, Budapest.

many other physician-analysts; Freud, Erich Fromm, and Wilhelm Reich published book reviews in the journal. In 1928, Ferenczi published his study "The adaptation of the family to the child" there (Ferenczi, 1980f[1928]). In 1929, a vibrant debate emerged about the effectiveness of psychoanalysis. The presence of psychoanalysis was so powerful that in 1935 the journal *Emberismeret* (Human Nature) turned to the important writers of the age with a question to elicit their opinion about "the extent to which psychoanalysis influences the thinking, world view, literature, and art of humanity" and about "the influence of psychoanalysis on writers and literature".[62]

Within this milieu, it is poet Attila József who figures as the emblematic figure of the intertwined nature of psychoanalysis and literature. In 1928, as a member of the group tied to the left-wing, liberal journal *Századunk* (Our Century), he met Róheim, whose writings and psychoanalytic approach to the study of the customs and rituals of indigenous cultures appealed to him. In 1929, during a period of crisis, Mihály József Eisler (1882–1944),[63] a member of the Hungarian Society, arranged his referral to a sanatorium. Later, he received treatment from the Stekelian Samu Rapaport for his psychosomatic complaints. Despite Jószef's repeated requests, Rapaport refused to see the poet for psychoanalysis although, according to today's diagnostics, he showed signs of borderline personality disorder. Then, during a newer crisis, István Hollós arranged for him to receive treatment from Edit Gyömrői, who had now found refuge in Budapest after fleeing Berlin and the fascism spreading in Germany. József's *Szabad-ötletek jegyzéke* (List of Free Ideas) is both a dramatic exercise in free association and a unique attempt on the part of the poet to renew his poetry and to elaborate on his passionate emotions (József, 1990). During his last crisis, he underwent psychiatric treatment with psychoanalyst Róbert Bak. A congratulatory piece he wrote for Freud's eightieth birthday is a beautiful example of the poetic embrace between literature and psychoanalysis.[64] Freud sent him a smart thank you note signed "Your Freud". *Szép Szó* published a thematic issue edited by Ignotus and József on the occasion of Freud's eightieth birthday to honour Freud and psychoanalysis on behalf of the literary world (*Szép Szó*, May 1936). It featured József's poem:

On Freud's Eightieth Birthday

> What you hide in your heart
> open up for your eyes
> and await in your heart
> what you foresee with your eyes.

> They say that love leads
> the living toward death.

Yet we crave pleasure
as we crave bread.

And all who live are children
longing for their mother's lap.
When not embracing, they're killing—
the battlefield is a marriage bed.

May you be like the Old One,
mauled by the young,
who, bleeding away,
sires a million sons.

The thorn that once stuck in your foot
has now fallen out.
And now even your death
drops quietly from your heart.

Let your hands fill
with what your eyes see ahead.
Either kiss or kill
the one you hide in your heart.

(Translated by John Bátki)

Ferenczi's study trip between 1926 and 1927 took place during this period of consolidation, made possible by an invitation from The New School for Social Research in New York. Ferenczi held lectures in New York, Baltimore, and Washington in psychoanalytic institutes and psychiatric clinics there and met people who thought similarly to him about the dynamic of social relations and their pathogenic functions. Of these, the interpersonal trend represented by Harry Stack Sullivan (1892–1949) would become the most influential later. According to Clara M. Thompson (1893–1958), Ferenczi was the only one that Sullivan trusted from among the European psychoanalysts (Silver, 1996). He was considered to be the ambassador of European psychoanalysis even by those who were sceptical about the field. Even Ferenczi himself considered his activities in the USA a mission of sorts, as suggested by his letter to Freud of 30 June 1927:

> I seem to have shaken the movement, at least temporarily, out of a state of indolence. Even the New York group, which usually has so little interest in the common cause . . . they want to hold meetings

more frequently than only once a month; they talk about courses, about founding an institute etc. (Brabant, Falzeder, & Giampieri-Deutsch, 2000, p. 311)

Indeed, only a few years later, having lured Radó from Berlin, the New York circle entrusted him with developing the training course at their institute. For Ferenczi, the journey to America was undoubtedly successful. This is indicated by the 100 students who attended his course at The New School and by the numerous lecture and dinner invitations he received. At the same time, Ferenczi had to overcome serious obstacles. Some critics accused psychoanalysis of mysticism and sexual prying and claimed that it lacked the seriousness of the cognitive sciences, whose results could be proved through experimentation. This antipathy was aimed in part at Ferenczi himself, having taken a stand against the medicalisation of psychoanalysis in the USA. After all, he had caused major ripples in the American waters of psychoanalysis when he openly supported lay psychoanalysts and encouraged them to establish their own association and fight to put the practice of psychoanalysis on an equal footing with that of medicine. In his interview with *The New York Times* on his departure, he stressed the indispensable role of lay analysts in treating neurosis (Ferenczi, 2000b[1927]).

Some of the criticisms, opposing views, and hostility, however, were much more intended as diplomatic messages to Freud. Ferenczi withstood these trials well, and even in intellectual duels that were meant to trap him (such was a certain dinner with US psychologist and founder of behaviourism John B. Watson (1878–1958)), Ferenczi still managed to convince his audience in his own kind and modest way "that one perhaps doesn't have to give up one's soul after all" (letter from Ferenczi to Freud, 30 June 1927, Brabant, Falzeder, & Giampieri-Deutsch, 2000, p. 294).

Having returned from the USA, he continued, after a ten-year hiatus, his earlier public lectures in Budapest with renewed vigour, outstanding events of which included six talks he gave at the conservatory of music with a consistent audience of 200.[65]

During this period, serious efforts were made in the Hungarian analysts' community to lay the groundwork for the psychoanalytic outpatient clinic as previously envisaged. The Hungarian Psychoanalytical Society established its training institute in 1926. In 1929,

Michael Balint, István Hollós, Imre Hermann, Zsigmond Pfeifer, Mihály Eisler, and Alice Balint participated in a theoretical training programme. Imre Hermann and Vilma Kovács held seminars on theory and case studies. In fact, the seminars led by Vilma Kovács at her villa in the quiet Naphegy section of Budapest became legendary as a forum in which one could express oneself, learn, and think with a free mind. István Székács-Schönberger describes this milieu in an interview:

> One got a style there somehow ... perhaps a turn of phrase ... Ferenczi's spirit was there ... in how we should treat the patient ... Naturally, the narcissism of the future analyst is constantly at the ready, and it expects to be wounded and corrected. Making the corrections, therefore, was essentially very important analytic work for those who asked the questions because they asked them in such a way that it should never be hurtful, that it should rather be about understanding and bringing things forward. If the candidate missed something, for example, because he didn't notice the significance of countertransference, then ... the senior members, Vilma Kovács, Alice Balint mostly, [Endre] Almásy, and [Zsigmond] Pfeifer ... were extraordinarily careful [in indicating it]. You couldn't see how they did it, but they were never hurtful. (Mészáros, 1997, p. 8, translated for this edition)

The institute opened its outpatient clinic in the autumn of 1929—borrowing Ferenczi's private surgery for this purpose at the time—and the Society developed the polyclinic in 1931. This news was published in the journal *Gyógyászat*,[66] which faithfully served the cause of psychoanalysis in Hungary for almost a quarter century. The earlier proposal made by Antal Freund of Tószeg had finally come to fruition: an outpatient clinic was established, where psychoanalysis became a method of therapy available to the poorest strata of society. Naturally, the complexity of reality was a great deal more nuanced than a simply joyous response to a piece of news. From a letter sent to Freud by Ferenczi on 31 May 1931 and another to Max Eitingon on the same day, it turns out that it had been a long, exhausting struggle with the authorities to establish the site for the polyclinic. It was set up in a five-room flat which they had rented "totally from our own means", a corner flat on the ground floor at 12 Mészáros Street in a leafy, residential section of Budapest's District I (Brabant, Falzeder, & Giampieri-Deutsch, 2000, p. 411).

After the death of writer and critic Jenő Rákosi (1842–1929), Ferenczi, now filled with the joy of having arrived, bought the writer's villa in Lisznyai Street (also in District I) with the money he had saved from his American journey. He shared his enthusiasm with his friend Georg Groddeck in a letter dated 15 June 1930:

> Now for the real news: we have bought a villa, consisting of two floors with a garden, over on the Ofner hill and will be moving in towards the end of this month. . . . It was a good buy (for approximately 70,000 Marks). . . . I look forward to getting fresh air and sun, which I greatly missed here. (Ferenczi [1930], Fortune, 2002, p. 93)

Ferenczi's most spectacular later writings were conceived in this villa, which saw the ripening of ideas from previous years that by today constitute essential elements of psychoanalysis with regard to the method of therapy, the dynamics of the genesis of trauma (in "Confusion of tongues between adults and the child"), and the responsibility of the analyst. This is where *Clinical Diary* was written,

Sándor Ferenczi and the sculptor Oscar Nemon, with the bust of Ferenczi in his villa at Lisznyai Street, in 1931.
Courtesy of Aurelia Young, Oscar Nemon's daughter.

which, besides methodological and metapsychological discoveries, led to dramatic recognitions due to unsparingly candid analyses of Ferenczi's feelings towards Freud:

> My own analysis could not be pursued deeply enough because my analyst (by his own admission, of a narcissistic nature), with his strong determination to be healthy and his antipathy toward any weaknesses or abnormalities, could not follow me down into those depths and introduced the 'educational' stage too soon. Just as Freud's strength lies in firmness of education, so mine lies in the depth of the relaxation technique. My patients are gradually persuading me to catch up on this part of the analysis as well. The time is perhaps not far when I shall no longer need this help from my own creations. (Ferenczi, 1988[1932], p. 62)

Ferenczi recognised that not working through negative transference destroys the quality of analysis and throws up stumbling blocks to key processes. In fact, Freud had also done this with others, as Freud's response to Ferenczi's criticisms suggest: "we were by no means so sure that these reactions could be expected in every case. At least, I wasn't" (letter from Freud to Ferenczi, 20 January 1930, Brabant, Falzeder, & Giampieri-Deutsch, 2000, p. 386). Unfortunately, the burgeoning conflict that overshadowed Freud and Ferenczi's relationship as well as the ever more powerful symptoms of Ferenczi's illness, pernicious anaemia, suppressed the joy offered by the lifestyle of a fine villa with a garden.

The ten-year period of expansion, which can only be considered transitory though it was still quite intensive, brought about an intellectual strengthening among the Budapest analysts and contributed greatly to the crystallisation of the way of thinking among the people who belonged to this community. Alice Balint's *The Psycho-analysis of the Nursery* (A. Balint, 1953) and Imre Hermann's Psychoanalysis as Method (Hermann, 1933) were published in the early 1930s.[67] Around 30–40 patients were treated at the polyclinic, the number of analyst candidates undergoing training was twenty-two, and, as we know from István Hollós's report, the Society held twenty-eight scholarly lectures between 1932 and 1934. Thus, an interested general public in Budapest and throughout the country could always expect talks by psychoanalysts.[68]

This development is clearly illustrated by the articles collected for a surprise volume in honour of Ferenczi's sixtieth birthday titled

Lélekelemzési tanulmányok (Psychoanalytic Studies) (Almásy et al., 1993 [1933]). Here, the Budapest analysts gathered all the knowledge appropriate to the special occasion with which they could give pleasure to Ferenczi, the colleague, the friend, and the tireless innovator. Unfortunately, it was published posthumously, since Ferenczi died several weeks shy of his birthday. As a result, the book reflects all that was present in Hungary in the mid-1930s in the method of therapy, in theoretical knowledge, and in applied psychoanalysis. Some of the articles—such as Mihály (Michael) Bálint's "Character analysis and new beginning", Imre Hermann's "The unconscious and the whirlpool theory of instincts", Alice Bálint's "The development of love and the sense of reality", and Vilma Kovács's "Training analysis and control analysis"—are considered among the classics of psychoanalytic literature. Intended as a gift, the volume includes studies, the newness of which reveals the capacity for innovation among the Budapest analysts. One of these is a paper by Lajos Lévy, perhaps the very first representative of psychoanalytic psychosomatics, entitled "What should we watch for in a cardiac patient's anamnesis?"[69] It comes as no surprise that the younger generation was drawn to relatively new topics. Thus, Fanny K. Hann wrote about countertransference, Klára Lázár (1900–1980) discussed educational guidance, and Lillian Rotter-Kertész (1896–1981) covered neglected issues of female sexuality.

Despite its intentions, the volume became a symbol of farewell with Freud's foreword and a collection of posthumous writings. The immediate responses following the shock and pain of Ferenczi's unexpected death—obituaries, appreciations, and essay-like remembrances written by his writer friends, students, and colleagues[70]—paint a faithful picture of Ferenczi's work as well as displaying the roots produced by Ferenczi and contemporary Hungarian psychoanalysis, roots that had spread throughout the international psychoanalytic movement and permeated Hungarian literary and intellectual thinking as well (Mészáros, 2000a). As Ignotus observed,

> [i]f psychoanalysis today is not merely a medical speciality and a survey of the mind, but rather a map of human nature, on which every scholarly field must be rebuilt—history, sociology, the law, education, and the study of art and religion—then, after his master [Freud], it is perhaps Sándor Ferenczi who has played the greatest role in this. (Ignotus, 2000[1933], pp. 39–40, translated for this edition)

Ferenczi died in May 1933, in the very month that books were being incinerated in bonfires, a clear sign that European civilisation was now in jeopardy. Freud, however, believed in the development of civilisation, and he believed that burning books and destroying the intellect represented a symbolic event, which substituted the desire for real destruction among people who spread undesirable ideas. Convinced that what had happened was a humanised version of aggression, he once mused, "What progress we are making. In the Middle Ages they would have burnt me: nowadays they are content with burning my books" (Freud, 11 May 1933, cited in Molnar, 1992, p. 149).

The burning of books, however, was far from a symbol of tamed aggression. In one of his last letters to Freud, written on 29 March 1933, Ferenczi voiced his concern for the future, noting that this state of affairs would spread to Vienna and, ultimately, to Budapest: "Short and sweet: I advise you to make use of the time during this not yet imminently dangerous situation and, with a few patients and your daughter Anna, go to a more secure country, perhaps England" (Brabant, Falzeder, & Giampieri-Deutsch, 2000, p. 447). Freud, however, saw the situation differently:

> It is not certain that the Hitler regime will also overpower Austria; . . . it will not reach the height of brutality here that it has in Germany. There is certainly no personal danger for me, and if you assume life in oppression to be amply uncomfortable for us Jews, then don't forget how little contentment life promises refugees in a foreign country . . . Flight, I think, would be justified only in the case of lethal danger. (Letter from Freud to Ferenczi, 2 April 1933, Brabant, Falzeder, & Giampieri-Deutsch, 2000, p. 449)

A few years and the psychoanalytic community in Budapest would be gripped by the dilemma expressed in the final correspondence between Freud and Ferenczi. To go or to stay? This choice—whatever it would be—had to be made in a timely manner.

Thus, in this period between 1920 and 1938, a sketch was made for a painting of the Budapest School on that long canvas that depicts the universal history of psychoanalysis. The Budapest analysts formed part of the international scholarly mainstream. Their writings had appeared in *Imago*, *Zeitschrift für Psychoanalyse*, and *The International Journal of Psychoanalysis*. Moreover, their participation at international conferences also signified a solid role for Budapest in the movement. Before the annexation of Austria, between 15 and 17 May 1937, Budapest hosted the Second *Vierländertagung*, a four-country conference organised with the participation of analysts from Hungary, Austria, Czechoslovakia, and Italy. The methodology and technique of supervision, the early phases of self-development, primary love, psychoanalytic pedagogy, and the significance of ego defence mechanisms in the process of psychoanalysis were all among the topics discussed. Anna Freud, Paul Federn (1871–1950), Eduardo Weiss (1889–1979), Otto Fenichel, Theodor Reich (1888–1969), Carl Landauer (1887–1945), and, from Hungary, Michael Balint, Alice Balint, Lillian Rotter-Kertész, and Imre Hermann spent this weekend together (Harmat, 1994). Few imagined that they would never meet this way again.[71] They now faced a future filled with immeasurable trials.

CHAPTER SIX

The USA's immigration policy: the sum of conflicting vectors

It was in the immediate wake of the Anschluss that the American Psychoanalytic Association (APsaA)[72] established the Emergency Committee on Relief and Immigration, as I will discuss in detail in a later chapter. Thus, the Emergency Committee sprang from a civil society initiative.

The significance of its establishment and operation can only be fully appreciated in the context of the US government's refugee and immigration policy. It is in the light of this that we can reconstruct the various domestic and foreign policy factors that determined and limited the organisation's room for manoeuvre. It is in this way that we can arrive at the answers to such questions as who the committee needed to co-operate with, how it managed to obtain support, who it could count on, and what resistance it met as it attempted to aid in the escape and resettlement of European peers in line with its set goals.

The backdrop of a restrictive policy

The immigration policy of the USA in the period preceding the establishment of the Emergency Committee on Relief and Immigration was shaped by four major factors:[73]

1. Restrictive immigration laws and regulations already in place.
2. The rigid attitude of the USA's State Department officials and their overemphasis on protecting American interests.
3. Anti-immigration sentiment among the American public.
4. The initial reluctance of Franklin D. Roosevelt (1882–1945), the president of the USA throughout this critical period between 1933 and 1945, to undertake political risks that necessarily accompanied humanitarian measures;

Traditionally, the USA has been a refuge for European emigrants and an advocate of religious and political rights. During the second part of the nineteenth century and the beginning of the twentieth, America permitted over 2.5 million Jews to enter. The growth in the number of immigrants, however, was accompanied by a gradual increase in the fear among the White Anglo-Saxon Protestant (WASP) American mainstream of racial and religious minorities—such as "blacks, Orientals, Roman Catholics, as well as Jews" (Breitman & Kraut, 1987, p. 7). Therefore, the government steadily imposed restrictions on immigration first against the Chinese and Japanese and then—after the First World War—against Europeans.

At the same time, America saw the emergence of the Red Scare tied to the spread of Bolshevism and anarchism, both of which were viewed as an import from abroad. Some of the immigrants—especially those who had joined strikes as members of trade unions—were deemed non-required radical elements and were often branded as being disloyal to their adopted country. Further, eugenics and poorly interpreted anthropology represented an influential form of racism disguised as science. A book published in 1916 by anthropologist Madison Grant (1865–1937), *The Passing of the Great Race*, reinforced this nativist racism, as did *The Dearborn Independent* newspaper a few years later. Published by Henry Ford (1863–1947), who had revolutionised the auto industry, this was an anti-Semitic weekly that frightened its readership with articles on the Red Scare and Jewish world domination.

Meanwhile, the Johnson–Reed Immigration Act, which had been in the works between 1921 and 1924, established an annual national origins quota for each European country. The criteria for the development of the quota system had clearly represented a value dimension in American society. One of the key goals of the policy was to effect a return to the country's earlier ethnic proportions. A quota system developed in 1921 set the proportions based on the USA's Census of 1910. It is fascinating to ponder what lies at the heart of the various criteria, considerations, and ideologies in a country's decision as to whom it can accept and in what number. At first, the US established the annual immigrant quota at a maximum of 3% of the total number of foreign-born Americans and, within this, the national origins composition reflected the presence of the various foreign-born nationalities based on the 1910 Census. In the end, however, the Johnson–Reed Act considered Census figures from 1890, since the proportions in that year favoured certain European national groups thought to be more diligent—that is, WASPs—and, thus, it was able to exclude those who were deemed as having difficulty assimilating or being unwilling to do so. These groups included, for example, the Slavs ("Every Slav is a Bolshevik agitator"), the Italians ("Every Italian is an anarchist"), and the Jews ("who have too much power in the US").[74] By the time the law was enacted, the initial 3% was reduced to 2%. The principle of national origins sparked heated debate. Nevertheless, the law went into effect in 1929, and, based on the quota system, an annual ceiling on the number of immigrants was set at 153,774 (Breitman & Kraut, 1987, p. 7).

Due to the Great Depression, the USA was forced to impose further restrictions. President Herbert Hoover (1874–1964) and the State Department—without approval from Congress—introduced a stricter version of the so-called Public Charge Clause in 1930,[75] which had first seen the light of day in a law from 1882 and had then re-emerged in the Immigration Act of 1917. This clause regulated people who were unable to work due to physical or mental disabilities and were, therefore, likely to become a public burden. In order to prevent this, people in these categories were not granted visas. This discriminatory law was first applied to Mexicans. In September 1930, however, it was expanded to include European immigrants as well. The restriction was justified by the argument that immigrants who were unable to work would be unable to find a job under current market conditions and therefore be unable to earn a living.

This tightening of policy, dubbed the Hoover Barricade after the previous president, was still in effect in 1933, when Jews were forced to escape Nazi Germany. Despite congressional debate, no new immigration laws were introduced in the 1930s. Inertia favoured advocates of tightened policies although the pro-immigration camp also included influential figures—among them Secretary of Labour Frances Perkins (1880–1965) and Felix Frankfurter (1882–1965), who was a Harvard law professor, an adviser to President Roosevelt, and a Supreme Court Justice.

While the number of Jews immigrating to the USA remained within the established limits, it gradually grew throughout the 1930s. However, between 1939 and 1941, the tendency reversed due to tightened regulations—precisely at the point that the Nazis had launched their mass deportation and annihilation of the Jews. The period of an even more restrictive policy lasted almost until the war's end. During the Roosevelt era, the American government focused on two significant issues: economic growth and defending the USA against the fascist enemy coalition. In the absence of presidential and congressional—that is, appropriate political—backing, few bureaucrats found saving persecuted foreigners to be compatible with protecting national interests.

Between 1933 and 1944, altogether 120,000 German and Austrian citizens immigrated to the USA. In the light of the number of immigrants escaping Nazism in other European countries, the total number of immigrants in this period can be set at 250,000. Great Britain permitted 70,000 to enter, but Canada allowed fewer than 5,000. The USA's performance is hardly the weakest, therefore, although the total annual quota of 153,774 was never met and the total number never even surpassed 54% of that quota. Also, the annual quota of 25,957 set for Germany was only rarely met. Tragically, many hundreds of thousands of the six million Jews killed during the Holocaust had applied for a USA visa even before the war had broken out—and had been rejected (Breitman & Kraut, 1987, p. 10).

Those who enforced the law did so rigidly, and the State Department placed enormous pressure on its consuls. As a consequence, it was impossible to use up the quotas permitted by the law. The State Department's exclusionary policies were already being served at the first stage of the system, since the consulates and consuls working abroad naturally did so under the aegis of the Department. The interests of State always stood in opposition to the policies of the liberal Secretary of Labour and, later, to the efforts of all the organisations that fought for a loosening of the quota and other prohibitive measures. We can only obtain a realistic picture of the circumstances and difficulties that the refugees and their supporters struggled against through an analysis of the relationship between these two federal departments. Their internecine rivalry was taking place at a time when every single step—indeed, every single delay—was, literally, a matter of life and death, yet the USA's refugee policy in the early days of Hitler's Germany (1933–1934) was characterised by pitched battles between these two institutions.

Initially, the USA wished to view Adolf Hitler as merely a factor in German domestic politics. Both news reports throughout the month following the Führer's rise to power and the reaction to them represented an accurate expression of the contemporary public mood. In the 14 March 1933 issue of *The New York Times*, the new Democratic administration announced the launch of a $2 billion aid programme to assist many millions of America's unemployed and declared an arms embargo on the world's troubled regions (Breitman & Kraut, 1987). The *Times* also reported on the persecution and arrest of members of the opposition in Hitler's Germany. However, as Breitman and Kraut observe, "there was no sign that the president of the United States had taken any particular interest in German developments" (p. 11).

Irving Lehman (1876–1945), a judge (later chief judge) on the Court of Appeals in President Roosevelt's home state of New York, attempted to draw the president's attention to the worrying German situation as well as to the fact that some of the Jews were being forced to flee their homes. The judge expressed his hope that the government would state its sympathy for the persecuted and that the president would amend Hoover's 1930 order on the strict enforcement of the Public Charge Clause.

Because of unemployment, however, the liberalisation of immigration would have posed a major political risk. The Secretary of State did not back the proposal that the German Jews should be granted visas above the quota—no matter how humanitarian this might have been. The administration had to bow to pressure, however. Thus, in a cabinet meeting on 7 April 1933, President Roosevelt proposed that prominent figures persecuted by the Nazis should be permitted to enter the country. This was backed by his Secretary of State, and the president charged Secretary of Labour Perkins with taking action.

The first female member of a USA cabinet, Perkins had to cope with a great many responsibilities during the Great Depression, yet her attitude toward the immigrants remained positive and understanding. She supported the émigrés throughout with her actions and recommendations. She and Felix Frankfurter, then a key adviser to President Roosevelt, drafted a proposal, which, if implemented, would have counted, rather hopefully, on the co-operation of the USA's consuls abroad. The purpose of the proposal was to institute new criteria in assisting the refugees while complying with the laws in force. Among these, the most important ones were:

1. Visa applications from people escaping racial or religious persecution should enjoy priority.
2. The Secretary of State should issue an order that the USA's consuls abroad should handle visa applications submitted by those fleeing racial or religious persecution in accordance with the procedures used prior to Hoover's 1930 amendment; that is, consuls should disregard the criterion of likely employability under current market conditions since this criterion was selective by its very nature.

However, the proposal was opposed by Secretary of State Cordell Hull (1871–1955),[76] and was considered an outright mistake by William Phillips (1878–1968), then Undersecretary of State. Therefore, as a result of the anti-immigration laws, the annual German quota remained unfilled, and, in President Roosevelt's assessment, no measures were necessary under the circumstances. Perkins strongly criticised Phillips's position because she believed that meeting the quota was rendered impossible by the strict interpretation of 1930. Moreover, it turned out that in 1930 the State Department had ordered its consuls to *reduce* the number of immigrant visas to 10% of the existing quota. The consuls were working under the authority of the State Department, while the enforcement of immigration laws fell under Labour. Was it possible to have a positive effect on the consulates in this environment?

Since the USA's government had not openly condemned Nazi Germany, the points of orientation came down to regulations created in the crossfire between the two departments. The Labour Department attempted to create acceptance for its humanitarian approach through economic arguments—seeing potential customers in the immigrants—but this supportive attitude stood in stark contrast to the line taken at the State Department, which rejected the proposal for fear of a larger confrontation. Officials at State acted as if they did not wish to understand what was actually happening in Germany. In their ostrich policy, they upheld their role in representing the interests of America's twelve million unemployed—although that particular socio-economic problem actually fell under the purview of Perkins and her department. Under these circumstances, positive change in small steps was the only thing that could be hoped for.

All Perkins could do was to extend existing visitors' visas and to continue bringing pressure to bear on State in the hope of assisting the refugees in finding a way to reach America. Finally, the State Department made a modest compromise. It ordered its consuls at least not to apply the Public Charge Clause quite so zealously when it came to foreign relatives of American residents. However, those who could not secure an affidavit from relatives or were unable to prove that they would be able to provide for themselves continued to fall under the effect of the limitations imposed by the Clause. The word *affidavit*, thus, was elevated to a special status, since the existence or lack of it could determine whether one lived or died.

Obtaining an affidavit represented an enormous task for every person and civil society organisation, including the Emergency Committee. Financial guarantees were required for every single immigrant, and a family of three or four required a deposit of $5,000 annually. This amount—which was double the annual income of the chief administrator at the Chicago Institute for Psychoanalysis and was equal to the yearly pay of a recently graduated physician at the same institute—had to be deposited in advance.

Initially, Roosevelt was politically more worried by the Third Reich threatening the interests of the USA than by the Holocaust specifically. Thus, the president sometimes wished to influence immigration policy with the aim of liberalising restrictions and at other times with the aim of tightening them until, in the end, he took a new tack and established the War Refugee Board in January 1944, which proved to be an effective solution—though one which was long overdue.

The ordeal of obtaining documents

Even in peacetime, it required massive time and effort to meet the requirements set by the Immigration Act of 1924. It listed the following requisite documents:

1. Proof that the individual has no criminal record.
2. Proof of military service.
3. Two copies of a certified birth certificate.

These documents could only be obtained from competent authorities at one's permanent place of residence, and that was no easy process. Victims of persecution who had managed to escape Germany and found temporary refuge were, therefore, unable to procure all of the paperwork. Nevertheless, arguing that criminals should not be permitted into the country, the State Department was unwilling to relax policy. In September 1933, it did little more than offer the option of "the most favourable treatment permissible under the law" (Breitman & Kraut, 1987, p. 18) to applicants facing a nearly impossible task. Within a few months, by the end that year, the situation had become so intolerable that the State Department provided the consuls the option of granting an exemption on the documents if an applicant was unable to produce them.

Another small step forward was a statement from the Labour Department known as the Public Charge Bond, with which it was sufficient for an immigrant to guarantee that she or he would not become a public charge.

However, the State Department protested and threatened to reduce the quota. It was outraged by the fact that Labour had placed hurdles in the way of the consuls' work, having tied their hands by preventing them from declaring applicants as potential public charges. As a consequence, in their view, the US would lose one of its security measures: consuls, as the "vanguard" of their nation, had up to then been practically competing with one another to reject immigrant visa applications. In 1933, therefore, the quota for Germany of 25,975 remained largely unfilled: a mere 1,300 applicants in Germany were issued immigrant visas that year (Breitman & Kraut, 1987, p. 23). Although the situation improved somewhat in the following year (in 1934, 4,000 refugees were granted immigrant visas under the quota), this still amounted to six and a half times *fewer* than the annual number of people who *could* have been offered the opportunity to resettle in the USA.

The immigration of the German Jewish refugees was, thus, limited by the State Department's understanding or interpretation of the Public Charge Clause. The strictness of the Clause could have been eased with the Public Charge Bond, but the Labour Department was unable to develop its plan thoroughly. Many government officials worried that if they gave a green light to immigration then unemployment would grow—and so would anti-Semitism. Public sentiment, and, therefore, Congress, preferred to back a restrictive policy.

Berlin up close (1933–1934)

The phrasing of the tightened immigration policy of the USA in the 1920s was developed by the Chief of the Consular Bureau, Wilbur J. Carr (1870–1942), and it was he who embodied the refugee policy of the 1930s. Between 1924 and 1937, he served as Undersecretary of State. As a model bureaucrat, he ran his office with an iron fist and placed absolute compliance with American laws above all else. Carr sincerely believed that he was doing everything possible to assist the refugees within the set legal framework. For various reasons and due to various convictions, top officials at the State Department generally fought vigorously against Perkins's liberal-minded and helpful attitude and against the efforts of Jewish organisations in the USA.

While the USA's government engaged in its conceptual battles, George S. Messersmith (1883–1960),[77] the consul general in Berlin, clearly grasped what awaited the German Jews based on his daily experiences. His German origins, proficiency in the language, and position all enabled him to nurture important ties with politicians and business people. When Göring was outraged at the media reactions in the USA to the German boycott of Jewish shops, Messersmith responded in his own restrained but determined way, making it known to the German military leadership that his country's government did not control the media and that, like many other Americans, he, too, was concerned about the persecution of the Jews. Messersmith cultivated good relations with the leaders of European Jewish organisations, and American Jewry also acknowledged his efforts. In fact, for his good deeds, the Nazis branded him a "half-Jew" (Breitman & Kraut, 1987, p. 41).

Messersmith saw clearly that the increasingly brutal measures taken by Germany pointed toward the annihilation of the Jews. Of the "enemies of the Third Reich", over 25,000 people were rounded up and hauled off to concentration camps as early as July 1933. In the autumn, Messersmith was already aware that the Nazis were preparing to deprive Jews of their German citizenship. By that time, it had become patently obvious that they were being made outcasts by law, plundered and penniless, their entire fortunes confiscated. This further weakened the chances for Jewish refugees to immigrate, since they were forced to rely on affidavits from others. Nevertheless, the consul general in Berlin followed the orders handed down to him and dropped the quota to 10%.

Messersmith trusted in the speedy collapse of the Third Reich and attempted to keep the American nation distanced from Nazi Germany. For example, he advocated that his country should boycott the 1936 Summer Olympics in Berlin. He saw the European Jews' immigration to the USA as a danger, but this view was informed by open nationalism, not by veiled anti-Semitism. As the number of applications grew, Messersmith was approached to help amend the Hoover order. However, he turned down the request, justifying it with the USA's unemployment and domestic political risks. Similarly, he opposed the establishment of the University in Exile[78] proposed by Alvin S. Johnson (1874–1971), which later became part of The New School for Social Research and employed numerous left-wing and Jewish staff who had had to flee Germany.[79] As Fermi observes, "[a]s a consequence of Hitler's laws, 1,678 lecturers and professors lost their jobs" (Fermi, 1968, p. 52). However, in a letter to Carr dated 5 July 1933, Messersmith argued as follows: "We cannot fill our own universities with foreign professors who are alien to our thought and will influence our youth in a direction not in line with our national policy and our cultural life" (cited in Breitman & Kraut, 1987, p. 44).

Clearly, Messersmith was worried that members of the left-wing intelligentsia did not have sufficiently strong ties to the American system and, thus, would be unable to reinforce feelings of patriotism in America's youth:

> The average Jew, for example, who desires to emigrate to the United States, will be very glad to be able to make a home for himself in our country and to fit himself into our picture; but these professors who feel that they have a mission in life may potentially be a danger to us. (Breitman & Kraut, 1987, pp. 44–45)

Lives depended on the personal judgement of the consuls, and Messersmith was a centrist. He considered it worth supporting clearly unproblematic people who—either presumably or certainly—posed no threat to the USA, while, with regard to the others, he was of the opinion that, even though they were being persecuted, their immigration visa applications had to be rejected.

European fascism gains strength, and the USA's visa policy is eased

After the Nuremberg laws were introduced in 1935, fascism gained strength in Europe, prompting the State Department to effect changes in policy. At the recommendation of the visa office, an affidavit would also be accepted from distant relatives of immigrants. In 1937, regulations were further relaxed: now, a consular officer could only reject an applicant that he deemed *highly likely* to become a public charge; the mere *possibility* of the applicant becoming a public burden was insufficient grounds for rejection.

Homer Brett (1887–?), consul general in Rotterdam, maintained that this "radical change" was due in large part to the efforts of Jewish organisations. As a result of the shift, the number of European immigrants rose to 6,987 in 1936, 12,532 in 1937, and 20,301 in 1938. However, let us not lose sight of the fact that 1938 was a watershed year for the spread of fascism in Europe. The occupation of Austria was a powerful warning sign even for those who had doubted the power of the Third Reich.

On 12 March 1938, the German army marched into Vienna, having experienced no resistance, and Austria was annexed to Germany. National Socialism now had a destructive effect on culture in Vienna. Creative intellectuals—independent-minded scholars and artists—were forced to flee. According to later figures, 36.25% of Austria's musicians left for the USA and 6.3% immigrated to the UK, while 37% of those involved in Austria's cinema and theatre escaped to the USA (Rathkolb, 1995).

On 13 March 1938, the second day of the Anschluss, the Vienna Psychoanalytic Society held a meeting, as an exception, in Freud's home at 19 Berggasse. It was a pivotal evening. The members voted to dissolve the Society and to re-establish it wherever Freud would resettle. The eighty-two-year-old Freud shook hands with every member and said goodbye with the following words: "There is nothing one can do about it" (Freud, 1938, cited in Molnar, 1992, p. 230).

Anna Freud was interrogated by the Gestapo. She had to prove that the IPA was neither a political group nor an international terrorist organisation. It was clear to her that she, her family, and all those close to them would either manage to escape or be fated to suffer a concentration camp and death. The psychoanalytic publishing house was seized. Three days after the Anschluss, on 15 March, the Freud family home was searched by a unit of SA brownshirts. The Freuds' passports were confiscated along with 6000 schillings, for which a receipt was left. Freud noted laconically, "I have never taken so much for a single visit" (Molnar, 1992, p. 231).

In a speech in Vienna two weeks later, Hermann Göring announced that the city would be purely German within four years. The Jews had to go. This statement not only referred to the 170,000 religious Jews there, but also to all "non-Aryans", amounting to the deportation of an additional 400,000–500,000 people—code for liquidation. The Nazis immediately began to assess and confiscate Jewish property. Deprived of their homes and loved ones, their property and human rights, the Jews had to leave their homeland within a set time period. Otherwise, they would be destined for the concentration camps at Buchenwald and Dachau. Within six months, a total of 50,000 Jews had left territories under Nazi occupation.

At the USA's consulate in Vienna, about 6,000 people were received daily between 9 a.m. and 10 p.m., and 500 interviews were conducted. The Nazis did not want to allow the Jews time to obtain visas for the USA, as this would have taken a number of months. They insisted on their immediate departure and threatened them with extermination in the name of de-Judification if they did not leave. The would-be émigrés were caught in a trap. How could they leave the country without their passports, which had been confiscated? Hundreds of thousands of people were in imminent danger, yet the USA's annual quota at the time permitted no more than 1,413 immigrants from Austria.

It became clear that America had to make a move. President Roosevelt himself backed a humanitarian strategy but preferably in such a way that it should not require the approval of Congress, which would surely have opposed any such plan. Vice President John N. Gardner (1868–1967) noted, "if it were left to a secret vote of Congress, *all* immigration would be stopped" (Breitman & Kraut, 1987, p. 58).

The Roosevelt administration was forced to find loopholes within the existing regulatory framework. Four suggestions were made to resolve the situation:

1. Roosevelt proposed a clever compromise to increase the quota limit for Austrian immigrants: since Austria had been annexed to Germany, the Austrian quota should be added to the German quota and this should hold valid for Austrian Jews. Thus, the number of potential Austrian immigrants, which had been below 1,500, was raised to 25,957.
2. The procedure for evaluating affidavits submitted by Americans should be simplified.
3. A new US organisation should be established to co-ordinate donations provided by private groups and individuals.
4. A new international organisation should be set up to assist the refugees in the face of the enormous opposition to the immigration of German, Austrian, and Czech Jews—and the 3.3 million Jews in Poland did not even figure in the equation at the time.

Roosevelt agreed to using the concept of political—and not racial or religious—refugees and also reminded Americans of their national traditions, primarily the humanitarian gesture of receiving immigrants. At the same time, he also encouraged the emergence of private organisations that could provide financial support.

However, the strict affidavit procedure remained unchanged. Messersmith, then Chief of the Consular Bureau, insisted on this position: only those who may be useful to the American state should be allowed to enter the country. Perkins's recommendation for relaxing the process was rejected. The following data illustrate the USA's public sentiment at the time: in January 1939, nine months after the Anschluss, 82% of the population was opposed to immigration (Breitman & Kraut, 1987).

The efforts of the US psychoanalysts on the Emergency Committee on Relief and Immigration to rescue their European peers and their family members should be located and evaluated within the context of the special circumstances of the age—against the backdrop of an American public opinion that was opposed to the liberalisation of immigration and harboured major reservations about it at best.

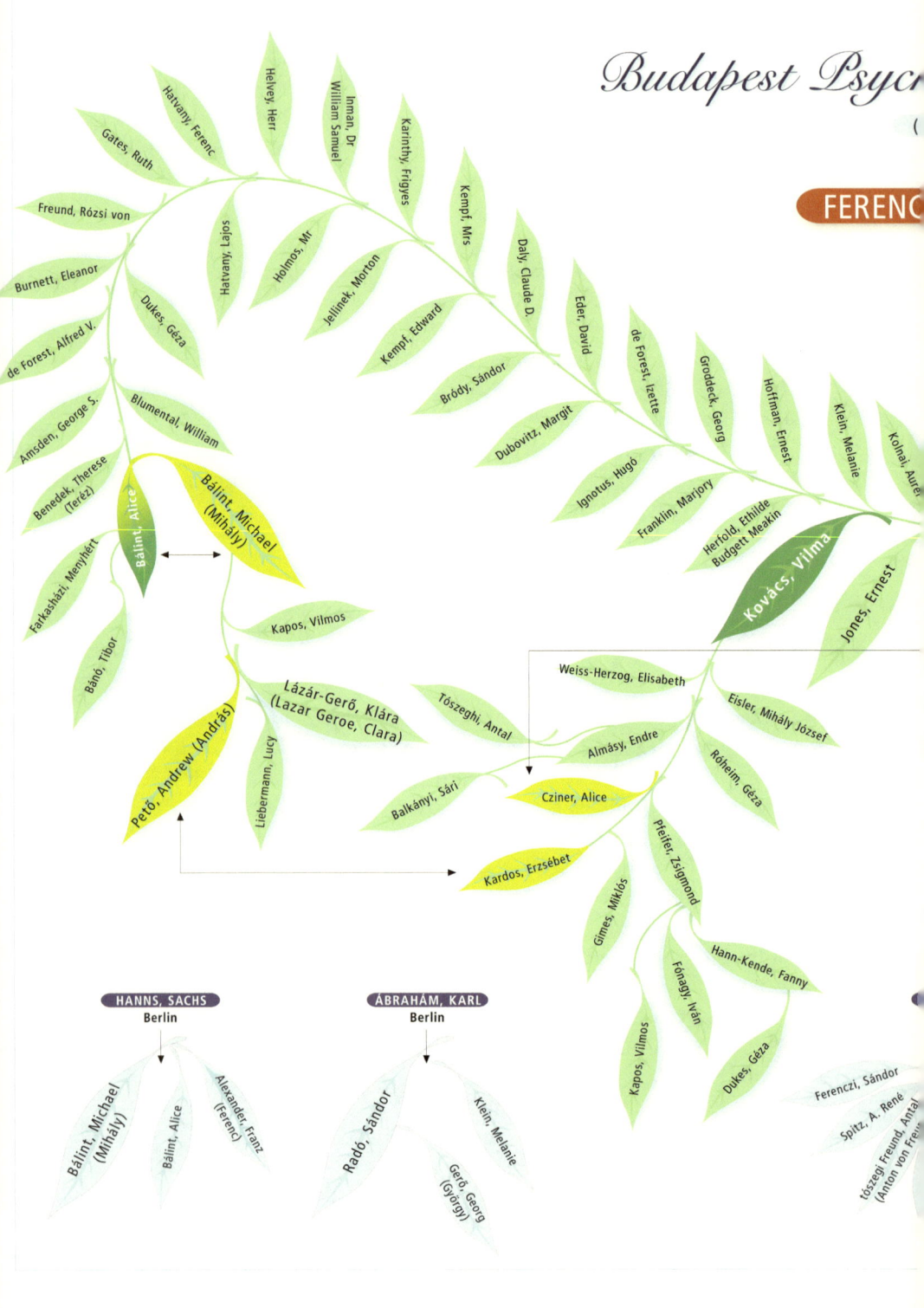

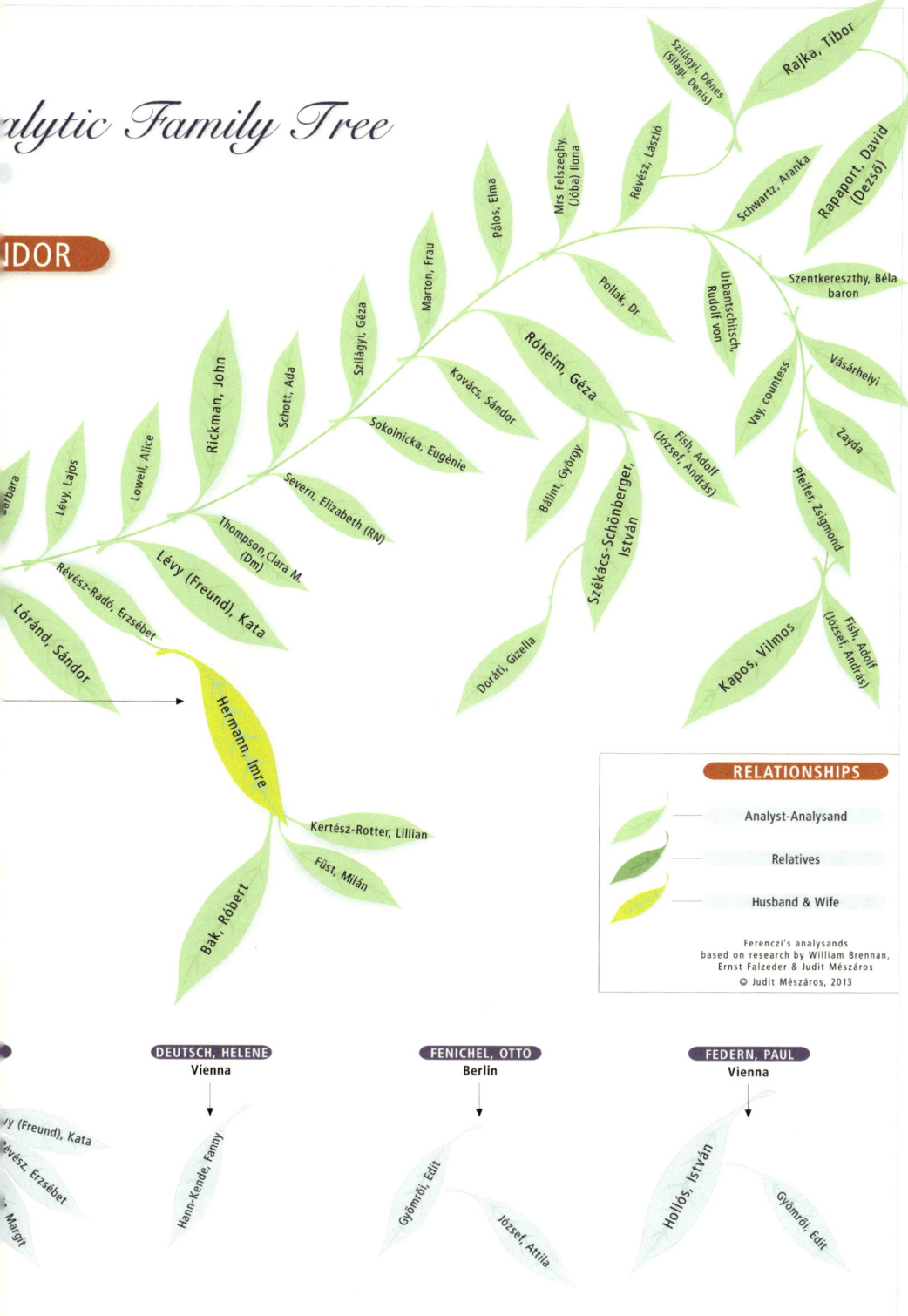

CHAPTER SEVEN

"Your Committee": the Emergency Committee on Relief and Immigration of the American Psychoanalytic Association

> "I can assure you that we will do all we can to secure affidavits
> ... for all of our colleagues who want ultimately to come here"
> (Kubie to István Hollós, 19 January 1939, Mészáros, 2008, p. 222)

On Sunday 13 March 1938, one day after the Anschluss, the American Psychoanalytic Association (APsaA) set up the Emergency Committee on Relief and Immigration. The work of this committee would play a central role in the history of psychoanalysis (Jeffrey, 1989; Mészáros, 1998b, 2012; Thompson 2012). Members of the committee were drawn from several different psychoanalytic societies in the USA: Dr Lawrence S. Kubie, Dr Bertram D. Lewin, Dr Sandor Rado, Dr Monroe A. Meyer, and Dr George Daniels from the New York Psychoanalytic Society; Dr Lewis Hill representing the Washington–Baltimore Psychoanalytic Society; Dr Helene Deutsch, Dr Henry Murray, and Dr M. Ralph Kaufman from the Boston Psychoanalytic Society; and Dr Franz Alexander and Dr Thomas French on hand from the Chicago Psychoanalytic Society.

The majority of the committee members had had considerable experience and personal relationships with the European analysts.

Many had undergone training in Berlin. In addition to Hungarians Rado and Alexander, who had resettled in the USA earlier, there were also Thomas French and Bertram D. Lewin, both of whom had been trained by Alexander at the Berlin Institute. Lewin's duties on the committee involved financial matters. The committee chair, Lawrence S. Kubie, had spent several years in London, while Helene Deutsch's own life history made her very much at home in Central Eastern Europe. She knew the members of both the Vienna and Berlin societies very well and was familiar with conditions in the region.

These are the people—along with committee co-chair and secretary Bettina Warburg—who would do the most in the coming years to keep the organisation mobilised so that it could play its historic role in rescuing the European analysts. Chair Kubie had a particularly enormous job in all this, as did Lewin and Warburg, who worked closely with him.

What was it that sustained the energy in the committee members, which they were able to channel into aiding so many peers in the years to come? A few lines about their histories might bring us closer to an answer and, more importantly, to the people themselves.

Lawrence S. Kubie (1896–1973) was a psychiatrist and psychoanalyst born in New York City. He began his studies at Harvard, taking courses in the law, politics, and economics, but in his second year he turned his attention to medicine, and to psychiatry in particular. In 1921, he earned his medical degree from Johns Hopkins University in Baltimore, Maryland. He won a research grant, which took him to London and work in neurology. Here, he saw Edward Glover for personal analysis between 1928 and 1930. A close friendship would develop between them after his return to New York. Kubie retained his strong ties to British and European psychoanalysis through Glover much as he upheld his keen interest in politics and the social sciences (Bartemeier, 1974). This certainly explains why he brought such outstanding service to bear in his position as head of the Emergency Committee (1938–1939). In fact, his efforts went well beyond the remit of his position. He was truly a man on a mission. In 1939, when he was elected president of the New York Psychoanalytic Society, he resigned from his post at the Emergency Committee but continued to work on behalf of the refugees.[80]

Bertram D. Lewin (1896–1971) grew up in San Antonio, Texas. He possessed outstanding skills in music and literature and also spoke several languages. He studied medicine at Johns Hopkins between

1916 and 1920. A life-long friendship developed between Kubie and himself as of 1917. His family had preserved the roots they had transplanted from Germany, and he began his studies in psychoanalysis in the 1920s with Franz Alexander at the Berlin Institute. He experienced his first taste of anti-Semitism and marginalisation in the USA when his outstanding student performance won him the opportunity to sail for Europe on Henry Ford's "Peace Ship" during the First World War but Ford would not permit him to come along because he was Jewish. He put his mathematical skills and extraordinary memory to the service of the committee as its financial officer.[81]

Helene Deutsch (1884–1982) was a physician and psychoanalyst. She was born Helen Rosenbach and grew up in Przemyśl, a town in Poland near its present-day border with Ukraine. She studied in Lemberg (Lviv in present-day Ukraine) and in Zurich and came into contact with members of the Polish radical intelligentsia at a young age. A committed advocate of equal rights for women, Deutsch earned her medical degree from the University of Vienna in 1913. It was a matter of enormous prestige for her, particularly as a woman, to work with the Austrian psychiatrist and future Nobel laureate (1927) Julius Wagner-Jauregg at his psychiatric clinic. Her husband, Felix Deutsch, was also a physician and psychoanalyst. Freud was Helene's first analyst between 1918 and 1919, and later, from 1923 to 1924, she saw Karl Abraham in Berlin. She began teaching at the Berlin Psychoanalytic Institute and then, after her return to Vienna, assisted in setting up the Vienna training institute, which she ran as of 1935. During her time in Vienna, her students included August Aichhorn, Anna Freud, Heinz Hartmann, Wilhelm Hoffer, Wilhelm Reich, Theodor Reik, and Richard and Edith Sterba (Roazen, 1985). Like many other European analysts, including Franz Alexander, she was invited to the First International Congress on Mental Hygiene to be held in 1930 in Washington, D.C. Alexander was the first to ask her to come to America, but she declined. However, she accepted Professor Stanley Cobb's invitation in 1935 and moved to Boston with her husband in 1936, prior to the Anschluss.[82]

Henry A. Murray (1893–1988), American physician, psychologist, and psychoanalyst, founded the Boston Psychoanalytic Society and taught for several decades at Harvard. In the 1930s, he went to Carl Gustav Jung for analysis and was strongly influenced by him. He developed the TAT (Thematic Apperception Test), a personality assessment procedure. The point of the test is for the participant to project fantasies on to a series of pictures through a projection mechanism.

M. Ralph Kaufman (1900–1977) was the president of the APsaA between 1949 and 1951.

We have already encountered Franz Alexander (1891–1964) several times so far. He was born in Budapest to an educated Jewish family. His father, Bernard, was a renowned philosopher. As a young man, Franz was involved in the intellectual renewal of Budapest in the 1910s. He started and completed his medical studies in Budapest, but also studied in Göttingen and Cambridge in the meantime. His psychoanalytic approach was shaped by his years at the Berlin Institute and by his early relationship with Freud, Ferenczi, and the Budapest analysts. Together with Sandor Rado, he gained enormous experience from his emigration from Hungary in the 1920s and his Berlin years, which would ready him for his work on the committee. He established the Chicago Institute for Psychoanalysis in 1931 and worked as its director for twenty-five years. He had a great impact on the development of psychoanalysis and psychoanalytic psychosomatics in the USA.

Thomas French (1892–1976) turned to medicine after having studied engineering. In 1920, he completed his degree at the Cornell University School of Medicine and specialised in psychiatry and psychoanalysis. He was trained as an analyst at the Berlin Institute with Alexander as his training analyst. When Alexander commenced his work at the psychoanalytic institute in Chicago, French was with him from the very outset. Although French and Alexander were individuals of completely different styles and temperaments, a working relationship that would span a lifetime developed between them. They published several books together. Among them, *Psychoanalytic Therapy: Principles and Application* (1946) was based on a review of 292 institute cases. After the last volumes of Ferenczi's complete work were published in 1939, French—unlike Freud and Jones—acknowledged the significance of Ferenczi's new approach to trauma theory (French, 1941). After Alexander's departure in 1956, French remained in Chicago and carried on his teaching and research.

Sandor Rado was one of the acknowledged leaders and teachers of North American psychoanalysis. From 1931 to 1941, he was founding director of the New York Psychoanalytic Institute. In 1944, he established the Psychoanalytic Institute at Columbia University in

New York City, which he ran until 1955. He assisted in the establishment of the New York School of Psychiatry at the State University of New York (SUNY), which he headed for ten years. He wrote a number of studies that are considered classics. He abandoned orthodox Freudian psychoanalysis and stressed the capacity of the personality to adapt and the importance of genetics.

Born in New York City, Monroe A. Meyer (1892–1939) was a psychiatrist and psychoanalyst. After earning his medical degree from Cornell in 1916, he saw service overseas in the First World War. In 1921–1922, he studied with Freud in Vienna and then returned to New York to begin his practice. He first worked as an adjunct psychiatrist at Mount Sinai Hospital in New York alongside his private practice. Later, as of 1932, he devoted himself to the aim of building up the New York Psychoanalytic Institute. He was also one of Lawrence Kubie's supervisors. He was very sensitive to questions of democratic and autocratic forces in the world and was highly motivated to assist "all who suffered, whether it was a patient or a nation" (*Psychoanalytic Quarterly*, 8: 139–140).

Lewis Hill (1894–1958) was born in Lima, Ohio. He studied medicine, graduating in 1916 from the Medical College of Virginia in Richmond, and began to specialise as a surgeon, but his interests soon turned to psychiatry and psychoanalysis. In 1925, he commenced his training in psychoanalysis at the Washington–Baltimore Psychoanalytic Society. In all likelihood, he attended Ferenczi's USA lectures in 1926–1927 because he sought Ferenczi out as his supervisor in Budapest in 1933. According to his obituary, "[t]his year in Budapest was not only fruitful from the professional point of view but was an enriching life experience which remained vividly with him" (Anderson, 1958, p. 741). In 1933, Hill returned to Baltimore. At the time the only psychoanalyst in the city, he pioneered the development of psychoanalysis in the Washington–Baltimore region. He was the president of the Washington–Baltimore Psychoanalytic Society between 1935 and 1938, and he was elected president of the APsaA in 1939. He began teaching at Johns Hopkins in 1944, a job he continued to do for the rest of his life, just like his work in training psychoanalysts at the Baltimore Psychoanalytic Institute and in teaching psychiatrists at the National Institute of Mental Health. His primary interests lay in schizophrenia and borderline cases. 1955 saw the publication of his book *Psychotherapeutic Intervention in Schizophrenia*.

On 13 March 1938, Kubie signed the one-and-a-half-page memorandum that set down the operating principles of the Emergency Committee.[83] It had already been discussed several months before that, based on experience accumulated with the immigrants from Germany, an organisation would be necessary to serve as a liaison between the APsaA and the International Psychoanalytical Association (IPA). In January, Rado, French, Hill, Daniels, Kaufman, and Kubie met in New York City as members of an APsaA special committee to discuss how to facilitate the immigration of their European colleagues into the USA most effectively and what solutions could be found to lessen the hardships tied to their resettlement. They came to the conclusion that the APsaA should set up a standing committee to deal explicitly with these problems and to seek out solutions for the integration of the European analysts. Their main points were as follows:

1. The relationship of the émigré analysts to the IPA and to the APsaA must be clarified.
2. Lay analysts must be offered the right to teach in compensation for opportunities available to them in the USA that diverged from European psychoanalytic practice. A review must also be made of the circumstances under which and with whom they would be able to practise psychoanalysis.

The primary goal of the January meeting was to maintain the number of émigré experts within certain limits; to direct them to less preferred professional communities instead of the more popular hubs; and to ensure that psychoanalytic training would continue to remain in the hands of highly qualified and recognised training institutes (Kubie, 1937–1938).

After the Anschluss, processes accelerated: setting up the standing committee—which was already thought to be necessary in January—suddenly became a matter of urgency because of the fate of Freud and the Austrian analysts. However, in the new situation, the criteria set down in the January meeting proved too narrow in scope. The options for émigrés had to be widened further. The committee hammered out the details for the "domestic" professional criteria, which it had retained and to which it added "foreign policy" duties. Indeed, the priority among the objectives was to produce the necessary financial resources to assist European peers in escaping. Setting up a regular channel of information between the two continents was indispensable.

News of Freud and his family suffering abusive treatment spurred President Roosevelt himself into action. On 16 March, having been directed by the President, the Deputy Secretary of State sent a cable signed by Secretary of State Cordell Hull to the USA's consul general in Vienna, John C. Wiley (1893–1967).[84]

> In accordance with the President's instruction, I have requested Wilson[85] in Berlin to take this matter up personally and informally with the appropriate German authorities and to express the hope that arrangements might be made by the appropriate authorities in Austria whereby Dr Freud and his family might be permitted to travel to Paris, where the President is informed friends are anxious to receive him. I appreciate that it is probably impossible for you under present conditions to take similar action in Vienna. I wish, however, you would telegraph the Department what the present status of the family may be and what arrangements, if any, are being made or can be made for them to leave Austria.[86]

Several days later, it became clear from another similar cable sent to Wiley that the Department of State was aware that Greek princess Marie Bonaparte[87] (1882–1962) had provided funds to aid Freud, his wife, and his daughter Anna in their escape. In that telegram, the representative from the State Department made his position clear: "To support sixteen persons is, of course, entirely beyond any resources at my disposal". He then went on to say, "But I doubt that even her [Marie Bonaparte's] resources would be sufficient to care for more than the professor, his wife, and [his] daughter, Anna".[88]

Meanwhile, psychiatrists in the USA sent a letter to the State Department signed by the president of the American Psychiatric Association in which it was stated that the nearly 2,000 psychiatrists that make up the association were ready to provide any assistance necessary for the Freud family.[89] A telegram sent to the Secretary of State by thirty-five members of the staff at New York City's Bellevue Psychiatric Hospital expressed solidarity with the Freuds and requested Secretary Hull to provide refugee status for Freud and his family in the name of humanity and to clear the way for them to cross the border safely.[90]

These disparate efforts clearly highlight how necessary and timely it was to set up the Emergency Committee to offer assistance in an

Telegram sent by US Secretary of State Cordell Hull, 16 March 1938.
Archives of the British Psychoanalytical Society, Refugee File.

efficient and co-ordinated manner. The aims of the Emergency Committee are clear from a memorandum from Kubie dated 13 March: the committee would provide aid to European psychoanalyst peers and their families in resettling in the USA and in rapidly integrating into their adoptive American professional communities. The committee would co-ordinate efforts among individuals and APsaA member organisations. It would also provide communication. In an effort to avoid overlapping efforts and lack of co-ordination, the committee would consult on individual letters of invitation and other similar steps. The Emergency Committee would update its European peers on specific conditions in the USA through the IPA and the national societies in Europe.

The Emergency Committee would also publish appeals for donations so that psychoanalysts in the USA could also aid their European colleagues financially. This collection served a dual purpose: first, to facilitate their departure from their respective countries by depositing money abroad for them to use for travel, by easing their efforts in crossing the border, and, in fact, by expediting the emigration of these endangered colleagues—irrespective of their final destination; second, to provide the resources to cover ongoing immigration. The committee set up a fund to pay for the issuance of affidavits and for the resettlement of the immigrants. Early on, this was called the Lewin Fund, since Bertram Lewin managed it.[91] The committee requested member organisations to call meetings and begin collecting donations in the light of the urgency of the situation (Kubie memo, below).

During its existence for over a decade, the Emergency Committee offered aid not only in the refugees' escape and resettlement, but also in subsequent support for those immigrants who could not find suitable work. In carrying out its complex mission from expediting the refugees' flight from European countries that had become a real danger to providing the personal guarantees required by the USA's immigration authorities to offering assistance in all phases of resettlement—from finding jobs to establishing a stable lifestyle—the committee was prepared to support those who needed it.[92] No less value should be placed on the significance of these humanitarian efforts when one considers that analysts in the USA who were providing aid had originally envisaged a more bilateral co-operation. No secret was made of the fact that, in addition to philanthropic concerns, the long-term professional consequences of this wave of immigrants were being taken into account and that the committee therefore insisted on the right to keep a check on it.

With Kubie as its chair and Bettina Warburg as its co-chair, the Emergency Committee rolled up its sleeves. It established contact

> On Sunday, March 13, 1938, the Committee of the American Psychoanalytic Association on its relationship to the International Psychoanalytic Society met and passed the following resolution:
>
> BE IT HEREBY RESOLVED that an Emergency Committee on Relief and Immigration should be established immediately by the American Psychoanalytic Association, – such Committee to be constituted as follows, and to have the powers outlined below:
>
> (1) That it should consist of the Secretary of the American Psychoanalytic Society as Chairman, and of representatives appointed by each constituent society.
>
> (2) That it shall act for all constituent societies in all matters pertaining to relief for psychoanalysts from abroad and their immigration to this country.
>
> (3) That all inquiries and appeals for information and help which are received either by members of the American Psychoanalytic Association individually, or by the various constituent societies, shall be referred to this Committee; or that the Committee shall at least be notified of all such inquiries and appeals.
>
> (4) That all invitations to European psychoanalysts, or offers of help and of information, should be made through this Committee; or where for special reasons such help, information, or invitations are extended privately, that notice of this should be supplied to this Committee in order to avoid reduplication and to coordinate all efforts.
>
> (5) That all European societies and individual analysts where they can be reached should be asked to work through this Committee.
>
> (6) That the Committee be empowered to issue a bulletin of information for prospective immigrants, advising them of the special conditions of practice in this country.
>
> BE IT FURTHER RESOLVED that each Society be asked to raise funds at once, – such funds having two purposes:
>
> (1) That an Emergency Fund be raised with all possible speed, to be put on deposit abroad for the relief of those who may have to leave troubled areas in great haste as political refugees, and with need for travelling and living expenses the moment they cross the border, irrespective of their ultimate destination.

Page 1 of a Memorandum by Lawrence S. Kubie, 13 March 1938
(The Archives & Special Collections of the A. A. Brill Library,
The New York Psychoanalytic Society and Institute).

with the State Department and the Consular Bureau and worked constantly with US government agencies. The chair took care of the lion's share of the committee's "foreign relations" work. Kubie was in direct contact with the IPA and with Ernest Jones, who at that time was the president of both the IPA and the British Psychoanalytical Society. It was through the two men's co-operation that the main emigration strategy for the European psychoanalysts was formed.

-2-

(2) Further funds to be placed on deposit here for the assistance of immigrants to this country, for the guaranteeing of affidavits of support, and the like.

All funds should be forwarded to Dr. Bertram D. Lewin, 25 Fifth Avenue, New York City, without tagging them for either purpose, so that he can allocate the money received to each demand as needed. It is urgent, however, that your society should raise funds with all possible speed for these purposes, both among your own members and in wider circles. We would ask you to call a special meeting for this purpose at once.

Arrangements are being completed that donations to this fund will be deductable from income taxes.

(Signed) Lawrence S. Kubie
Sec., American Psychoanalytic Assoc.

Page 2 of Kubie's Memorandum of 13 March 1938.

The committee maintained regular contact with psychoanalysts in the USA through APsaA member organisations. Warburg met the immigrants, interviewed them, and, if necessary, lent a hand in resolving the practical matters of everyday life. She was aware of anything that refugees might require, whether alone or with their families (Jeffrey, 1989). The Emergency Committee attempted to co-ordinate donations and streamline all processes to ensure that operations ran smoothly. It also sent reports on its meetings to APsaA member associations. In a genuine reflection of the spirit of this undertaking, the committee made regular reference to itself as "Your Committee", not merely to point out that it had been created by the APsaA, but to make clear that all along it was representing the USA's psychoanalysts in its work.

In the chair's letter of 19 March, the committee provided an early detailed account of the status of the Freud family as it suffered harassment at the hands of the Nazis and of the situation in Vienna that made it extremely difficult for the Emergency Committee to carry out its humanitarian work. It turned out that the authorities had confiscated Jews' passports immediately after Austria's occupation, and then, as part of a systematic effort, they had begun to impound their personal possessions right in the middle of official formalities. News of cruelty on a mass scale had not yet reached America, but there had been word of body searches. According to an Emergency Committee bulletin,

> Through diplomatic channels efforts are being continued to win a special permission for Professor Freud to leave. These efforts are being conducted largely through Dr Ernest Jones, who is still in Vienna. For the rest, at present, no Jew is allowed to leave Austria under any circumstances, nor is it settled what form of passport or travelling permit will be issued to replace the former Austrian passport. . . . [I]t [is] highly unlikely that anyone will be allowed to emigrate for several weeks.[93]

This news contradicted consular news that stated that, due to Nazi pressure, official documents were urgently required so that the Jews could leave the country. In an annexed Austria, the Jews had become prisoners in their own country without a passport and with their possessions confiscated. If they found no way to free themselves from this trap, they would certainly end up in concentration camps.

As noted in the previous chapter, the USA's State Department conducted a restrictive policy with all the means at its disposal. This stood in stark contrast to the dictates of common sense and the ethics of humanitarian aid, which press one to provide immediate assistance to those in need. This dilemma can be seen in the following excerpt from a letter from Kubie. Socialised in America in a far more trusting era, he almost instinctively believed one could and indeed should count on the co-operation of the country's authorities:

> In the State Department there is *great eagerness to help*, but at the same time to avoid missteps or impulsive acts that may hurt someone in Austria. That there are some risks in delay are [sic] obvious; but the Department feels certain that no amount of haste will enable anyone to escape on whom the new regime has already centred its resentments. They came in prepared with detailed lists of those whom they wanted, and went systematically about the process of taking them into custody. The only chance for such a person to escape would be hiding and secret travelling; no formal steps with rapid passport papers and visas would solve such a problem. For this reason, and because no

legal travelling permits are being issued anyhow, no harm can be done by deliberate action. (My italics)

A belief in the rule of law and in the good intentions of the State Department seemed sufficient as a rational explanation for the delay: Kubie went on to say,

[T]here are certain advantages in delay. With better organisation there will be less danger that emigrants with proper papers will be ruthlessly turned back at the border, less danger of their having valuable papers destroyed and confiscated, less danger of physical violence to refugees en route, and probably increasing freedom to bring out at least their personal possessions, clothes, libraries, etc. This was the experience in Germany and a similar development is expected by those who are watching the present situation.

Kubie communicated the American consulate's criticism of sending the letters of intent to provide aid, the official documentation, and the affidavits to those they wished to help escape. After discussing methods to be followed in future, the Emergency Committee agreed with the consulate as follows: affidavits and necessary documents would be sent to the consulates, where they would be used when it was deemed most timely and appropriate.

Kubie exhibited a certain common sense in noting in this letter: "Naturally each individual is entirely free to send his affidavit as he wants". However, the most important practical question remained unanswered: how much would be required for the guarantee? According to Kubie, "It is extremely difficult for anyone in the State Department to indicate a definite amount of money as the basic amount required to guarantee a year's support for an immigrant" (Kubie, 1938, cited in Kurzweil, 1992, p. 344). Here was a difficult question to answer. Why did all this fall under the scope of the State Department and not the Labour Department? And in 1938—when there was the benefit of experience with the immigrants from Germany—what was the source of all the difficulty? Kubie wrote: "The only approximation which I could get, was that for a family of three or four, who could not be expected to earn any material sum of money within a year, they would want a guarantee of about $5,000" (cited in Kurzweil, 1992, p. 344).

It should be borne in mind that this amount was double the annual pay of an executive assistant at an institute or a young physician just starting out. All of this must be taken into account in assessing the sheer determination that must have lain behind the generous issuance of affidavits.

In a letter dated 31 March, Kubie requested urgent additional assistance, citing the situation in Vienna that had changed so dramatically. Nevertheless, the authorities failed to loosen the ban on the emigration of Jews. As an exception, it was permitted to cross the border for 20 schillings, or four dollars. Thus, Jews were faced with the threat of annihilation on one side of the border and, on the other side, with the fate of the penniless refugee at the mercy of others.

Thanks to the solidarity of the American analysts, however, this humiliating last resort was very rarely necessary. The Emergency Committee had managed to secure affidavits for a large number of their psychoanalytic peers in Austria, according to a letter from Kubie. So, he went on to say, as soon as the emigration ban was lifted, those not headed for other European countries would be given the option of obtaining a US visa.

Thus, as long as the Nazis maintained the blockade against leaving the country, there would be no visa. And if there was no visa, there would be no permission to leave the country. In a letter dated 8 June 1938, the USA's Consul General Wiley informed Messersmith in Vienna of what he had observed: "Nazi officials were not content to wait a number of months until individual Jews received visas to the United States; they insisted on immediate expulsion" (Breitman & Kraut, 1987, p. 54).

This sort of political doublethink was tantamount to a death sentence for hundreds of thousands of Jews. The lack of a visa provided a good excuse for authorities to continue ridding the country of Jews in the concentration camps—where the labour of the inmates could still be used in the service of the Third Reich. They could well say that it would be a shame not to take advantage of the opportunity. After all, the Jews were the authors of their own fate. Why had they not left in time? And why had they not been taken in anywhere else? Indeed, as we saw earlier, Hitler sent a message to Göring to the effect that if the Jews failed to get out of Austria then the Nazis would take care of their removal. As Wiley observed to Messersmith: "If there is war, Heaven alone knows what will happen to these unhappy and wretched people" (p. 54).

Kubie could do little else in New York than he had already been doing: to ask his fellow psychoanalysts to donate money to save their

European colleagues and their family members from an intolerable situation so that, if they obtained a visa with the affidavits with which they had been provided, they would be able to arrange for food and shelter on the other side of the border and to buy tickets for the train or ship that would take them to freedom.

What happens next?

This is the question that occupied everyone, both those forced from their home countries and those who took them in. They were well aware of the fact that if they managed to avoid danger in one place they would still have to face the complications of resettling in a new place. They would need to assimilate into the culture and local professional community of their new country, not to speak of the primacy of their quality of life. All of this laid a certain financial burden at the door of those who had taken the immigrants in. After all, they were sharing what they had.

The American psychoanalytic community had been glad to receive their European peers as guests in the early 1930s. Indeed, there was a demand for their expertise: for example, when Rado was lured away from Berlin. In December 1930, A. A. Brill, president of the New York Psychoanalytic Society, urgently invited Rado to come to the USA as a founding director of the New York Psychoanalytic Institute and develop its training structure based on the Berlin model. Brill referred to Rado as "a leading figure and the most admired teacher at the Berlin Psychoanalytic Institute" (Jacobs, 1983, p. 29). Rado arrived early in 1931, and the institute was already opening its doors nine months later. It was in the same year that Franz Alexander was also invited from Berlin. After 1933, however, there were suddenly too many Europeans in America's psychoanalytic communities.

Kubie described the situation in a letter to Jones dated 26 April 1938:

> Our larger centres, where well organised societies and institutes already exist, are well supplied with trained analysts and students in training; and this number has already been increased by immigrants from Germany. On the other hand, there are many large cities where there is a need for psychoanalysis and where there are literally no psychoanalysts.[94]

Aware of all this, the Emergency Committee developed a potential script and resource in which, through Jones and the IPA, it informed those intending to immigrate of their options—without sparing them the anticipated practical difficulties.

According to one of the key considerations, it was desirable for newly arrived, experienced analysts to resettle in cities where psychoanalysis was as yet unknown. Some younger analysts, both from America and from among the new émigrés, could also be brought along to such "less developed" areas, where their work could be supervised. Thus, not only would the experienced analysts find stability again, but the seeds of psychoanalysis could also be planted in as yet uncultivated areas. The Emergency Committee promised assistance in selecting locations that could potentially be developed as well as financial aid for the early period. In return, it expected that "those who accept our assistance will cooperate with us and follow our recommendations" (note 93)

The committee took the position that it was "unnecessary and undesirable" (note 93) for the IPA "to grant" (note 93) colleagues who had escaped from Europe membership-at-large or, as they themselves called it, to register them as "Nansen" members, to retain their IPA memberships.[95] It is sobering to consider the void in which the analysts had suddenly found themselves professionally after their European associations had been dissolved. After Berlin, Vienna's society was also broken up in 1938, and, thus, all those who had belonged to these organisations lost their membership rights as analysts. Indeed, according to the IPA Rules, only members of national associations were eligible for IPA membership—a rule that continues to be in force to the present day. If there was no national society, therefore, there was theoretically no chance for membership.

Certainly, a solution had to be found for this volatile situation. It seemed that the most obvious answer was to exempt the refugees and allow them to join the IPA as independent professionals in their own right. However, this very much conflicted with interests in the USA. According to the APsaA position, the refugees would have needed to bring documentation of their qualifications with them and apply for membership in an APsaA member organisation. Thus, every émigré analyst would be assessed according to the USA's norms. However, their norms differed from those of Europe.

One stakeholder in this conflict was Erich Fromm (1900–1980), sociologist, psychoanalyst, social scientist, and one of the founders of psychoanalytic social psychology.[96] On 25 March 1936, Fromm turned to Jones with the following request from New York:

> Since there is no alternative, I accept the fact of giving up my membership in the German Psychoanalytic Society. Though I am in close connection with the Washington–Baltimore Psychoanalytic Society, where I gave a course of lectures last year, it would be against their principles to accept a non-physician as a member, and I would rather not press the matter. This being the case, I would prefer to become a "Nansen" member of the International Association and would be very grateful to you, if you would take the necessary steps to arrange it.
>
> Yours sincerely,
>
> Erich Fromm[97]

In 1936, Jones was still able to respond to Fromm's request as follows: "in the way of being accepted there, then, I can offer you the direct 'Nansen' membership in the International Association" (Jones, 1936, cited in Funk, 2000, p. 192). However, the Viennese analysts did not benefit from the same exemption after their exodus. This was the very question on which the American analysts were upholding their right to decide, a right they made completely clear in their bulletin.

The status of European analysts without a medical degree became very difficult since the USA's legal system only permitted physicians to practise psychoanalysis on adults. Among the committee's plans was a compromise by which specially trained lay analysts of repute could be granted the status of "honorary guest" on the condition that they would not be involved in training lay candidates. In other words, they would need to accept the conditions of physician-directed psychoanalyst training. Unless they wanted to look for another line of work, this meant that lay analysts could only earn a living in accredited education or child therapy—and even those jobs could only be done under supervision at the beginning.

Kubie put the principle of mutual benefit into practice. In a letter, he promised to reduce the workload of the immigrants and recommended rapid consolidation. The Emergency Committee clearly felt that psychoanalysis could also be introduced in large cities where it was as yet unfamiliar by putting analysts from Europe to work there. However, this plan would relegate the immigrants to professional isolation. One would have had to be young and ambitious to cope with such a sequestered life.

Teaching provided lay analysts with a living that represented the sort of intellectual challenge to which they were most accustomed. However, if they wanted to practise psychoanalysis, analysts who arrived with a medical degree had a difficult task ahead: to have their degrees recognised in their new home country. At the time, this represented a daunting process, and it stopped many a career short. It was no mean feat for American psychoanalysts to generate job offers or to create appropriate jobs for the newcomers. Early on, those forced to emigrate certainly thought only in terms of any employment opportunities that they were offered. These conditions posed the greatest challenge for all of those who had to make the life choice of whether to stay or go, but it provided the strongest disincentive for the older generations, not to mention the fact that a key instrument of psychoanalysis is the word: everyone had to face some degree of difficulty with the new language—even those who knew English well. Indeed, language is an essential element of communication in the field. It remains the most important tool in therapy even if the messages of the unconscious are often expressed by non-verbal communication. All hidden references in the work of psychoanalytic psychotherapy, whether intended or not, can only be understood in terms of the system of symbols in the spoken language. Naturally, non-verbal communication becomes extraordinarily useful, for example, in treating borderline or psychotic patients. Still, we must not forget the primary importance of language in the standard psychoanalysis or psychoanalytic process.

The Emergency Committee decided that it would make all the information available in one bulletin for those undertaking to immigrate. Kubie asked Jones to make use of all informal and formal channels possible to provide their European colleagues with the *facts*. Certainly, with the difficulties involved in resettling the analysts from Berlin fresh in their minds, they took great care in drafting this document.

The saying "The devil is in the details" inevitably springs to mind in this context. If a would-be refugee already had an MD under her or his belt, a perusal of these four pages of information might well have left the reader gasping for breath, since having a European medical degree recognised in the USA—at least on first reading—appeared to be almost completely unfeasible. According to the bulletin, it was virtually impossible for a foreigner to obtain a medical licence in twenty-one states of the USA either because of state regulations or procedural practice there. As becomes clear below, the twenty-one states listed in the bulletin actually translated to seventeen, including the District of Columbia: Arkansas, Delaware, the District of Columbia, Florida, Georgia, Illinois, Kansas, Kentucky, Louisiana, Michigan, Minnesota, Mississippi, Nebraska, Nevada, New Jersey, New Mexico, Pennsylvania, South Dakota, Tennessee, Utah, and Vermont. It was impossible to have one's degree confirmed in these places for a number of reasons: either citizenship was a condition of taking the medical board licensing examination (the boards) with the process of becoming a citizen lasting six years, or one was required to present documentation of accredited USA medical training in registering for the boards, or one was expected to complete a year of residency at a designated hospital before even being allowed to sign up for the examination. If one did manage to find such a job, then, after a year, one could submit an application to have one's degree recognised. This was, in fact, possible in four states: Illinois, New Jersey, Pennsylvania, and Vermont. It is unclear why these four were listed among the twenty-one with the impossible conditions in the bulletin, but the most likely assumption for why they were mentioned twice in the document is that it was simply an oversight. It is clear, therefore, that it would have been pointless to try one's luck in seventeen states and that there was a chance in four states after a hospital residency.

According to the bulletin, foreigners were permitted to take the boards in twenty-eight states: Alabama, Arkansas, California, Colorado, Connecticut, Idaho, Indiana, Iowa, Maine, Maryland, Massachusetts, Missouri, Montana, New Hampshire, New York, North Carolina, North Dakota, Ohio, Oklahoma, Oregon, Rhode Island, South Carolina, Texas, Virginia, Washington, West Virginia, Wisconsin, and Wyoming.

Based on unfortunate past experience, the editors of the bulletin also broached a delicate topic. They asked their peers who were planning to emigrate "to look upon their relationship to [their newfound] communities as real obligations". In other words, they were requested to prepare to remain for several years in the location that had been designated for them even if that became difficult, except, naturally, if it became intolerable. They made no secret of the fact that they had

had a number of experiences with immigrants suddenly changing their plans, failing to keep the promises they had made to the members of their community, and leaving their psychoanalytic work unfinished.

Having taken these conditions into account, the committee undertook to provide the utmost assistance for everyone in finding the optimum location and to arrange for financial backing in the early stages. The care taken by the Emergency Committee is characterised by the standard CV points that tend to present so much trouble for everyone everywhere—but especially for those from another cultural and linguistic context. An appendix to the bulletin offered a system of fourteen points, thus providing a model for newcomers on how to summarise their qualifications, experience, and skills, which would be so essential for their future.

By June 1938, it had become obvious what the Anschluss meant for the American psychoanalytic community. The APsaA held its annual meeting in Chicago, where a key point on the agenda was the experience of the Emergency Committee. The minutes provide the first glimpse into the gap that had grown between the original goals of the committee and the philanthropic outlook that later became inevitable. In January 1938, the committee's brief was to endeavour "to restrict and control immigration" (*Bulletin*, 1938, p. 65) and to direct the newly arrived analysts towards less populated communities while consistently safeguarding the training system that had evolved in the USA. After the Anschluss, however, humanitarian criteria also had to be considered, even though they often clashed with earlier aims.

Looking from today's vantage point at these reports with their factual, straightforward, and accurate figures, two aspects become clear: the first stems from the particular approach and training process shared by the Viennese analysts and the other from the immigration figures, which were far below the anxiety-ridden vision of a mass wave of Austrian analyst émigrés.

Difficulties arose due to a proportion of the Viennese analysts who were generally seen to have been kept far removed from America

> by the traditional isolationist policy of that group, by its old antipathy to the medical world, and by the hostility to America which had long been inculcated from many sources, some old and historical, some more recent. (p. 66)

Freud felt an aversion to American psychoanalysis, and he encouraged others to keep their distance from America. He also took Ferenczi's one-year sojourn in the USA amiss, as well as the move many analysts had made from Europe. In his view, every key individual who left the European continent weakened the psychoanalytic movement there.

Training models in Europe diverged from one another, but this also represented a healthy diversity that stemmed naturally from different cultures and experiences. Lay analyst training was backed in Vienna and Budapest, while this was not the case in Berlin or in American training, which laid emphasis on the Berlin model. The Budapest School owed its many characteristic features to its interdisciplinary openness, and there were also many lay analysts working in Vienna. Freud himself supported the opening up of psychoanalysis beyond physicians' circles, and Ferenczi openly stood behind a lay group during his nearly one-year stay in America. These oppositions came to the fore during the emigration and became a considerable source of conflict when the Austrian analysts were suddenly forced to leave their country behind and the USA appeared to them an ideal final destination for their escape.

When it turned out that the influx of newcomers would not be on such a mass scale as they had originally believed, the American psychoanalytic community experienced somewhat of a calming of "intense feeling . . . not without . . . elements of conflict and confusion" (p. 65). The committee had listed the names of seventy-five analysts who were thought to be potentially seeking refuge in the country. However, it soon turned out that twenty of them had no intention whatsoever of coming to the USA and that they had found another country in which to resettle in the meantime. A further fifteen of the fifty-five remaining Viennese analysts were unable to leave their place of residence because they were "from countries other than Austria, in which the quotas have already been applied for in advance" (p. 66).[98] Therefore, there were actually potentially only forty Austrian analysts to prepare for. A total of 5–6 of these forty were highly skilled lay analysts. It sounded reassuring that seven were young physicians, their training already under way when they were forced to leave their country, and the remaining twenty or so were qualified psychiatrists or neurologists. By June, twenty potential immigrants already had an affidavit in their hands thanks to the efforts of relatives or friends.

The committee saw that further measures were required in two areas: jobs had to be created and affidavits had to be issued to potential immigrants. The committee was being sent requests for aid from "Paris, Switzerland, Budapest, Czechoslovakia, the Scandinavian countries, London, Antwerp and Austria" (p. 67). By June, $10,000 had been deposited in the committee's account. Two thousand dollars of that was wired to Jones so that he could help in rescuing the European analysts (p. 68).

In late November 1938, the committee was already reporting that, of the twenty-nine individuals requesting assistance—of whom two were medical students who had begun their analyst training, three were lay analysts, and many were psychoanalysts with a medical degree—fifteen had been found jobs in psychoanalyst communities in various parts of the country. Featured on the list were institutes in urban centres ranging across the country from the east to the west coasts: Boston, Worcester, Brooklyn, Newark, the Washington–Baltimore area, Detroit, Chicago, Kansas City, Los Angeles, and San Francisco.

The report also makes mention of a fourteen-member group whose fortunes would, they hoped, take a turn for the better in the New York area. The city enjoyed an exceptional status, and the committee even noted its special features.[99] It had always stood out as a major urban hub with a particularly cosmopolitan culture and set of customs founded on a variety of European traditions. As we will see later, many of the Hungarian analysts also resettled in New York.

Why New York?

1. This was the place where a traveller entered the country and where a refugee was likely to come across the most friends and countrymen. This was the city, therefore, where the sense of loneliness and isolation was potentially the least painful.
2. The boards could be taken relatively quickly there, while a physician's licence obtained there also granted one the right to practise in a number of other states based on the principle of reciprocity.
3. It was more economical to remain there until one took the boards rather than shifting from one location to another.
4. Inexpensive courses were organised to prepare refugees for the boards.

5. Moving on often demanded more strength than many émigrés could muster. According to an Emergency Committee report,

> immediate further migration becomes psychologically and emotionally impossible, arousing great anxiety and depression, and endangering the ultimate happy adjustment to this new environment. For such émigrés it is important to give them time to catch their breath before urging on them their duty to scatter through the land.[100]

Most psychoanalysts who were forced to emigrate benefited from changes made in 1938 in numerous states to state board requirements. At the end of November, the Emergency Committee announced welcome news: "Your Committee has prepared a new digest of the States' laws, and of the reciprocity relationships" (note 99). Now, in a number of states,[101] if someone had graduated from a Class A foreign university and already held a licence to practise, she or he could take the boards without having to wait for citizenship or even being required to go through a year of residency.

By 1 November 1938, the Emergency Committee had collected nearly $13,000 and paid out $7,600 in aid.

It was not only the USA's immigration policy and states' regulations that threw up hurdles for the Emergency Committee in its efforts to rescue the European analysts. It was also internal professional tensions that had divided the psychoanalytic movement from the very outset. These conflicts were only strengthened during the waves of forced emigration in the 1920s and 1930s, and while they took the form of no more than rivalry most of the time, they also led to serious threats to one's very livelihood in extreme cases.

Within Europe, a controversy arose primarily in London, that is, between Melanie Klein and Anna Freud, a situation that was only heightened by Jones's ambitions for power. Jones never made a secret of the fact that he wanted to establish a little psychoanalytic empire in Britain, and he had gained Freud's backing for his plans. Then, after the Anschluss, a combination of the forced flight of the Viennese from their homeland, Freud and Anna Freud's escape to London, and Freud's death shortly thereafter absorbed the professional conflicts that had been brewing between Melanie Klein and Anna Freud. Klein, who had been living in London since 1926, had seen her views on psychological development rejected by the Viennese. This is why she encouraged Jones to place pressure on them. It was at that time that Anna Freud, who was living in London by now, began to hint that Melanie Klein should be forced out of the international association. Their bitter conflict also split the British analysts. Those who stood behind Melanie Klein criticised Anna Freud and the Viennese analysts for attempting to determine which undertakings were in line with those of Freud's, which ones were not, and who could be considered his intellectual heirs. Others saw the line represented by Anna Freud as the only possible continuation of Freud's way of thinking (Steiner, 2005).

What appeared to be an irreconcilable conflict was also raging between the APsaA and the IPA. The Americans felt that the IPA was towering over them and chipping away at their efforts toward autonomy. They also believed that it failed to acknowledge that the American psychoanalytic movement had diverged in its development from that of the Europeans'. This conflict had become so severe that, in the winter of 1938–1939, Jones, the IPA president, and Edward Glover, the IPA secretary, indicated to APsaA representatives that they planned to discuss these issues during their visit to the USA and that a solution had to be reached to overcome the current differences of opinion. An agreement was reached on the date of the meeting (9 May 1939) and the members of the negotiating committee. The escalation of the war, however, brought a halt to the meeting—but it did not quash the intention to arrive at a potential compromise. In a letter to Kubie, Glover communicated Jones's recommendations for resolving the tensions in a letter to Kubie dated 31 August 1939:

> I realise that situations might arise due to legitimate differences in local conditions when a too close organisation might have its disadvantages *to both sides*. . . . If there is to be any international organisation, it must be in a position to do all it can to further the interests of psychoanalysis and of psychoanalysts in all countries. And it seems to me that for this reason alone, it is very desirable that whatever can be, should be done to solve the perplexing problem of [the] 'migration' of analysts originally recognised as competent by their own competent branches. This may not be a problem for all time, but it is certainly a problem of the present day. (Glover, 1940, p. 30)

Jones sent a summary of his recommendations, which consisted of organisational changes to the IPA. A crucial point is the following: the international association should split into two independent organisations, the American Federation and the European Federation. With this act, Jones was simply confirming an already existing situation. At the same time, it also included the notion that the two federations should remain united, operating within the framework of the IPA, under the same conditions, and according to the rules of the international body.

The third serious difficulty was brought about by the presence of the European psychoanalysts in the USA. The immigrants behaved with an air of European superior knowledge, as if they were the transmitters of authentic psychoanalysis. For their part, their colleagues in the USA tended to look down on the lay analysts who had become such a key feature of the European landscape. Furthermore, through USA law, the Americans did not even permit them to practise psychoanalysis. The Europeans reacted to this restriction with criticism that they felt was justified: they felt psychoanalysis in the USA had become medicalised and that this approach diverged in principle from Freud's original intentions. Brill and Jones were among those who opposed lay analysis. In rebuttal, Freud wrote a book on the issue, which was published in English in 1927 as *The Problem of Lay-Analyses*. Freud also sent a disappointed-sounding letter about this development to Ferenczi on 22 April 1928:

> The inner development of Ψα everywhere runs counter to my intentions, away from lay analysis to the purely medical specialty, which I sense to be ominous for the future of analysis. Actually, I am *only* sure about you that you share my point of view without reservation. (Brabant, Falzeder, & Giampieri-Deutsch, 2000, p. 339)

In 1938–1939, then, during the wave of Viennese emigration,[102] but before the larger exodus of the Hungarians, these issues were being argued passionately, for example, at both the New York Psychoanalytic Society and the Institute.

One of the key players in the conflicts was Karen Horney (1885–1952), whom Alexander had brought to Chicago to work with him but who later moved to New York in 1934 for a position at the New York Psychoanalytic Institute. Horney emphatically rejected the priority of Freud's biological instinct theory and stressed instead the personality-shaping power of environmental and cultural factors. Horney found followers, among them Ferenczi sympathisers (Harry Stack Sullivan) and even students/analysands of Ferenczi's, such as Clara Thompson. At the same time, among those diametrically opposed to this view were analysts of Hungarian descent right there in New York, such as Rado.

Horney was fundamentally opposed to Kubie and Rado's clinical "orthodoxy" and accused them of overly influencing the intellectual development of New York's candidates with their views. Horney gave voice to the conviction that it was more effective in many cases to deal with a patient's present in order to understand her or his past than to begin psychoanalytic therapy by urging someone to acknowledge some repressed issue from the past in order to make that person understand current problems. Horney's opponents believed that she taught nothing but her own views and failed to introduce candidates to classical Freudian theory. Such was the din of battle at the Institute that the recently arrived former Viennese analyst Eduardo Weiss felt compelled to write a letter from the Menninger Clinic in Topeka, Kansas, to inform Jones:

> I was told [by] a group of psychoanalysts of [sic, from] Vienna that Dr Rado used very irreverent expressions toward some of Freud's theories and ways of proceeding in psychoanalysis in his . . . course . . . . I was present at some lessons of Rado['s] and didn't like them.
>
> [Paul] Federn complains of not being allowed to teach. In my opinion, all psychoanalysts should collaborate even if they do not agree in every detail and even if there arise great differences in their conceptions.[103]

In contrast to his view of the situation in New York, Weiss had a very favourable opinion of the Chicago Institute for Psychoanalysis headed by Alexander: "In Chicago, I found much better conditions. The psychoanalytic group directed by Dr Alexander is nicely organised and there is a friendly collaboration of all colleagues" (note 102).

For his part, Kubie painted a clear picture of the current situation at the New York Institute in a letter to Glover in November 1939:

> I think I hinted to you that this [new] curriculum was the fruit of a pretty violent struggle, in the course of which I was quite unwillingly erupted into the presidency of the Society and into the midst of a

rather unpleasant scrap. The situation which lay behind it was briefly that we were developing four cliques not only among the Society members, but among the students: a group of students who were under exclusive Horney influence—another group under exclusive Rado influence—another group under Kardiner's influence—and a group that had a more general classical training. Each group was more or less hermetically sealed from the others, and you can imagine how much confusion, lopsided and inadequate training, and mutual distrust and hostility all of this generated.

This curriculum was designed in order to insure some kind of reasonable orderliness in the sequence of the students' studies—and to make it certain that every student would have to be exposed to all possible influences. (Kubie, 1939, cited in Kurzweil, 1992, pp. 348–349)

This was the context in which the Hungarian analysts made their request for aid.

CHAPTER EIGHT

The time has come (1938–1941): the second wave of emigration

The Hungarian analysts and their emigration struggles—constraints and opportunities

"Though our recent situation is not yet so difficult . . . its turn
to the worst can be expected in a very short time"
(Hollós to Lawrence Kubie, 9 January 1939, Mészáros, 1998a, p. 211)

In the weeks following the Anschluss, the first anti-Semitic "Jewish law" came before Hungary's Parliament with the ultimate aim of "putting economic restrictions in place in the spirit of the *numerus clausus*" (Ránki, 1999, p. 119, translated for this edition). This term, meaning "closed number", refers to a Hungarian Act of Parliament in 1920 that imposed a quota on university admissions for Jews but which had become virtually defunct by 1938. This "first Jewish law" in 1938, soon reinforced by a second one, would prove to be a harbinger of far more dire things to come in Hungary.[104] On 29 May of that year, Parliament passed Act XV of 1938 on Securing a More Effective Balance in Social and Economic Life. With its ominously sanitised name, this legislation determined who was a Jew on religious grounds and, based on that, drastically cut to twenty per cent the number of Jewish members of professional associations tied to the press, the theatre and film, the law, medicine, and business. This set of measures put most of Hungary's college-educated Jews in an impossible bind because it was illegal to practise a profession without being a member of the relevant association. Passed on 5 May 1939, the "second Jewish law", known as Act IV of 1939 on Restricting the Expansion of Jews in Public Life and the Economy, determined Jewish identity based on *race* in the spirit of Germany's Nuremberg Laws. Thus, individuals were judged to be Jews if they considered themselves to be Jewish or if they had one parent or two grandparents who were Jews. Hungary's second anti-Jewish law reduced the twenty per cent figure set down in the first legislation to the six per cent quota that had been established earlier in the *numerus clausus* and set the upper limit of Jewish people employed in trade and industry at twelve per cent. Furthermore, it completely banned Jews from public service. According to estimates, the first anti-Semitic law directly affected the lives of around 15,000 people, while the second one had an impact on at least 200,000 (Romsics, 2000, cited in Losonczi, 2005, p. 82). If one considers the families of those people, the latter law effectively sealed the fates of over 600,000 people.

In a letter dated 9 January 1939, István Hollós, president of the Hungarian Psychoanalytical Society, turned to Lawrence S. Kubie to request aid for Hungary's analysts. Kubie sent a copy of Hollós's letter to IPA president Ernest Jones (Mészáros, 1998a):

Dear Dr Kubie:

During the Paris meeting in August 1938, I communicated to our colleagues that our Hungarian members had decided to stay under every possible circumstances in their country, and so continue their work here, as far as that would be possible. . . .

Though our recent situation is not yet so difficult . . . its turn to the worst can be expected in a very short time [my italics]. I made the same statement to Dr Jones as well and he gave me the advice in his very encouraging and detailed letter, to let also you know the present condition. I feel it as my duty towards our member[s] to let you know our circumstances and beg you to get in touch with the competent members and in agreement with them to consider our difficult position. . . . [I] ask you to inform us about the possibilities, difficulties and the means [and] ways we should try. A list of about 15 persons will be too sent to you for your disposition.

Believe me sincerely

Yours

Signed: Dr Hollós[105]

P.S. Please address your letter to H. Meng, Basel, Angensteinerstr. 16.

Hollós's letter can be found in the British Psychoanalytical Society Archives.[106] But who exactly were the analysts who would have required assistance? Where are their names? Since Kubie was the recipient and he only sent a copy of the letter to Jones—as becomes clear in the upper left-hand corner, "For Dr Ernest Jones, From Dr Lawrence S. Kubie, Date: January 19, 1939"—it is not inconceivable that Kubie did not pass on a copy of the enclosure to Jones. The clues thus point to New York.

But will a search through North America's archives bear fruit? Can the fates of the analysts—filled with their hopes, disappointments, and fateful turns—which are hinted at in the partial documents within the British Psychoanalytical Society's records be uncovered on another continent? The questions raised by the missing enclosure in the Hollós letter can only be answered if we follow the clues.

The second wave of emigration from Hungary was sparked by the first anti-Jewish law, though this was no more than the culmination of an ever more tangible anti-Semitism in Hungary, while Hitler's expansion, neighbouring Austria's annexation, and Hungary's close economic and political ties to both Hitler's Germany and Mussolini's Italy certainly boded ill for the future.

Kubie responded to Hollós's letter ten days later. Clearly written with the greatest care, Kubie's reply covered every possible detail and potential difficulty, including the discouraging fact that the quota on visa applications from Hungary was "over-applied-for already for a matter of ten or more years". A visitor's visa entitled the bearer to a six-month stay and could be extended several times for a further six months or more, but did not give one the right to employment. Furthermore, submitting an application for permanent residence meant that a person could not request a visitor's visa.

Some degree of hope was offered by the possibility that anyone who had received an invitation to teach in the USA could obtain what was called a "special teacher's non-quota visa" (see letter from Kubie to István Hollós, below), which fell outside the quota system. A precondition of that, however, was that the applicant should have at

Letter from Lawrence S. Kubie to István Hollós, 19 January 1939. Archives of the British Psychoanalytical Society, G07/BJ/F01/25.

least two years' "active teaching experience in a school which is recognised as a teaching organisation in Hungary" (see reproduction of letter, below). This requirement clearly excluded any teaching done for the psychoanalytic society. Kubie wrote that though many had been issued this sort of visa, there were some who had been denied.

THE TIME HAS COME (1938–1941): THE SECOND WAVE OF EMIGRATION   137

- 2 -

 The third possibility is to put in an application to come to this country, and then to move temporarily to another country while waiting for one's turn to come to this country under the quota. In order to put your name on the waiting list it is necessary, however, not only to register your application at the Consular office, but also to secure from someone in America a paper that is called an "affidavit of support". This is a promise on the part of an individual in this country not to allow the immigrant to become a public charge, – that is, a promise to support the individual who is coming into this country in case he gets into financial difficulties. I can assure you that we will do all we can to secure affidavits of that nature for all of our colleagues who want ultimately to come here. This takes a little time, however, because as you can imagine many people have given many such affidavits, and the law does not permit one to give more than a certain number in relation to one's own income.

 In order to make out such affidavits we need to have the following data on every prospective immigrant: Name, address, place of birth, age and occupation, for every member of the family.

 Finally it will be of assistance to us in placing our colleagues to have specific details on their professional education. For this reason I am enclosing a Curriculum Vitae, which I would ask you to have every prospective immigrant colleague fill out as completely as possible, and forward to me.

 I think that this about covers the information for which you ask in your letter. If there are further facts which you would like to have, please get in touch with me.

 With warm greetings, as always, I remain,

    Very truly yours,

       Lawrence S. Kubie, M.D., Chairman,
       Emergency Committee on Relief and
       Immigration.

LSK:eb

Continuation of letter from Kubie to Hollós.

In any case, his advice to anyone who wished to teach was to list all courses taught, locate the original documents, and send him a certified copy of each one.

As a third option, Kubie recommended that applicants should indicate the USA as their destination but move to another country temporarily and wait there for the quota system to enable them to enter the USA, that is, to let themselves be placed on a waiting list. Despite all these hurdles, Kubie wrote encouragingly, "I can assure you that we will do all we can to secure affidavits of that nature for all of our colleagues who want ultimately to come here" (letter from Kubie to Hollós). He also enclosed a list of items to be included in the CV, which should be attached to the application.

On 28 March, two weeks after the Germans occupied Austria, Géza Róheim wrote a desperate-sounding letter to John Rickman (1891–1951) in London. There must have been some exchange beforehand, because he opens it as follows:

> My dear John!
>
> Of course Vienna comes first, I knew that, it is quite obvious. The point is that everybody is trying to get away from here before something happens, and it may be too late. . . . Maybe this is only a group psychosis but one never knows. Now there is just one thing you can do for me. Please let me have a fictive invitation to give lectures at the Institute of Psychoanalysis say for a year, so that I can use this if I want an English [visa] suddenly. . . . Thanks at any rate and I quite understand about the Vienna people.
>
> With kindest regards to you both,
>
> Yours ever,
>
> Géza

Róheim's wife, Ilona, also added a note to the letter, lending emphasis to her husband's request:

> The things look too bad and very little hope. God knows what brings the next future. We are all very sad about the [Viennese] people and know very little about them. Please if you can do something try it. . . . Best regards [to] both of you from Ilona (see reproduction of letter below)

On 29 May, Róheim again put pen to paper, since there had been no response to his previous letter. He made an effort to enquire about everyday matters: had Rickman received the corrected proof? Had the document for Schönberger reached him? However, a sense of tense anticipation and repressed despair was palpable, particularly when he remarked: "I suppose there is no news regarding the migration to England or Australia".[107]

THE TIME HAS COME (1938–1941): THE SECOND WAVE OF EMIGRATION 139

DR. GÉZA RÓHEIM
BUDAPEST
XIV. HERMINA-ÚT 35. B.

CRB/10/04

28. III. 1938

My dear John!

Of course Vienna comes first, I knew that, it is quite obvious. The point is that everybody is trying to get away from here before something happens, and it may be too late, and we shall be in the same plight. Maybe this is only a group psychosis, but one never knows. Now there is just one thing you can do for me. Please let me have a fictive invitation to give lectures at the Institute of Psychoanalysis say for a year, so that I can use this if I want an English visum suddenly. Are Jewish circles

Page 1 of letter from Géza Róheim to John Rickman, 28 March 1938. Archives of the British Psychoanalytical Society, CRB/A0/05; cf. Steiner (2000, p. 115).

Rickman must have received the letter—after all, it was among the documents in the archives—but he was delaying his response because he was loath to send an outright rejection to Róheim with regard to Britain. Rickman could have invited Róheim without Jones' approval, but that would have sparked a conflict because Jones—for both general and personal reasons—did not back the idea of Hungarians resettling in London. A general reason—the tensions in London,

> doing anything for the Vienna people? By which I mean will they, if we are in the same situation, do anything for us? As Dr Eder is dead I suppose the only Jewish analyst whom you could ask about this would be Dr Franklin
>
> Thanks at any rate and I quite understand about the Vienna people
>
> With kindest regards to you both
>
> Yours ever
> Géza
>
> Dear John!
> The things look too bad and very little hope — God knows what brings the next future. We are all very sad about the Vienna people and know very little about them. Please if you can do something try it — I am not quite well. Best regards both of you from Ilona

Page 2 of letter from Róheim to Rickman.

which were discussed earlier—clearly did not favour taking in additional refugees, but in this case personal motives played an even more crucial role.

In all likelihood, one of the reasons was that Róheim was a lay analyst and not only that but one from a fairly distant field, ethnography. He was far more interested in the metapsychology of psychoanalysis than in clinical practice. Furthermore, it was Sándor Ferenczi and Vilma Kovács who had been his training analysts. Róheim's greatest transgression in Jones' eyes was certainly the fact that Róheim was considered a follower of Ferenczi's, that he had begun his training analysis with Ferenczi, and that Ferenczi had strongly backed his Australian expedition. It is common knowledge that Jones was tireless in his efforts to seek out any potential negative aspects of Ferenczi's mental state. On 28 May 1933, a few days after Ferenczi's death, Róheim wrote a letter to Jones which was presumably a response to a request for information and in which he said that he had known Ferenczi well, had been analysed by him between 1916 and 1917, and thought of Ferenczi as, "in a sense, part of my life".[108] He added that, beyond the fatigue and difficulty in concentrating that had developed as a result of his pernicious anaemia, he had experienced nothing pathological in Ferenczi's mental functioning (Mészáros, 2003).

What follows is part of Róheim's letter to Jones:

28th of May, 1933

Dear Dr Jones!

Thank you for your letter regarding this very sad and unexpected loss.
. . .

Ferenczi had been suffering from pernicious anemy [sic, anaemia] since some time. He was unwell at Wies-baden and afterwards but picked up in autumn and worken [sic, worked] all through the winter. At Easter he had to give up analysing [analysis] because he was too fatigued by his illness to concentrate. Then things seem[e]d to be improving again but he was in bed most of the time. He had regained his blood count when on Monday without feeling specially unwell previously he suddenly died after lunch. . . . He seems that the damages done . . . the spine or something (you know more exactly than I can t[e]ll you) had [gone] too far. He was expecting to recommence to work in August and they intended to go to Zürich to a specialist, but delayed it because his feet would not carry him. . . .

Britain had already closed its doors to Róheim, a fact borne out by another document. According to this letter, written by an unknown author and addressed to Jones, Róheim had planned to emigrate to Britain years before and had made inquiries about his options. The letter writer goes on to make the cutting remark that he had already seen that Róheim was ill-suited before his suspicions were confirmed:

I told him that the fact that he was a training analyst in Budapest would not make him a training analyst in England and that I for one would not send him private patients, until he has had more personal analysis, as I considered that his gifts lay in other directions than in clinical practice.[109]

Openly negative in its assessment, the letter was written after Róheim had migrated to the USA in the autumn of 1938 with the help of his friends and started working at the Worcester State Hospital in Worcester, Massachusetts. The author of the letter made the sarcastic comment,

Since he has been at the Worcester State Hospital I have received several letters dealing with practical matters of proof, but he also has found occasion to make a number of derogatory remarks about the doctors at the Worcester State Hospital (without mentioning names) from which I deduced that he was not in a very cooperative frame of mind and that his analyses of these same people was not likely to be successful. (Note 108)

Róheim had not aspired to do clinical work. His hospital job, a necessary evil, further deteriorated his situation since it was not a match for his training or his previous experience, and neither was he sufficiently motivated for the work. He did not possess the patience or the tolerance to accommodate even temporarily to his circumstances. The fact is he had longed for a university career. He soon left his position at Worcester, moved to New York City, and took a position as a lecturer at the New York Psychoanalytic Institute.

Like Róheim originally, Michael Balint and his wife Alice wanted to stay in Europe. They were prepared to emigrate, however, and with the annexation of Austria Balint made the necessary arrangements: "[I]t was time to go. I did not want to be caught up in it. I tried to make all sorts of contacts; I mobilised Jones and John Rickman. . . . John Rickman was very helpful. Jones too, but John Rickman especially" (Swerdloff, 2002, p. 394).

It should be borne in mind that these lines are from a 1965 interview. If we take into account the conflicts between Jones and Ferenczi and between Jones and Balint[110] as well as Balint's diplomatic temperament, the way Balint says "Jones too, but *John Rickman especially*" (my emphasis) takes on a particular significance. It turns out that Jones was not at all pleased that Rickman was supporting the Balints. He had no wish to see these people—followers of Ferenczi's—in London. This is ultimately why Michael and Alice Balint did not resettle in London.

The Balints had lived in a fifth-storey flat at No. 12 Mészáros Street in a leafy residential district of Budapest. The building is not merely of interest to us because this is where Michael grew up, within walking distance of Werbőczy Grammar School, which he and so many other great Hungarians, including Attila József, had attended. Neither is it merely worth noting because this is where he lived later with his wife Alice after they had married. No, it is in this building, on the ground floor, that the Hungarian Psychoanalytical Society's Polyclinic had commenced operation in 1931. After Ferenczi's death, Balint was its director from 1933 to 1938 and practised there with numerous other analysts, including his wife.

Mihály Bálint and Alice Bálint, ca. 1935. Archives of the Sándor Ferenczi Society & International Ferenczi Centre, Budapest.

One of Alice Balint's patients,[111] a teenager at the time, was visibly moved some sixty years later in recounting the period prior to the Balints' emigration. In fact, she spoke of it with the self-reflection of an analyst (Mészáros, 1998b).

> TB: When she already knew she was going to Britain, Alice first recommended Klári Lázár [Clara Lazar-Gero], whom I knew already because I had seen her at the Mészáros Street clinic. Klári took me on but then soon told me that she was planning to immigrate to Australia. At the time, I felt I had been tricked. After all, when she took me on, she never said a word about wanting to leave.
>
> JM: Had Alice said she wanted to emigrate?
>
> TB: I knew they were planning to go to Britain.
>
> JM: What did Alice say about it?
>
> TB: First, she said that I should try leaving too and that this was no place to live. A great many people were considering emigrating at the time.
>
> JM: How did what Alice said affect you?
>
> TB: She promised that she wouldn't stop working with me until she left. We said our goodbyes at her flat . . . and then I went to the railway station too.
>
> JM: Do you remember your last meeting at the flat in Mészáros Street?
>
> TB: There were no formalities: we just shook hands and parted ways. . . . Like me, she was deeply moved. She didn't say that I should see her off. In fact, she said we should say goodbye right there. But I went [to the railway station] anyway. I remember humming a tune the whole time as I was heading down Rákóczi Road toward Eastern Station. When I got there, I watched Alice, her family, and the group that had accompanied them. She saw me and came up to me, so we said goodbye again.
>
> JM: What was the tune that was going through your head?
>
> TB: A Spanish dance. I hummed it the whole time I was there.
>
> JM: Could you sing it now?
>
> TB: It starts like this: [hums] I couldn't stop, I was incapable of letting go of it. It just kept going through my head . . . it was obviously compulsive behaviour.

JM: Did you cry?

TB: [There is a long silence, during which she is visibly struggling with her feelings.] ... I stood there discreetly, a great distance from them. ... Some people I didn't know brought flowers. ... They stood there by the train. Alice had told me when the train was going to leave. ... And I just stood there ... I stood there, I didn't want to ... and then she came over to me.

JM: Did she embrace you?

TB: No. But I got a letter from her from Britain. She wrote about how I could find some kind of work, about how I could get by as a waitress or in some other way [in Britain]. But, well, things were very tough. It even took a long time for them to get an entry visa. The British weren't really encouraging immigration. (Mészáros, 1998b, pp. 108–109, translated for this edition)

Michael and Alice Balint left Hungary early in 1939 (in January or February) with their young son, János. They resettled in Manchester, an industrial hub in the north of England. We know why they did not go to London, but not why they ended up in Manchester. Presumably their old friend and compatriot Michael Polanyi had something to do with it, just as he had the first time they had emigrated, when they had been forced to flee to Berlin. After much hesitation, Polanyi had emigrated from a Germany ever more tightly in the grip of Nazism in the spring of 1933 and resettled in Manchester, where he finally accepted a post at the physical chemistry department (Frank, 2002). Thus, it is likely that the aid of their friend Polanyi played a role in the Balints' choice of location, once London had been ruled out. Balint would later say, "[f]irst we *had to* settle in Manchester. It was a very provincial, small-minded place then" (Swerdloff, 2002, p. 394, my emphasis). In the meantime, Alice died suddenly of a ruptured aneurysm. According to Balint, "as soon as I could, I came to London. ... I joined the Tavistock Clinic" (Swerdloff, 2002, p. 394).

In 1945, Michael Balint resettled in London, and he joined the Tavistock Clinic in 1948. In the six years prior to this move, he remained in "provincial" Manchester, where he was the director of a clinic that cared for at-risk children.

The move to London marked a shift of fortune for Balint. Hungary and Manchester had each been the scene of some great loss in his life.

The forced emigration itself had been accompanied by a series of other losses, culminating in the unexpected death of his young wife—and closest colleague—soon after they had resettled. Balint had viewed their work as a collaborative effort—no matter whose name it was published under—since it always stemmed from an ongoing exchange of ideas between them. However, the series of personal losses did not end for him there. The following year saw the death of Balint's mother-in-law, Alice's mother, Vilma Kovács, who was not merely a close relative, but also a key figure in Hungary's psychoanalytic movement: she had been a training analyst and supervisor for numerous young people as well as a strong supporter of the society whom many saw as its "guardian angel". Thus, a year after the death of his wife, Balint also lost his mother-in-law. This suffering was only heightened by the news of his own parents' death: fearful of the Nazi menace and their own arrest, they had committed suicide in Budapest.

In the Swerdloff interview, Balint was clearly not willing to recall the anguish of the Manchester years. Not even giving his interviewer a chance to broach the subject, Balint steered the conversation in another direction: "In London I joined the Tavistock Clinic. Now we are [already] talking about modern history" (Swerdloff, 2002, p. 394). Indeed, it was in London that Balint's life finally took a turn for the better.

In early 1939, Hungary's tiny psychoanalytic community was pondering emigration. Dr Lilly Hajdu Gimes[112] wrote a letter to Kubie dated 27 January 1939, in which she used "Dear Sir" in the salutation, perhaps because she felt she did not know how to address him. "Time is come, when I must appeal to you, though it is not easy to beg, specially for me as someone unknown to you." She made reference to István Hollós's suggesting she should write the letter. She was primarily interested to find out what options there were for a psychoanalyst with experience in psychiatry, the main area of endeavour of which lay in the study and treatment of schizophrenia. She was also suited to research work, borne out by studies she had published in Hungarian medical journals. She introduced herself as follows:

> In my analytical practice I am mainly engaged in the treatment of insane persons, viz. of persons suffering from schizophrenia or from manic-depressive psychosis. The research work done by me up to now relates in the first place to the aetiology of schizophrenia, in the second

place to the technique of the analysis of [the] insane. . . . [O]n all these problems I held a number of lectures in the Psychoanalytic Society.[113]

It comes to light from the brief CV she included as part of the letter that she had earned a medical degree in 1914 and that she had had six years of experience as a training analyst (1927–1933).[114] We also learn that she had done training analysis between 1930 and 1933 and had become a regular member of the Hungarian Psychoanalytical Society in 1933 as well as a training analyst in the Society in 1938. She closed the letter with the following note:

> After this [curriculum vitae] my request is as follows: I should like to find a post at a hospital for mental diseases, where I could carry on with my research work and where [I could earn a living for myself and my family]. My husband is a [medical] doctor too and analyst candidate. I have two children: a daughter of 18 and a son of 21. An early reply would greatly oblige me.
>
> Yours truly
>
> Dr Lilly Gimes Hajdu [Hajdu Gimes]
>
> Budapest V. Honvéd u. 8.
>
> Hungary (see note 112)

The fates of Lilly Hajdu (1891–1960) and her husband, Miklós Gimes (1889–1944), are emblematic of both the interpenetration of psychoanalysis and twentieth-century history and of the many paths of life taken by their contemporaries so filled with misfortune. Both Hajdu and Gimes had graduated with degrees in medicine and belonged to the Galileo Circle—indeed, Lilly had been elected its president. This is where she met Ferenczi. In 1918, she contributed to plans for reform at the university. Her interest as a psychiatrist and later as a psychoanalyst turned to the pathography of schizophrenia and to the care of mentally handicapped children. After she bought the Frimm Institute, a private therapeutic facility in Óbuda on the hilly outskirts of Budapest, she developed her own institute, calling it the Therapeutic Institute and Children's Recreation Area, which remained in operation until 1933. The family's friends included: the Hungarian writers Frigyes Karinthy, Dezső Kosztolányi, and Jenő Heltai; the Polányis, the family that produced the great scholars John (János) and

Michael (Mihály) Polányi; and, from among the psychoanalysts, István (Székács) Schönberger, Lillian Rotter-Kertész, and the Balints. Participants at the seminars that Lilly Hajdu held at her flat during the Second World War included Imre Hermann and Alice Hermann, István (Székács) Schönberger, Endre Almásy, István Hollós, and Lillian Rotter-Kertész. Hajdu's husband was deported after the German occupation of Hungary in 1944 and perished in a concentration camp at Leitmeritz (Litoměřice) in the present-day Czech Republic. After the war, Hajdu worked at the National Institute for Neurology and Psychiatry and served as its director between 1954 and 1957. Her son, Miklós Gimes, Jr, a journalist, who for ideological reasons had turned against psychoanalysis in the early 1950s and then felt equally compelled to back Prime Minister Imre Nagy during the Hungarian Revolution of 1956, was imprisoned, put on trial—as part of the show trial against Nagy and his supporters—and, finally, executed in 1958. Hajdu's daughter, Judit (Juca) Gimes (later Juca Gimes-Magos), and her brother Miklós's young son managed to escape to Switzerland in 1956. Although Lilly had been a member of the Communist Party since 1945, her application for a visa to visit the surviving members of her family in Switzerland was repeatedly denied by the Hungarian authorities. After her third visa application had resulted in a "permanently denied" stamp, she finally committed suicide in 1960.[115]

By 1939, the following Hungarian analysts had submitted an application, according to documents held in the British Psychoanalytical Society Archives: Edit Gyömrői-Újvári, Dr Lilly Hajdu Gimes, Dr Imre Hermann, Dr István Hollós, Dr Elisabeth (Erzsébet) Kardos, Dr Klára Lázár-Gerő (Clara Lazar Geroe), Dr Andrew (Endre) Pető, Géza Róheim, and Dr Stephen Schönberger (István Székács). Also listed are the names of several people whom we know to have left Hungary in the first wave of emigration. These include Dr Georg (György) Gerő, who was hoping to leave Denmark in 1939, and René A. Spitz, who saw that this was the time to leave Paris. According to the documentation from 1939, Imre Hermann was planning to go to Holland, while there were several possible destinations for István Hollós. It was recommended that István Schönberger go to America, whereas Klára Lázár-Gerő, Erzsébet Kardos (?-1945), and Edit Gyömrői-Újvári all indicated New Zealand as their destination.[116]

The energy that Jones personally devoted during this period to assisting members of the Hungarian and other European psycho-

Psychoanalyst Lilly Hajdu Gimes and psychoanalytic candidate Miklós Gimes
with their children, Miklós and Judit, Budapest, 1929–1931.
Archives of the Sándor Ferenczi Society & International Ferenczi Centre, Budapest.

analytic communities is remarkable. Gyömrői's leftist political connections were common knowledge—this has already been discussed—so she was in particular jeopardy both as a Jew and as a communist. Jones knew exactly what this meant. In a letter to Kubie dated 27 April 1938, he laid strong emphasis on the fate of the Budapest community, especially on Gyömrői's situation, and he expressed his great respect for Hungary's analysts: "The courage of the Budapest Group in facing what seems to me to be an inevitable and frightful fate commands one's highest admiration". He also pointed out that Gyömrői had been forced to flee Berlin immediately after the Nazis took power there and that since the same situation could arise in Hungary—and it was common knowledge that "the Gestapo never forgets"—Gyömrői had to leave the country as soon as possible. Jones was actually requesting aid from Kubie in Gyömrői's escape:

> I am assured that the sole reason for the migration is one of the past record for years and that as a colleague they value her highly and will regret her going. I am also assured that she has not taken part in politics and is not intending to do so of course in America.[117]

This could be interpreted as Jones undertaking a guarantee on Gyömrői's behalf[118]—with the clear goal of saving a life. Jones knew the Berlin psychoanalysts very well. He would certainly have been familiar with the circle of Marxist analysts surrounding Otto Fenichel who attended the clinical seminar for young analysts, or *Kinderseminar*, between 1924 and 1933. He would have known that Gyömrői was also there. In the course of nearly a decade, according to notes taken during their sessions, the group met 168 times, always at somebody's home. Among its regular members were Wilhelm and Annie Reich, Barbara Lantos, Georg Gerő, and Edith Jacobson. This workshop on psychoanalytic technique blended with Marxist political debates with the express aim of forming "a bridge between psychoanalysis and historical materialism" (Brecht, Volker, Hermanns, Kaminer, & Juelich, 1985, p. 40).

Gyömrői wrote several letters to Jones in which she asked him not to send money to her but to forward it to foreign addresses indicated by her. Jones apparently expressed his displeasure at what he perhaps saw as non-transparent transactions because Gyömrői next wrote the following on a ship bound for Ceylon (Sri Lanka):

> I am mainly writing you now to clear up the misunderstanding about the US address I gave you. I was unable to do this from home for safety reasons. Mrs Lazar-Gero wanted to pay me the equivalent of the £100 in Budapest.

What had happened was that Gyömrői had asked that the aid being offered to her be sent to an address in the USA, a request of which Jones obviously disapproved. To complicate matters, Gyömrői then changed her mind about the address, requesting that the money be sent to a new address in London:

> It was very important to me to clear up this matter for you because I would certainly not like you to doubt my honesty even for a moment. I beg your pardon if I have caused you any irritation due to these ambiguities. It is so difficult for me to express myself in writing these days. You cannot imagine what it means to us to have regained our human freedom.[119]

Thus, with money (£100) drawn from a fund to aid Europe's analysts, which was ultimately channelled through Jones at her request, Gyömrői had managed to leave the country. Ceylon (Sri Lanka) represented not only a safe haven for her, but also the chance for a new life. She did not leave Hungary empty-handed. As Mrs Edith U. Gyömrői,[120] she came equipped with a certificate issued by the Hungarian Psychoanalytical Society and signed by its president, Dr István Hollós, and its secretary, Dr Zsigmond Pfeifer.

In January 1939, István (Székács) Schönberger (1907–1999) also turned to Jones for aid in a letter dated 26 January, in which he recounted correspondence between himself and an Australian colleague, Dr Roy Winn (1890–1963). According to the letter, Canberra seemed a potential destination for those who had "dropped out of the New Zealand expedition". Since Dr Winn shared Schönberger's view that some pressure might be brought to bear on the Australian Medical Board, Schönberger requested Jones to support his application to enter Australia as a physician.[121] Jones' reply has not remained to us, but in all likelihood he did answer because, in a letter dated 4 February, Schönberger thanked him for his promise to send a letter of support.

Letters written to Jones also document the extent to which the idea of emigration occupied so many psychoanalysts at the time. Erzsébet Kardos, for instance, sought his opinion on alternatives to New Zealand and Australia, Kata Lévy wanted to know if she could accompany the group as a physician who was not an analyst, and Schönberger informed him that Vilmos Kapos also wished to join them.[122]

The CV Schönberger sent to London contained the following information: he had completed secondary school in 1925 and earned his medical degree in Budapest in 1932. Between 1927 and 1935, he conducted research on the chemistry of haemoglobin under Professor Pál Hári at the university's biochemistry institute and published numerous studies. He started his training analysis in 1934 and began practising as an analyst in 1936. Schönberger received his training in psychoanalysis from Géza Róheim, and he was one of the young psychoanalyst candidates who attended Vilma Kovács's legendary theoretical seminars and case study discussions at her home in Orvos Street in the smart Naphegy section of Budapest. As he would later retell: "Kovács's assistants were there ... whom I owe an enormous debt ... Alice Balint, who was extremely important to me. The other one was Zsiga [Zsigmond] Pfeifer, from whom I also learned an enormous amount" (Mészáros, 1997).

According to the CV he sent to Jones, Schönberger had become a full member of the Hungarian Psychoanalytical Society in 1938, and that same year he had given a paper at the 15th IPA congress in Paris entitled "A dream of Descartes: contributions to the unconscious origin of science".[123] His wife, Anna Dénes, studied chemistry, physics, and mineralogy at the university in Budapest, earning her degree in 1929 and defending her doctoral dissertation in 1930. She, too, underwent analysis for several years and attended seminars which the Society organised for educators. Given her background in the natural sciences and her scholarly ambitions, she was certainly someone who could find work anywhere in the world; at the same time, she felt close to the psychoanalytic community right there in Hungary.

After some initial optimism, Schönberger wrote a downhearted letter to Jones on 13 May to inform him that the visa application he had submitted to the Australian authorities on 6 April 1939 had been denied. He made no mention of the reason. However, he went into great detail in describing the Australian Medical Board's criteria for evaluating physicians' applications for permanent residence. They were, apparently, only able to issue licences to a total of eight qualified physicians annually—a process that required a personal interview. The immigration law also gave priority to individuals who could show evidence of outstanding professional qualifications or experience in teaching or research.

Through the intercession of an Australian colleague, Schönberger turned to Australia's home secretary to ask him to back the immigration of psychoanalyst physicians to British Commonwealth countries, such as New Zealand and Australia. Schönberger very much regretted not being part of the effort to introduce psychoanalysis to Australia, as one of his Hungarian colleagues was. His intention to emigrate did not change even after his application had been denied by the Australian authorities. He simply altered his plans by considering another continent, North America. In a bittersweet closing to a letter to Jones, he said that he hoped he could continue to count on him "in the rather improbable case when, owing to a sort of Deus ex machina, I could leave this country" (see reproduction of letter, below). The summer of 1939 proved to be a period of uncertainty for Hungarian analysts preparing to emigrate. Two couples, Dr Klára Lázár and her husband, Dr Vilmos Gerő, as well as Dr Erzsébet Kardos and her husband, Dr Endre Pető, decided they would make a go of the option to resettle in Australia. They were all medical graduates, thus increasing their chances. Lázár's correspondence with Jones bears witness to efforts made among officials, colleagues, and friends in London, Sydney, Melbourne, and Canberra. A reader today may just detect the signs of a constant feeling of vulnerability behind the disciplined lines of her letters. For instance, Lázár does not seem to be able to thank Jones enough for his efforts (see reproduction of letter, below).

On 24 September 1939, Kardos finally received her Australian visa. On 9 July 1939, Lázár was also informed that she would be allowed to travel to Canberra with her husband and son. In the meantime, Edit Gyömrői was already living in Ceylon (Sri Lanka).

In 1939, the lives of the Budapest analysts were filled with tough choices, tensions tied to preparations for emigration, hopeful anticipation, and unhappy disappointments. Ferenczi's death had not caused a break in terms of the Hungarian psychoanalytic legacy since Ferenczi had made sure to transmit it, and the first generation of analysts—István Hollós, Zsigmond Pfeifer, and Imre Hermann, among others—had then passed it down. The next generation to be fortified by Ferenczi—Michael Balint, Vilma Kovács, and Alice Balint—stood at the ready to pass on the theoretical and practical knowledge of the Budapest School that had accumulated over the decades: the countertransference phenomenon in psychoanalytic

Kossuth Lajos-tér 14-1
Budapest,V.
13th May,1939.

G07/BJ/F01/14

Dear Dr.Jones,

I am very sorry to inform you that my appl. cation for a Permit to enter Australia,has been refused on 6th April /under No.39/3/512./;it was not until yesterday that I got the official note.

Curious enough,that with the same mail there came a letter of 28th April,sent by Dr.Winn by air-mail,partly very favourable to me.Though I am afraid it is of no use for me any more,still I may communicate with you about it with regard to my colleagues,who may still have the chance of getting a Permit.

Dr.Winn admits,that he "was misinformed by the secretary of the B.M.A.concerning the 8 graduates;it is not meant to limit the number who will be allowed to practise without doing the last 3 years of the medical course,but applies to all;in other words only 8 medical graduates from foreign countries will be allowed registration per year,some whome, however,may be registered immediately if specially qualified,/the intention of the Act being to make use of any possessing outstanding ability,particularly in teaching or research/."Applications for registration at the M.B.must be made personally;there are already 15 applications in the hands of the Secretary of teh M.B.,so that I should not be able commence the Fourth Year before 1942,unless I were granted the right to practise immediately,under the regulations which applies to those with special qualifications.Among th applicants is Dr.S.Fink an associate member of the Swiss Society. He "had many months previously made inquiries on the possibility of psycho-analysts being admitted -soon after receiving Dr.Jones first appeal- and an officer of the Commonwealth after interviewing me stated that he would report favourably on the matter." "In accordance with the suggtion of Mr.Duncan Hall,who has recently been in Au.I have written a letter to an official of the Department of the In terior /Mr.A.R.Peters/advocating the admission of analysts and associating with that appeal the names of two well know Sydney psachiatrists.Also I have written to Dr.Elwell of Brisbane asking him to send a similar joint letter on the part of psychiatrists and others interested in Qeensland. And have asked Dr.Paul Dane of Melbourne not only to do the same for Victoria,but also to write to Dr.Hone and Dr Fry of Adelaide." This part belonged to Drs.Lázár,Kardos and Pető,as well,whose coming would be much welcomed by him.He further to the M.B.,where he has many friends,stating,that "the registration of psychoanalysts would not injure the interests of the medical profession as a whole,because of the limited number of patients that it is possible for an individual analyst to treat." The N.S.W.branch of the B.M.A is opposed to practising without being registered,but there is "no legal reason,why a psycho-analyst should not practis provided he did not described himself as a medical practitioner";"it should be regarded as a private arrangement". Nevertheless,"it would certainly be advisable not to go cou

Letter from István Schönberger to Ernest Jones, 13 May 1939. Archives of the British Psychoanalytical Society, G07/BJ/F01/14.

SCHÖNBERGER ISTVÁN LEVELE ERNEST JONESNAK, 1939. MÁJUS 13. P. 2.

ter to the B.M.A.because that body could use its influence to oppose you,and that would tend to interfere with the standing of Psycho-analysis in the future."Assuming that I am not registered immediately,he is working - indeed in an almost touching manner - to get a job for me as a biochemist,and he provided two patients to me,as well,in order to xxxxxxxxxxxxx enable me to make living during the pursuit of the medical cours He further asked for particulars concerning my qualifications as a training analyst;I was entitled by Dr.Hermann to state, that the T.C.was just considering my registration as a trainin analyst,and he personally -and I am in the position to add that Mrs.V.Kovács as well- were supporting this.Moreover Dr.Hermann gave me recently opportunity of getting experience in leading seminaries..

I cant help repeating wht a pity it is,that a plan,supported with so great efforts by you and Dr.Winn,so well founded both as to doing pioneer-work for Psycho-analysis in Australia and as to securing me a living for the time of the medical course,should fail.

I should like to express my thanks for all that you have done so far and I wish I could count on your kind help also in the rather improbable case when,owing to a sort of Deus ex machina,I could leave this country.

Yours sincerely,

Dr Stephen Schönberger

Continuation of letter from Schönberger to Jones, 13 May 1939.

theory and practice; the personality-shaping powers of the early mother–child relationship and the new perspectives it offered via the object relations approach; Ferenczi's interpersonal and object relations view of trauma; psychoanalytic psychosomatics; new understandings and discoveries in psychoanalytic pedagogy and psychoanalytic anthropology. The talented members of the youngest generation then—among them Róbert Bak, Fanny Hann-Kende, Vilmos Kapos, Endre Pető, Tibor Rajka (1901–1980), and István (Székács) Schönberger—proved responsive to all this.

When the Balints left Hungary in the early months of 1939, the second emigration wave of the Budapest School had begun and the

Budapest. VI.
Vilma királynő ut 50,

31st May 1939.

Dr. Ernest Jones,
81, Harley Street,
LONDON. W.1.

Dear Dr. Jones,

We have had no answer from Australia as yet, but - as you know - Dr. Winn referred in writing to Dr. Schönberger to our letter and has very kindly promised to be of assistance to us.

Meanwhile we have been informed by our Australian friends that the Delegate of the Department of Interior, Mr. G a r r o t , has recently arrived in London and that he supervises the applications at the Australia-House.

Our friends suggested to try to take up contacts with Mr. Garret. Which way do you think could this be done the best? May we perhaps venture to ask you to intervene on our behalf? (Our applications have also been filed with the Official Secretary, Australia House, with all the necessary documents).

Please forgive our trespassing on your kindness and accept once more our heartfelt best thanks.

Yours sincerely,

Dr Elisabeth Kardos,
Dr Andrew Pető,
Dr William Gerő & Clara Lázár-Gerő

Letter from Clara Lázár-Gerő to Ernest Jones, 31 May 1939.
Archives of the British Psychonalytical Society.

opportunity to carry on this building project in Hungary evaporated. This wave put an irreversible process in motion for both the future of those involved and the fate of psychoanalysis in Hungary. Many had been able to return from the Weimar Republic, but now all roads through a Europe in the clutches of Nazism led simply out and away—permanently.

THE TIME HAS COME (1938–1941): THE SECOND WAVE OF EMIGRATION   157

Continental shift

In his letter to Kubie of 19 January 1939, Hollós made a reference to the fifteen people listed in an enclosure who were requesting assistance to leave Hungary. Hollós clearly brought it to Kubie's attention that "Dr Jones ... gave me the advice in his very encouraging and detailed letter, to let also you know the present condition".[124] We have already seen in earlier chapters that it was part of Jones' and Kubie's co-operative agreement to keep one another up-to-date. Clearly, Jones had done a great deal for the Hungarian analysts. (See, for example, his correspondence with Gyömrői, Schönberger, and Klári Lázár-Gerő.) At the same time, it is also abundantly apparent that he restricted his assistance to the sort that would keep the Hungarian analysts far away from Britain. The USA and the Commonwealth countries, therefore, represented a convenient solution. Documents from the British Psychoanalytical Society bear witness to the fact that many of the analysts forced to emigrate from Budapest after 1938—such as Géza Róheim, the Balints, Imre Hermann, and Edit Gyömrői—would have preferred to remain in Europe. However, it was only the Balints that managed to resettle in Britain. There was a small group that was able to find its way to Australia: it was not only the Lázár-Gerő couple and their child that obtained Australian entry visas, but also the Kardos–Pető couple.

What we know as a certainty is that the following Hungarian psychoanalysts left the country in 1939: Michael Balint, Alice Balint, and their son, Géza Róheim; Edit Gyömrői-Újvári and her husband at the time, Laszlo Újvári, and Klára Lázár with her family. All the rest had was hope. But how would they manage to leave Hungary and Europe, where would they resettle, where would they find work, and how would their lives change after they emigrated?

In my research, I found no trace of the enclosure to Hollós's letter, but I did manage to unearth a very telling document in a jumbled box stored in the Payne Whitney Archives that provided a link between other documents and various and sundry bits and pieces towards understanding the process of emigration and immigration.[125]

It was a cable sent from Zsigmond Pfeifer, the Hungarian Society's secretary, to the Emergency Committee, on 29 April 1941, with the following message: "Telegraph whether immigration for members [and] candidates[,] some with children over 18[,] possible on superquota [non-quota visa] and also help for [residence permit]. [Potential applicants for] [s]uperquota [non-quota visa] about eight" (see note 124).

The Emergency Committee requested the National Refugee Office to have their representative contact Pfeifer while they reviewed their own committee documents. In April 1941, the following information was available on the Hungarian analysts:

Eligible for non-quota visas: 5

Dr Imre Hermann
Dr István Hollós
Dr Zsigmond Pfeifer
Dr László Révész
Dr Lillian Rotter-Kertész

Requiring affidavits: 12 [sic, 14]

Dr Renee Amar	Kata Lévy
Dr Margit Dubovitz	Dr Margit Ormos
Dr Melchior [Menyhért] Farkashazi	Lilly Perl-Balla
Dr Miklós Gimes	Zelma Sulamith Rubin Farber [Farber Rubin]
Dr Lilly Hajdu-Gimes	Dr Stephen [István] Schönberger
Dr William [Vilmos] Kapos	Dr Julius [Gyula] Szuts
Mrs Imre Major	Dr Róbert Bak

Have affidavits secured by the Committee: 3

Dr Géza Dukes
Dr Elizabeth [Erzsébet] Kardos
Dr Andrew [Endre] Pető

This list from 1941 was accompanied by the following remark:

Although we are uncertain at the present time about the route over which these people could leave Hungary, or indeed whether they can leave at all, we are advised by the Migration Department of the National Refugee Service that every effort should nevertheless be made to secure affidavits and to be in readiness to pay passage should the opportunity arise for them to leave.

It becomes clear from this document that Géza Dukes, Erzsébet Kardos, and Endre Pető were all given the green light to immigrate to the USA. In addition, Imre Hermann, István Hollós, Zsigmond Pfeifer, László Révész (?-1944), and Lillian Rotter-Kertész were all possible candidates for the non-quota visa. Nevertheless, of the people on the list, it was only Róbert Bak who availed himself of the help offered.

However, the following comes to light from another document:

> In response to a request from Dr István Hollós, the Emergency Committee tried to secure affidavits or teaching invitations for the following members and students [analyst candidates] of the Hungarian Psychoanalytic Society:
>
> **Members**
>
> Dubovitz, Dr Margit
> Dukes, Dr Geza [Géza]—Analytically trained lawyer. Affidavits were sent to him.
> Hajdu Gimes, Dr Lily
> Hermann, Dr Imre
> Hollos, Dr Istvan [István Hollós]—Living in Switzerland
> Levy, Dr [sic] Kata F. [Kata (Freund) Lévy]—Training analyst
> Pfeifer, Dr Zsigmond
> Revesz, Dr Laszlo [László Révész]
> Rotter-Kertesz, Dr Lillian
> Szuts, Dr Julius [Gyula Szücs]
>
> **Associate members**
>
> Amar, Dr Renee
> Hirsch, Marguerite [Margit]—Did psychological work with problem children
> Hermann, Dr Alice—Wife of Dr Imre Hermann; lay analyst, teacher
> Major, Mrs Imre—Child analyst
> Patzay, Mrs Lucy [Lucy Liebermann Pátzay]—M.D., analysed teacher [sic]
> Peto, Dr Andrew [Endre Pető]—Affidavits were sent to him in 1940
> Schonberger, Dr Stephen [István (Székács) Schönberger]
>
> **Students [analyst candidates]**
>
> Dric [sic], Mrs Susanne [Zsuzsa Déri]
> Farkashazi, Dr Melchior [Menyhért Farkasházi]
> Fisch, Adolf [Wolf],[126] PhD—Rabbi. His case was referred to the National Refugee Service.
> Gimes, Dr Mklos [sic, Miklós]—Husband of Dr Lily Hajdu Gimes

Kapos, Dr William [Vilmos]—Affidavits sent by relatives in the United States
Kerenyi, Dr John [János Kerényi]
Ormos, Dr Margit
Perl-Balla, Mrs Lilly—Child analyst
Peto, Dr Elizabeth [Erzsébet] Kardos—Wife of Dr Andrew Peto [Endre Pető]
Rubin-Faber [sic, Farber Rubin], Dr Zelma[127]

This extraordinarily detailed document contains the names of Hungary's analysts and analyst candidates who applied for immigration and requested assistance from the Emergency Committee.

The section that follows is a review of those Hungarian psychoanalysts whose names can be found on the membership lists of psychoanalytic associations in the USA in the years to follow and of those who managed to reach the USA without the aid of the Emergency Committee. It will also explore the question of what motivated those who ultimately decided not to set out on the journey.

The New York Psychoanalytic Society and the Hungarian newcomers

In 1937, according to Thompson, "the society had 71 members ... a decade later, in 1948, its membership was 152, with 51, a full third, being émigrés ... [who] had an enormous and long-lasting impact on the educational and intellectual life of the New York Psychoanalytic Society" (Thompson, 2012, p. 24). Among these were a number of Hungarians who, as training analysts for the new generation, also played an important role in the further development of psychoanalytic theory and practice as well as serving as presidents of the society. The reader will find more on the impact they had in the next chapter.

Róbert Bak (1906–1974) started studying law in 1925 but left it behind after one term, turning to medicine in 1926.[128] He completed his residency at the Hungarian Royal Institute for Neurology and Psychiatry (1933–1935) and then took a position (1935–1940) at the Neurological and Psychiatric Clinic on Balassa Street in central Budapest. His decision to specialise in psychiatry was largely motivated by his brother Miklós's condition (schizophrenia). His interest

Róbert Bak (right) and his older brother Miklós, Budapest, early 1930s.
Archives of the Sándor Ferenczi Society & International Ferenczi Centre, Budapest.

in psychoanalysis was aroused by Zsigmond Pfeifer, his brother-in-law, who also introduced him to Géza Róheim—who would become a lifelong friend (Stewart, 1975). These early influences took root and grew into a keen interest within psychoanalysis in the treatment and theoretical approach to schizophrenia.

Bak's first scholarly article discussed insulin treatment for schizophrenia (Bak, 1934). Although he was also well read in other areas, he always maintained his focus on disorders tied to early object relations and on the pathological processes involved in the archaic layers of instinct. He also integrated psychoses and perversions into the system. In fact, in keeping with Ferenczi's very early position, Bak even incorporated the feeling of love into the category of borderline condition. Ferenczi interprets the experience of love as a "border area" between the sick and healthy states of a person's mind in one of his very early articles "Love in science" (Ferenczi, 1999f[1901], p. 78). Seventy years on, in a study published in 1971, Bak describes the phenomenon as follows:

> '[B]eing in love', a borderline condition, usually transitory, in which the distortion of reality is due to overestimation of the object when self-representations are deprived of their cathexis and the anticipatory function of the ego is impoverished. (Bak, 1971)

Bak did his training analysis with Imre Hermann and attended Vilma Kovács and Alice Balint's seminars on case study discussions at the Kovács family home in Budapest's fashionable Naphegy section. Róbert Bak, István Schönberger, and Endre Pető formed a triumvirate of sorts, both as a matter of friendship and as a professional association: after the seminars they would linger and discuss what had been said.

A student of Ferenczi's, Vilma Kovács was an extraordinary person who managed to create an atmosphere during the seminars, in which, as István (Székács) Schönberger later recalled, "even a criticism made during the case reports, which were taken very seriously indeed, was a light caress" (Mészáros, 1997, translated for this edition). They worked in a creative and anxiety-free environment. Bak, too, was socialised in this professional milieu, though he never actually handled his own students with kid gloves. Stanley Ricklin, who had studied under Bak in New York, once turned to his teacher at a seminar and asked, "Dr Bak, I've read your article, and there's something I don't understand." Bak cut him off and, without any further explanation, simply said, "Why don't you read it again?" At the same time, Bak would speak with great tolerance about pathological conditions, psychoses, and perversions, always striving to make these serious conditions as real as possible for his students (Mészáros, 1999b, p. 166).

When Edit Gyömrői was having difficulty with the poet Attila József's psychoanalysis, her uncle, István Hollós, the president of the Hungarian Psychoanalytical Society, hurried to the aid of his colleague and niece. Hollós asked the young Róbert Bak to take over the great poet's treatment. Since then, numerous articles and book-length studies have examined Attila József's mental state (Bak, 1938; Németh,

2000; Stark & Bókay, 1980; Valachi, 2005). As his articles testify (1971, 1973), Bak spent the rest of his life diagnosing his famous patient's condition as schizophrenia and was happy to quote his poems for his American students.

Róbert Bak became a professionally mature psychoanalyst at a historic moment. He was admitted to the Hungarian Society in June 1938. Two months later, he was already presenting a successful paper at the psychoanalytic congress in Paris entitled "Regression of ego-orientation and libido in schizophrenia", which to this day figures among his often-cited studies (Bak, 1939). In all likelihood, it was the Hungarian-language version of Róbert Bak's Paris talk—a talk that was soon published in the IPA journal—that had also been his inaugural lecture when he assumed membership in the Hungarian Society.

The years to come would see a change of fortune. With the youngest generation of the Hungarian Society having enjoyed their successful debut before the international professional community at the Paris congress, they would see their names again, three years later, on the list of those requesting aid from the Emergency Committee. Hungary had set up a system of forced labour known as the Jewish Labour Service, which had an impact on many analysts and two of the Bak brothers. In 1940, Róbert and his older brother Loránd were taken as part of the labour service to Transylvania (in today's Romania), a portion of which had been ceded to Hungary that same year. Through Róbert's careful planning, a certain Professor Benedek (who will be discussed later) hid Robert's sick brother Miklós in the Siesta Sanatorium in Budapest on several occasions. As their family later recalled,

> [a]s a company physician in Transylvania, Robert was being put up in some sort of peasant house, so he once simply declared that a country where a person is forced to be without a bathroom is one where, sooner or later, he might just as easily be beaten to death. . . . That's a place you have to leave. (Mészáros, 1999b, translated for this edition)

Therefore, Róbert decided to emigrate, although actually implementing this plan would be tricky since he would be unable to leave the country while subjected to the Labour Service. However, his father managed to secure him a passport through his foreign ministry connections. With his wife, an actress named Pepa Kántor, he travelled to Spain, where he had a relative.[129] With his assistance, the couple embarked on the now legendary last ship of the war to sail from Casablanca to America. Dr and Mrs Bak arrived in Manhattan on 7 June 1941, six months before the USA entered the war.

Robert Bak also received support from the Emergency Committee in the sum of $200.[130] In April 1943, he joined the New York Psychoanalytic Society and experienced nearly instant success. In 1944, he became a lecturer at the New York Psychoanalytic Institute. In 1945, he accepted Rado's invitation to become an adjunct professor at Columbia's Psychoanalytic and Psychosomatic Clinic, which Rado had established the year before.[131] In 1947, Bak became a training analyst and then president of the New York Psychoanalytic Society a decade later (1957–1959). The USA made him one of her own very quickly, and for his part he became a real New Yorker in no time. His elegant office at 985 Fifth Avenue on the Upper East Side proved a memorable spot for both students and patients alike.

The Emergency Committee list above even includes the name of an analyst, Endre Pető, who also took the opportunity to immigrate to the USA, albeit not in the early 1940s. He, too, left Hungary, though in a later phase in history, in 1949, and eventually managed to arrive in New York and, in another sense, within the New York Psychoanalytic Society as well. The course of his life reflects a different approach to that of Bak and the other whizz-kids of his generation.

Pető was a mild-mannered man who was ever willing to seek compromise; his was the life's path typical of a middle-class Jew in Central Europe in the twentieth century, full of its particular hopes and disappointments. In an interview with Hanna Pető, his second wife, she answered the question of why he had chosen not to set off with his first wife, Erzsébet Kardos, when he had had the opportunity. After all, Australia and the USA had flung their doors wide open to them, and their staying in Hungary would come with a grave consequence: the death of his wife. What was it, then, that prompted Peto to leave Hungary in 1949, at the age of forty-five?

Endre Pető (1904–1985) was born into a Jewish family in Budapest in 1904. He was not admitted to the medical course at Budapest because of the *numerus clausus* laws. This was the first time he would experience the pressure of circumstances, and so he left the country to study medicine in Germany, Switzerland, and Austria, and finally complete his studies in Budapest in 1926. He was involved in paediatrics and neurology, but it was psychoanalysis that became his great passion. He saw Michael Balint for training analysis between 1935 and 1938, and—like Schönberger and Bak—joined the Hungarian Society in 1938. Naturally, Pető also attended the Paris congress in 1938, so, if he had been unaware of the fate of his peers in Vienna following the Anschluss, he certainly learned of it at that congress. Indeed, he had already experienced discrimination and lived the life of a foreigner. So, then, why did he still remain in Hungary?

Pető's second wife—who had by now changed the long Hungarian *ő* in her name to a simple *o*—provided an answer to this question in a 1996 interview:

> Hanna Peto: So there was some congress [the 15th International Psychoanalytical Congress held in Paris] . . . and they [Endre Pető and Erzsébet Kardos] were over there for two weeks and it came up then, but they had just been married and they had everything all ready. The flat was newly furnished, the office was ready . . . 1944 was still a long way off. Bandi [Endre] was very much attached to his mother, and Ákos [his brother] was already on the Russian front. Circumstances were such that they couldn't stay away. If they had, they would have had to stay away for good and they did not yet have a sure place to go at the time. They hadn't got their Australian visa yet . . .
>
> Mészáros: Do you know anything about why they applied to immigrate to Australia?
>
> Hanna Peto: Because Bandi had a lot of friends in Australia, people he had worked with at the Jewish hospital. They had gone to Australia in 1938. Klári Lázár [Clara Lazar Geroe] was there, so he had some notion that there was something out there, but he hadn't thought it through. He didn't have the will to leave the country. . . . Bandi's first wife was Erzsébet Kardos, who was an analyst, and in 1944 both Bandi and Bözsi [Erzsébet] were lying low, using forged papers. They felt that it was somehow safer for them to stay in two places, they didn't want to go to the same place together, and unfortunately somebody saw Bözsi and reported her. They killed her along with all the others she was with in the usual way. . . . Incidentally, there was some sort of Swedish immunity, but that didn't matter under the circumstances.[132] (Mészáros, 1996)

Endre Pető left Hungary with his second wife, Hanna, and Hanna's young child in 1949. The dissolution of the Hungarian Psychoanalytical Society[133]—and all that this entailed—created a dramatic situation for them:

Then Bandi [Endre] said his life was over if he could not be an analyst. To which I said, if a lawyer had to go clean toilets under this regime, that's a much worse offence than Bandi Pető going back to being a paediatrician. . . . 'Well, if you don't understand what this means to me, then there's nothing more to talk about.'. . . He didn't speak to me for three days. (Mészáros, 1996)

In 1949, the Petős had great difficulty leaving Hungary. In the end, after several years of delays, they managed to reach Australia, which they left for New York City in 1956. Peto taught from that point on until 1974 at the Albert Einstein College of Medicine of Yeshiva University in the Bronx. In 1958, he became a member of the New York Psychoanalytic Society and then a training analyst. He was even honoured by his peers in New York by being elected president of the society, in which capacity he served for two years (1975–1977). These were extraordinarily prolific years for Pető, with the publication of over forty studies. He was particularly interested in archaic thinking, the early ego functions and associated disorders, and a psychoanalytic approach to cultural and socio-psychological phenomena (on this topic, see Pető, 1958, 1959, 1961, 1963, 1975).

None of the Emergency Committee lists above includes the names Tibor Ágoston, Sándor Feldman, Fanny Hann-Kende, David (Dezső) Rapaport, or Géza Róheim. Nevertheless, all of them left Hungary and migrated directly to the USA, and all of them enjoyed the support of the committee.

Tibor Ágoston (Wirkman) (1904–?) arrived in the USA on 24 September 1940, already a psychiatrist and qualified psychoanalyst. He had earned his degree at the medical university in Budapest in 1928. All of the documents that verified Ágoston's medical training had the name Wirkman on them, according to a letter from Bettina Warburg to Samuel Atkin,[134] but, since he had reportedly experienced problems with the German name, he changed it.[135] Another document sets down that he was Roman Catholic.[136] This leads us to conclude that Ágoston first converted to Christianity because of Hungary's anti-Semitic laws and then left the country with his wife and their daughter, who was barely three years old at the time. Actually, Ágoston had already had some experience of living abroad, having worked in psychiatric clinics in Munich and Vienna. He became a member of the Hungarian Psychoanalytical Society on 16 February 1940, in the same year that he left the country.

Dr Samuel Feigin[137] and Bettina Warburg evaluated him at the request of the Psychiatric Advisory Board. Both of them gave him a very positive report. Warburg recommended him as a well-trained psychiatrist and psychoanalyst, who had also been involved in child psychology, and concluded that he was a completely capable physician with a good character and a pleasant appearance.

Ágoston quickly decided that he would take the boards and integrate into the New York Psychoanalytic Institute. Bettina Warburg seems to have taken him under her wing, because the day after he arrived she sent a letter of introduction to Dr Samuel Atkin, the head of the institute. Warburg also requested that some patients be referred to Ágoston "so that he can support himself during this first difficult period" (First letter from Bettina Warburg to Samuel Atkin, 25 September 1940).

We know Ágoston must have been struggling early on because, on the same day, Warburg sent another letter to Atkin requesting two patients for Ágoston to assist him in paying his rent, reassuring the director that, while the Hungarian's "spoken English is somewhat halting", he ultimately "seems like a reasonably reliable fellow". Warburg's justification for her request was that Ágoston's

> relatives here seem to be taking an unpleasant attitude toward him, and I think it would be better if he could finance his own living rather than try to get on relief with the National Refugee Service as they are cutting down the number of people they will support while studying for examinations. It might be difficult to get them to accept him because he has relatives who could support him if they wanted to. (See reproduction of letter, below)

In all likelihood, Ágoston's situation showed no improvement, because Warburg turned to Atkin again in a letter dated 24 January 1941, to request that the New York Psychoanalytic Institute send patients for several European analysts. According to her letter, they were looking for patients

> who can pay a low fee and who are too difficult for students to handle. It is of course important that the analysts who have not yet got licences should not be sent patients who may become psychotic, commit suicide, or get in trouble with the law.[138]

THE AMERICAN PSYCHOANALYTIC ASSOCIATION
A FEDERATION OF AMERICAN PSYCHOANALYTIC SOCIETIES

A. A. BRILL, M.D., HONORARY PRESIDENT
88 CENTRAL PARK WEST, NEW YORK CITY

DAVID M. LEVY, M.D., PRESIDENT
136 EAST 57TH STREET NEW YORK CITY

GEORGE E. DANIELS, M.D., VICE-PRESIDENT
129 EAST 69TH STREET, NEW YORK CITY

JOHN M. MURRAY, M.D., SECRETARY
82 MARLBOROUGH STREET, BOSTON, MASS.

HELEN V. McLEAN, M.D., TREASURER
43 EAST OHIO STREET, CHICAGO, ILL.

September 25, 1940

Dr. Samuel Atkin
The New York Psychoanalytic Institute
324 West 86 Street, New York City

Dear Sam

Enclosed is a copy of a letter of introduction which I have just given to Dr. Agoston for you. I also enclose a copy of an excerpt of my interview with him yesterday.

His spoken English is somewhat halting, but he says that he reads and writes without difficulty. He has just taken his language examination. He seems like a reasonably reliable fellow, and I wonder whether it would be possible to send him one or two patients as any money that he can make would help him to pay the rent.

His relatives here seem to be taking an unpleasant attitude toward him, and I think it would be better if he could finance his own living rather than try to get on relief with the National Refugee Service as they are cutting down the number of people they will support while studying for examinations. It might be difficult to get them to accept him because he has relatives who could support him if they wanted to.

Thank you very much.

Yours sincerely,

Bettina Warburg

Second letter from Bettina Warburg to Samuel Atkin, 25 September 1940. The Archives & Special Collections of the A. A. Brill Library, The New York Psychoanalytic Society and Institute.

and neither, indeed, should they be sent anybody who would jeopardise the chances of a physician who is currently unlicensed from obtaining a licence in the future. This is why Warburg recommended that unlicensed foreign physicians work together with their licensed peers. She suggested that Ágoston be given priority because, of all the Europeans, he was the one most in need of money.

The name Fanny Hann-Kende (or Fanny von Hann-Kende) (1891–1952) cannot be found on the Emergency Committee list sent by Hollós, but it becomes clear from another archival document that the

Emergency Committee was also sponsoring her. She came from the same milieu that István (Székács) Schönberger described so vividly in an interview once. Naturally, it was not only "the boys" (Bak, Pető, and Schönberger) who attended Vilma Kovács's seminars, but also young women analysts who were hungry to learn. The men of the "triumvirate" wrote off those women in the group whom they perceived to be unpleasant or stupid as "society ladies". However, Hann-Kende was spared from being placed in that category. As Schönberger put it, "Fanny was a great lady. . . . You could tell she was aristocratic. She didn't speak much. When she said something, it was clever" (Mészáros, 1997, translated for this edition). Indeed, this clever lady, as previously mentioned, had already seen her study on transference and countertransference (Hann-Kende, 1993[1933]) published in the surprise volume put out in honour of Ferenczi's sixtieth birthday.

Hann-Kende entered the USA with a temporary visa in April 1938. She launched her USA career as a guest lecturer at the New York Psychoanalytic Institute. She had applied for the position in a letter to Dr Adolf Stern.[139]

Hann-Kende's career is outlined in documents found at the New York Psychoanalytic Society. She received her medical degree at the University of Budapest in 1914. A psychiatrist and neurologist, she saw Helene Deutsch in Vienna for psychoanalytic training (1927–1929). She became a member of the Hungarian Psychoanalytical Society in 1930. Between 1932 and 1938, she worked at the psychoanalytic polyclinic in Budapest. From 1935 on, she was a training analyst for the Hungarian society. As of 1943, she was a member of the New York Psychoanalytic Society. Sandor Rado must also have thought her a clever lady because, in 1948, he took her on at the department he had established at Columbia. That same year, the New York Psychoanalytic Institute invited her as an instructor.[140] However, the most noteworthy of her achievements is the fact that she developed an "abbreviated" method of psychoanalytic therapy (Anon, 1952).

Sándor Feldman (1891–1973) completed his medical studies at the University of Budapest in 1915. He gained medical experience in hospitals in both Hungary and Austria. During the war, he served in Bosnia in a hospital ward that cared for patients with neurological conditions. During Hungary's brief Soviet Republic period, he worked as an assistant with Ferenczi at the university's psychoanalytic clinic. He completed his psychoanalytic training at the

Hungarian Psychoanalytical Society between 1919 and 1921. Later, according to Feldman, he underwent four years of personal analysis between 1935 and 1938, also in Budapest.[141] Interestingly, Feldman made no mention anywhere of who his training analysts were. In all likelihood, his relationship with Ferenczi deteriorated when he joined the "active analysts" tied to Wilhelm Stekel. In 1938, Feldman wanted to move to Canada to be with his brother there. This did not come to pass for reasons that remain unclear. In April 1939, he touched soil in New York City. The anguish that this forty-eight-year-old physician endured in obtaining his licence is typical of the experience émigré physicians undergo in their efforts to negotiate the bureaucratic maze of their adoptive country. He travelled from New York to another brother in Pittsburgh, Pennsylvania. He then submitted his application for a licence to practise in that state, and the licensing board exempted him from his one-year internship—which represented a rare exception. However, he failed the boards. Therefore, he returned to New York City and submitted his application there. The Emergency Committee then transferred him to Rochester, in upstate New York. Nevertheless, Feldman remained in New York City until he managed to pass the boards in New York State in August 1941. It had taken him two and a half years until he was able, at the age of fifty, to carry on his work as an analyst. At that point, he did resettle in Rochester, where he established a thriving analytic practice and became professor of psychiatry at the University of Rochester School of Medicine.[142]

The Menninger Clinic and David Rapaport

David (Dezső) Rapaport (1911–1960) grew up in a middle-class, college-educated, Jewish family. As a young man, he joined a Zionist youth organisation, of which he became the Hungarian group's leader and spokesman. Since the organisation was not entirely legal—its mission not being in line with government policy—Rapaport, who proved to be a powerful orator, found himself in trouble on a number of occasions. He studied mathematics and physics in Budapest. One anecdote, which is a favourite of his biographers, emerges from his university years. Despite sharing the same family names, David Rapaport and the well-known neurologist and psychiatrist Samu Rapaport—who was also Attila József's doctor—had nothing in common whatsoever, whereas there were a number of differences between them. The latter could not write, the former could. They supposedly co-authored two books, but David (still Dezső at that point) preferred to remain invisible rather than see his name on a book cover (Knight, 1961). After graduating, he joined a kibbutz through his organisation in what was then still Palestine, lived there for two years, and even established a family. He eventually returned with his wife and baby to Budapest, charged with running the organisation's Hungarian group again. Between 1935 and 1938, he continued his study of psychology in Budapest at what had been renamed Pázmány Péter University during the interwar years, where he earned a PhD with a dissertation "On the history of the concept of association" (Rapaport,

David Rapaport, late 1930s. Archives of the Sándor Ferenczi Society & International Ferenczi Centre, Budapest.

1939). It was during this period that he completed his own training analysis with Tibor Rajka (Gill, 1967). In 1938, when the first of a series of ever more harshly anti-Semitic laws was enacted, Rapaport was presented with a difficult decision to make: where should he go now? Should he choose Palestine and carry on his work at the kibbutz or move to the USA? He opted for the latter and arrived on the shores of North America in December 1938.

The Emergency Committee sent out over 200 letters in their determination to find Rapaport a position. This figure illustrates well the tireless efforts made by members of the committee to assist their peers. First, Rapaport worked at the Macy Foundation, a New York-based philanthropic organisation that promotes training among healthcare professionals, and then, in 1939, at the Osawatomie State Hospital, a psychiatric facility in Kansas that serves patients regardless of their ability to pay. The Emergency Committee supplemented his income with a thousand-dollar stipend, since his contract at Osawatomie was in jeopardy. It seemed the Kansas Medical Society was protesting his being given a position there on the grounds that he was neither a physician nor a citizen of the USA. In fact, the society was merely bringing pressure to bear on the hospital, but not enough for it to terminate its contract with Rapaport. In the end, it was Rapaport who had had his fill of the tension and decided to leave.

The major breakthrough in Rapaport's life came in 1940. He found a job that matched his qualifications perfectly, a research position at the Menninger Clinic in Topeka, Kansas. Apparently, just as Rapaport was looking for a way out of the tense situation in which he had found himself, Karl Menninger (1893–1990), a co-founder of the clinic, happened to track Rapaport down. It had come to Menninger's attention that a brilliant mind was at work at Osawatomie, and he knew that the Menninger Clinic, which was still taking shape, was sorely in need of creative and innovative staff. Karl Menninger, whom everybody called KAM, was curious about Rapaport and thus asked him to prove his diagnostic skills: Menninger had Rapaport administer the Rorschach test on Menninger himself and evaluate the results. It was after this that Menninger hired Rapaport at his clinic, where he was immediately charged with setting up and running the research section there.

The research was very wide-ranging: there was work being done on hypnosis and developmental psychology and testing on expressions of normal and pathological personalities in perceptual phenomena, but most important of all was the application of projective and intelligence tests in clinical practice. In fact, between the 1940s and the 1960s, Rapaport had such an enormous effect on psychology in the USA that diagnostic testing became a very important function among clinical psychologists and "psychoanalysis was the dominant ideology" (Mészáros, 2000a). The Menninger Clinic established an unparalleled reputation for diagnostics based on testing research. According to one of Rapaport's students, Herbert J. Schlesinger, the results of psychological tests enjoyed the same priority in case studies "as the pathologist's report at a medical Clinical Pathological Conference" (Mészáros, 2000a).

The Menninger Clinic provided Rapaport with an opportunity to grow and to pursue a brilliant career. His natural leadership abilities, his qualifications (in mathematics, physics, and psychology), and his writing talent had already made an impression based on his work in Budapest. Now he managed to capitalise on these strengths in establishing and operating the research section at the clinic. Rapaport wanted to develop a theoretical system of psychology that was capable of linking psychoanalytic theory to general processes of thinking and perception, or, in current parlance, to find links between psychoanalysis and the cognitive sciences. He devoted all his effort to incorporating ego psychology and social psychology into a common framework. As Csaba Pléh put it, Rapaport was "a very interesting proponent of a biologically based Freudian metapsychology" (Pléh, 2008, p. 53). In 1940, he was made an associate member of the American Psychoanalytic Association (APsaA), and in September of that year he was invited to the New York Psychoanalytic Institute to speak on the testing programme at the Menninger Clinic.

Rapaport invested incredible energy into his work. He was also happy to involve others in the creative process, and the feeling was reciprocated: everyone's total commitment was required in the common project. Rapaport's second year at the Menninger Clinic was punctuated with a monograph called *Emotion and Memory* (Rapaport, 1950[1942]), his first major work, which discussed "the relationship between experimental and psychoanalytic theories of forgetting" (Pléh, 2008, p. 29). Not long afterward, he collaborated with two colleagues at the clinic to write *Diagnostic Psychological Testing*, a standard work that is now regarded as a classic (Rapaport, Schafer, & Gill, 1945–1946).

Rapaport's students both admired and feared him, according to one of them, Henry J. Schlesinger, who would later become a colleague:

> He demanded as much of his students as of himself. He read our examinations and papers carefully ... correcting our English as well as our thinking. Many of my classmates felt terrorised by him and several had anxiety attacks in relation to going to his classes. These were bright people in the ordinary sense of the term, but their undergraduate education was in the American psychology of that day and their general cultural education had little of the breadth that DR took for granted would be second nature to a university graduate, i.e., of a European one. Freud, dynamics, holistic thinking, continental philosophy, and the philosophy of science all of which were interwoven in DR's lectures were totally foreign to them. (Mészáros, 2000b, translated for this edition)

The Menninger Clinic was considered liberal in that conservative Mid-western state. It was practically the only place in the region where analysts who had fled Europe could expect help. The fact that Menninger's analyst was Franz Alexander—another assimilated Jewish intellectual from Europe—might have played a role, and so the European way of thinking was not alien to Menninger. Rapaport had already been working at the clinic for several years when the correspondence below was taking place between Menninger, president of the American Psychoanalytic Association, and Ernest Jones, president of the British Psychoanalytical Society. The excerpts below illustrate well the emotions and concerns felt by those who took in the émigrés from Europe.

Jones opened a letter to Karl Menninger dated 13 May 1943, as follows:

> To be frank, I have been a little disappointed by the relatively small contact it has been possible to maintain between British and American psychoanalysts since the war began. This feeling relates particularly, it is true, to the refugee analysts who, after reaching America, seem to have forgotten all about this side of the water and all that we did for them then here. (Faulkner & Pruitt, 1988, p. 383)

Menninger responded to Jones on 19 August 1943 with the following thoughts:

> I fully agree with you that the psychology of the refugee analysts has sometimes been very disappointing. You say that many of them who came by way of England to America seem to have forgotten all you did for them there. I think I could add that they are not here very long until they have forgotten all we have done for them here; this applies to some of them, not to all of them. One cannot help but be a little irritated at this, but it still remains an interesting psychological problem, and I don't know the answer to it. At the clinic we have had a score of refugees, eight of whom are still with us; most of the others are now in private practice for themselves and are grateful, I believe, and, in fact, grow more grateful as they realise what we have done for them and how difficult they were for us in some respects at the beginning. These are not the refugees that I am disappointed in. . . . Much more serious I think is the fact that the private practice of psychoanalysis in this country has been a great temptation to the character of some of the foreign analysts. In the first place, some of them came over with a very authoritative, eloquent attitude as if they were about to instruct the benighted American savages in the highlights of European science. When more refugees came, those who got here first turned their sadistic trends toward the newcomers and played politics with the Americans. Of course, gradually the real assets and liabilities of the individuals became known, and it was next in order for some of them to turn their attention to playing politics with the American public or with the medical profession at large or the social workers or the anthropologists. . . . What distresses me is a more fundamental problem, and that is the fact that the great lure of making money has destroyed the incentive of so many of the older analysts to do teaching. (Faulkner & Pruitt, 1988, pp. 390–391)

Menninger complained to Jones that not long before, six people for whom both Jones and he had had great admiration were asked to teach at the clinic for $10,000 a year, a salary for which they would have had to do nothing but teach. They had all turned down the offer. Menninger went on to explain that they could earn $15–20,000 or even more with patients, and then asked the rhetorical question: "why should they want to give it up and go back to a job of teaching psychoanalysis?" (Faulkner & Pruitt, 1988, p. 391)

Although Menninger had great respect for Rapaport, he was not prepared to raise his salary despite Rapaport's complaints about the low pay at the clinic. According to Schlesinger, "[e]veryone at Menninger's was underpaid at the time. . . . Nobody liked it, but we knew we were at the best place in the world for what we did and the honour was payment enough in those idealistic days" (Mészáros, 2000b, translated for this edition).

However, in 1948, Rapaport and several other colleagues from the Menninger Clinic left to work at the Austen Riggs Centre in Stockbridge, Massachusetts, a tiny private psychiatric treatment facility. Rapaport set up the research department there. He was fascinated by thought disorder in schizophrenia, and it was the findings from this line of research that led to his book *Organisation and Pathology of Thought* (Rapaport, 1951).

Rapaport had earned unprecedented respect at the Menninger Clinic—both for himself and the clinic. Thus, Menninger made the unusual gesture of inviting him back to teach. Schlesinger described the situation as follows:

> KAM viewed every departure of a staff member (even some who, in effect, he drove away) as an act of disloyalty, a defection, and a personal rejection, and he broke off all relations with most of those who had departed, usually expecting the rest of us to do the same. That David Rapaport was invited back to teach says much about the respect KAM had for him as well as the wishes of the rest of the staff who revered him. Also, I never heard David Rapaport say an unkind word about KAM, trying though KAM could be. I believe Rapaport regarded him as one of the key people, if not the key person, that made it possible for him to have an illustrious career in the US, and he was always grateful. (Mészáros, 2000b, translated for this edition)

George Gero's saga

One can be forgiven for thinking that the efforts made by the Emergency Committee on behalf of Rapaport were the exception, but the case of Georg/George Gero (1901–1993) thoroughly refutes this.

He was born in Budapest and lived as György Gerő until he first emigrated. The course his life would take is emblematic of the history of psychoanalysis in Europe and provides the reader with a personal insight into its points of crystallisation. In the early twentieth century, grandmothers rarely thought to give their grandchildren a book by Freud, yet that is exactly what happened to Gerő as a teenager. As he recalled, "it starts when I was fifteen or sixteen years old. My grandmother was a very wise woman who didn't have any formal education but was enormously well read and gave me the first Hungarian translation of Freud's *Interpretation of Dreams*" (Pareja, 1986).

This was a decisive moment with regard to his choice of career. His mother's side of the family was part of a layer of intellectuals that professed liberal or socialist views, while his father's side of the family was of a conservative bent. Gerő identified with liberal principles and, after graduating from high school, emigrated from Horthy's Hungary. He studied sociology, psychology, and philosophy in Vienna and Berlin. At the psychological institute at the University of Berlin, he heard lectures by such outstanding figures of experimental psychology as Kurt Lewin (1890–1947) and Wolfgang Köhler (1890–1947). In Cologne, he received a degree in philosophy and psychology in 1925. In 1924, he had attended the psychoanalytic congress in Salzburg, which exercised a great influence on him. This is when he decided to begin his own training analysis at the newly founded Berlin Psychoanalytic Institute. He happened to go to Sándor Radó for personal analysis, who encouraged him, among other things, to study medicine. This is how he became a medical student at Modena, Vienna, and Heidelberg. He received his medical degree from the last of these universities in 1931. After this circuitous route, he completed his training at the Berlin Psychoanalytic Institute between 1930 and 1932 and became a member of the Berlin Psychoanalytic Society in 1933.

As I mentioned previously, Gerő was a member of a group of Marxist analysts surrounding Otto Fenichel in Berlin. It came to light once in a conversation how important it was to those involved in training analysis what the political views of their analyst were. Like Gerő, Fenichel had also ended up with Radó for personal analysis, but he was somewhat mistrustful. On one occasion, he simply shot out: "'How can I talk to you? You might be a Horthy Magyar.' When Radó burst out laughing, Fenichel was assured that now he could talk with him" (Pareja, 1986). After Hitler came to power in 1933, there was little doubt that Gerő, like so many others, would be forced to leave Germany as quickly as possible. But where should he go? His choice was not tied to a person, or to a destination. He said, "I was interested in Wilhelm Reich's new ideas, and wanted to work with him. And he went to Copenhagen. So I joined him there" (Pareja, 1986). Gerő held lectures and seminars at the psychiatric clinic of the university at Copenhagen and worked with residents but never received a permanent work permit. After the dissolution of the Berlin society, he—like Erich Fromm—was registered as a "Nansen" member. However, he was among the few who was recognised as a training analyst by the International Psychoanalytical Association in 1936. Eventually, Hitler's expansion in Europe included Denmark, with Germany's troops occupying the country on 9 April 1940. After this, Gerő had to escape a third time. He had previously thought of leaving Europe. Dr Smith Ely Jelliffe (1866–1945), the founding vice president of the New York Psychoanalytic Society, had issued an affidavit in March 1938, but Gerő informed the Emergency Committee that it would do him little good since, as a Hungarian citizen, he would not be included in the normal country-based quota that had been filled years in advance. According to the Emergency Committee's report, the committee had made "innumerable efforts to find a teaching position for him" so that it could obtain a non-quota visa for him (see the section on Gerő in the Summary of Individual Services Rendered by the Emergency Committee (1938–1948)). Lawrence S. Kubie reinforced the invitation from the New York Institute in a letter dated 27 September 1938 and signed it in his capacity as the chairman of the Emergency Committee: Gerő should join the teaching staff at the institute. According to the letter, "[w]e look forward eagerly to your coming here, and hope that this will assist you in this direction".[143]

The American consul in Denmark, however, followed the restrictive immigration policy set by the State Department and rejected Kubie's letter on the grounds that it had not been approved by the Department of Labour. Through extensive correspondence, the Emergency Committee attempted to bring pressure to bear on the State Department. Even though these efforts might have seemed a waste of time, it still persisted for years. The Committee endeavoured to find a position at an accredited university or college and finally, in 1940, it obtained a letter of invitation to teach psychology and German at the New Mexico State College of Agriculture and Mechanic Arts. However, two years of his salary had to be put on deposit for the affidavit, which amounted to no less than $4,000. To cover this, the Emergency Committee and the Rockefeller Foundation each lent half the sum. The Committee also provided Gerő and his wife with $1,000 more to cover their travel costs. After Gerő was no longer able to enter Germany, he travelled through Sweden, Finland, and the Soviet Union to reach the Pacific Ocean on the Trans-Siberian Express. In this, his fourth exile, Gerő and his wife traversed half the globe to reach San Francisco via Japan. Through his long wanderings, he had learned to fight for what he hoped to achieve. Now miserable at his agricultural college in New Mexico, he was determined to leave as soon as he could. All of his acquaintances from Berlin and Vienna were in New York, among them Rado, Annie Reich, Edith Jacobson, and Heinz Hartmann. His feeling was that he wanted to join the group, like a family member (Pareja, 1986). In 1943, he resettled in New York, and, in the long remainder of his life, he never moved again, living and working for nearly half a century in that great city, a place his colleagues and friends had also undergone so much to reach. Early on, his theoretical interests had lain in the psychogenesis of depression (Gerő, 1936); later, he turned his attention to a new structural theory of the origin of neuroses and to symptom formation (Gero, 1953, 1962).

As becomes clear, the Emergency Committee assisted those in need with both persistence and circumspection, tailoring its aid to individual needs. A special feature of the manner in which the Emergency Committee operated, which had a powerful, long-term impact on the psyche, was the fact that any financial support that was provided for an individual was considered a *loan*. In that sense, money given to an individual—the recipient's circumstances permitting—needed to be repaid. The Committee's 1948 report, to which reference has already been made several times,[144] contains the name of each recipient, the amount received, and a follow-up report on the recipient with details on how the loan was settled. Repayment could vary: a previous recipient might return the money to the Emergency Committee's fund or pass it on to a peer who was unable to support himself or to the peer's family. This represented more than a gesture. Erstwhile recipients felt that this made them independent, autonomous, and self-sufficient members of a professional community; indeed, it was elevating to be able to mark their status as equal partners in this way.

According to the documents, of the Hungarian analysts who had immigrated to the USA, the following received funding from the Emergency Committee: Dr Tibor Agoston, Dr C. Robert Bak, Dr Sandor Feldman, Dr Georg Gero, David Rapaport, PhD, Dr Fanny von Hann-Kende, and Geza Roheim, PhD.[145]

Financial support for the Hungarians ranged between $200 and $7,900. On average, they received a few hundred dollars, but an enormous sum had to be paid to aid Gero in his escape and resettlement.

According to the final report issued by the Emergency Committee, all the Hungarians repaid their loans.

Of those who ultimately remained behind in Hungary, the majority were not held back by any external force or by the hopelessness of having no help or nowhere to go. They stayed because of some other personal consideration. István (Székács) Schönberger was possibly the only one who did not receive a visa to Australia or the USA because, being a committed communist, he was not welcome anywhere. No doubt, the younger generation was able to leave home more easily. In 1939, István Hollós was already in Switzerland (see above the address on his letter of 19 January 1939, sent to Kubie), where he found a job at a hospital. It is unclear why he returned to Hungary, since he would not have experienced any language difficulty. Research shows that all of the Hungarian analysts who perished in the Holocaust had received an Emergency Committee affidavit: Zsigmond Pfeifer, László Révész, Géza Dukes, and Erzsébet Kardos. Funding was also available for the Hajdu-Gimes family.

The value of the Emergency Committee's efforts in aiding the European analysts in their escape is incalculable. In its most active years, between 1938 and 1942—in spite of the restrictive measures that made immigration to the USA so very difficult—it assisted 254 individuals in making their way to North America: analysts and, if necessary, their families as well as others who were close to the psychoanalytic circles.[146] Further efforts on the Committee's part also enabled the émigrés to integrate into American society and into the psychoanalytic community as rapidly as possible. In fact, the Committee was supporting those it felt were entitled to receive aid simply by virtue of their membership in the psychoanalytic community. There was no internal selection of any kind or any "brain drain" policy. Existing personal conflicts and rivalries were laid aside to focus on the job at hand of saving lives, even when clear personal and professional interests were at stake for both the refugees and their sponsors. Priorities had shifted. Saving life had overshadowed personal or professional antagonism.

Table 2 provides a glimpse of the Budapest psychoanalysts who fled the country between 1938 and 1941.

Table 3 provides the names of the analysts who left Hungary in the first or second wave of emigration and then resettled in the USA, where they set to work in various psychoanalytic institutes between 1925 and 1942.

Table 2. The second wave of emigration from Hungary (1938–1941).

USA	Australia	UK	Ceylon (Sri Lanka)
Ágoston, Tibor Bak, Róbert Déri, Susan Feldman, Sándor Hann-Kende, Fanny Rapaport, David (Dezső) Róheim, Géza	Lázár-Gerő, Klára	Bálint, Alice Bálint, Michael (Mihály)	Gyömrői, Edit

Table 3. Hungarians at psychoanalytic societies and institutes in the USA (1925–1942).

New York Psychoanalytic Society	Chicago Institute for Psychoanalysis	Topeka Institute for Psychoanalysis
Agoston, Tibor Bak, Robert Feldman, Sandor Hann-Kende Fanny Lorand, Sandor Mahler, Margaret Peto, Andrew (arrived in 1954) Rado, Sandor Roheim, Geza Spitz, René A.	Alexander, Franz Benedek, Therese	Gero, Georg Rapaport, David Devereux, George (arrived in 1959)

CHAPTER NINE

Emigration: losses and gains

> "Hungarians were aware that psychoanalysis was a two-way street"
>
> (Roazen, 2001)

The two waves of emigration embarked on by the Budapest School affected the domestic and international development of the psychoanalytic movement in myriad ways.

In 1918–1919, numerous, essentially long-term, programmes were launched at the initiative of the Budapest analysts and/or domestic supporters of analysis. Taken together, these signify an internal maturing of the Hungarian psychoanalytic movement.

Because of the destabilising effect of the political changes at the time, these initiatives ended up either becoming non-viable or being implemented in cities other than Budapest. The psychoanalytic publishing house was established in Vienna along with its first English-language journal, the *International Journal of Psychoanalysis*, which continues to be the most significant international publication in psychoanalysis to date. Berlin saw the establishment of the first psychoanalytic institute in 1920, where a new training model emerged that fundamentally departed from the previous tradition of educating lay analysts. Thus, psychoanalytic training took a new direction in Europe, since it was a prerequisite in Berlin to have a medical degree—unlike in Vienna and Budapest. It took another twenty-five years, however, before psychoanalysis was once again incorporated into university education: after the Budapest university department had reached the end of its mayfly's lifespan, it re-emerged in medical training at Columbia University in New York City.

The most important characteristic feature of the first wave of emigration is that Hungary's émigrés remained within Europe and thus enjoyed the opportunity to return home during the country's period of political consolidation (1924–1938)—if they wished to avail themselves of it. After what were undoubtedly major professional losses, Ferenczi managed to carry on his work without interruption; he also oversaw the launching of a new generation with the involvement of a few very talented analysts who had returned—and here I am thinking in particular of Michael and Alice Balint. Together with the Balints, Ferenczi and his student Vilma Kovács, who conducted training seminars later, represented a profound professional force, which soon brought about substantive results. At the same time, this period witnessed the emergence of a group of ambitious, talented young people, which included Robert Bak, István (Székács) Schönberger, Andrew (Endre) Pető, Fanny Hann-Kende, Clara (Klára) Lázár, and David (Dezső) Rapaport.

From the perspective of Hungarian psychoanalysis, the second wave of emigration (1938–1941) effectively constituted the loss of the majority of this young, innovative generation. The chances to return to Hungary were completely lost. This also represented losses for Europe—with the exception of the Balints and Melanie Klein, who had resettled in Britain earlier. Due to the operation of the Emergency Committee on Relief and Immigration, refugees escaping the destruction of fascism were offered a real chance in life. Despite their difficulties, those who did resettle managed to integrate relatively soon into the communities at America's psychoanalytic institutions and associations and, thus, into American society as well. With this European exodus, the second wave of emigration also swept along Hungarian analysts who, during the first wave, had moved from Budapest and resettled in Vienna, Berlin, Leipzig, and Paris—among them Margaret Mahler, Therese Benedek, Georg Gerő, and René A.

Spitz. These were specialists who had studied in Hungary and come in contact with psychoanalysis before the 1940s.

How was the emigration of the Hungarian analysts significant for the development of psychoanalysis today?

The past twenty to twenty-five years have seen the publication of a series of landmark books and studies[147] both on Ferenczi and the most outstanding analysts who had once worked in Hungary and were tied to the Budapest School through their education, culture, and psychoanalytic perspective. Here I am thinking primarily of research on the work of Ferenczi and Michael Balint by André Haynal (Haynal, 1988, 2002), the publication of Ferenczi's unpublished works, including his *Clinical Diary*, the extraordinarily important Freud–Ferenczi correspondence, the thematic journal issues on the career and work of Alice Balint and Michael Balint by Judith Dupont (Dupont, 1997–1998; 2002–2003), and a biography of Sandor Rado by Paul Roazen and Bluma Swerdloff (Roazen & Swerdloff, 1995), along with research on Ferenczi published in Hungary.

Despite the restrictions to length in this book, it is important to note the areas in which the later impact of the former Budapest analysts has proved to be definitive and to elaborate on the future of the dynamic perspective that was perhaps the most important innovation from Budapest. This is no less than the integration of countertransference into the process of therapy, due to which psychoanalysis has become a psychotherapeutic process based on interpersonal relational dynamics. According to our contemporary way of thinking, countertransference is unquestionably part of the methods used in the dynamic psychotherapies from psychoanalysis to short-term dynamic psychotherapy—Ferenczi's role as an innovator can also be demonstrated in the development of the latter.

Another reason for discussing countertransference is that it is through such a discussion that it illustrates the maturation process through which a phenomenon initially considered to be negative came to be an accepted, then a desirable, and, finally, an indispensable element in therapy, which also forms a shared point of connection among the Budapest analysts.

Before we delve into an exploration of the psychoanalytic approach that rests on interpersonal dynamics in the psychoanalytic process, let us explore where the innovations introduced by Ferenczi and the Budapest School can be located. These represent relatively well-defined areas such as the model of early object relations, psychoanalytic psychosomatics, a validated countertransference process in the interpersonal dynamic between patient and analyst, institutionalised forms of psychoanalysis, and a new approach to trauma theory.

Towards the model of early object relations

From a theoretical perspective, the early mother–child relationship is of crucial importance as is the impact it has on the formation of personality. In his *Clinical Diary*, Ferenczi noted that one should probe deep during analysis, "right down 'to the mothers'" (Ferenczi, 1988 [1932], p. 74); this statement illustrates the attitude towards therapy taken by the analysts of the Budapest School. Ferenczi, Alice Balint, and Michael Balint maintained that the earliest phase of one's psychic life is centred on objects—although these object relations are passive. If you like, this is the only period in human development when, ideally, the baby may enjoy the love directed towards him or her unconditionally—along with optimal maternal care—which is the most ancient desire and the ultimate aim of all erotic drives: "I shall be loved and satisfied, without being under any obligation to give anything in return" (M. Balint, 1949a, p. 269).

Ferenczi referred to this state as *passive object love*, a term which Michael and Alice Balint later replaced with the expression *primary love* or *the archaic relationship*. Therese Benedek, who, according to our current knowledge, made the first observations of mother and infant (1920), concluded that a powerful affective and cognitive relationship—today we would call it a reflective relationship—develops in the early communication between mother and child. Benedek found that infants demonstrate the symptoms of their mothers (Mészáros, 2004a). Today, according to Gergely and Watson, "the dominant biosocial view of emotional development holds that mother and infant form an affective communication system from the beginning of life . . . in which the mother plays a vital interactive role in modulating the infant's affective states" (Gergely & Watson, 1996, pp. 1186–1187).

"No more than necessary", "optimal", "good enough"

Michael Balint asserted that primary object love is not tied to any erogenous zone, "but is something on its own" (M. Balint, 1949a, p. 270). One of the central figures of early object relations is the mother:

> Libidinally the mother is receiver and giver to the same extent as her child; she experiences her child as part of her own body and yet as something strange and hostile in the same way as the child regards the body of its mother. (M. Balint, 1949a, p. 270)

He also asserted that they are both active: "The fact must be mentioned also that contrary to common parlance the child is not suckled; indeed it sucks actively" (p. 269).

In contrast to the contemporary English school (and Melanie Klein, who had a major impact on this segment of the school), Balint maintained that the infant is not primarily narcissistic and is not a little creature filled with early sadistic and aggressive drives; the infant turns out that way if the world does not love it enough and does not satisfy it properly. According to Balint, narcissism is a reaction to this early void: "if I am not loved sufficiently by the world, not given enough gratification, I must love and gratify myself" (M. Balint, 1949a, p. 269). The particulars of the most advantageous parental attitude were noticed quite early in Budapest, and it was believed that, in order to achieve optimal development, it was necessary not to engage early on in efforts aimed at preventing frustration and compensating dissatisfaction to determine the functioning of the young personality. As Ferenczi put it,

> Good children have become hypocrites themselves. 'Enfants terribles' are in revolt (perhaps to an extreme) against hypocrites, and exaggerate simplicity and democracy. Really favourable development (optimum) would lead to the development of individuals . . . that would be neither mendacious (hypocritical) nor destructive. (Ferenczi, 1988 [1932], pp. 149–150)

Ferenczi wrote a great deal about the importance of there being no more repression than necessary, the basis of which is that the parent is able to provide optimal freedom for the child. This idea soon returned with Margaret Mahler in her ideas about the optimal individualisation–separation process and in her use of the expression *optimal symbiosis* between mother and infant, which refers to the cradle of appropriate individualisation. The expressions "not more than necessary" and "optimal" soon became quite popular in a new term introduced by D. W. Winnicott (1896–1971): "good enough mother". Although Winnicott never cited Ferenczi, a number of his ideas display powerful parallels to Ferenczi's earlier work (Borgogno, 2007a). Clara Thompson maintains that

> Ferenczi also believed that love is as essential to a child's healthy growth as food. With it, the child feels secure and has confidence in himself. Without it, he becomes neurotically ill. Ferenczi even thought that children are actually more prone to disease and often die because of lack of love—in short, that lack of being loved is at the root of all neurotic disturbances. . . . Today, other analysts—notably Fromm and Sullivan—have presented similar ideas, but I believe Ferenczi was quite alone in Europe around 1926 in this type of thinking. (Thompson, 1988, p. 187)

Winnicott describes the same phenomenon as follows: "A baby can be fed without love, but loveless or impersonal management cannot succeed in producing a new, autonomous human child" (Winnicott, 1971, p. 108).

Early on, Ferenczi and Balint noted a series of disorders stemming from a state of lack. One of the basic concepts developed by Balint within his theory was what he called the *basic fault* (M. Balint, 1992 [1968]). This, in fact, signifies a series of dissatisfactions, anxieties, and frustrations stemming from the lack of primary object relations at the level of development in which a relationship takes shape primarily between two beings—the mother and her infant—and in which no third being has yet emerged or any conflict in the psychological sense of the word. This void leads to the feeling of being lost, empty, lifeless, and unwanted. The series of ideas related to the basic fault "have survived in Kohut's (1913–1981) deficit theory of the various self-disorders" (Ornstein, 2002, p. 32). Balint worked regularly as a guest lecturer at the University of Cincinnati in Ohio, and this was the beginning of an increasing openness in the USA to new ideas of replacing the theory of primary narcissism with that of primary object relations. According to Paul Ornstein, it was with the concepts of primary love, the basic fault, and the new beginning that "Balint further developed the original Hungarian object relations theory" (p. 33).

The serious pathological consequences of the deficit in the early object relations, as Ferenczi deduced, according to which a child without love might even die, was later borne out by experiments and observations by René Spitz (1887–1974). After having earned a degree in medicine at the University of Budapest, frequented Ferenczi's lectures, and seen Freud for analysis for a few months in 1911 at Ferenczi's recommendation, Spitz became known through his work on the primary relationship between mother and infant. Spitz left Hungary in 1919 during the first wave of emigration. He was a member of the Vienna Psychoanalytic Society between 1924 and 1928, but he often visited the Society in Berlin and moved to Paris in 1932. Forced to flee a Europe in the ever tighter grip of fascism in the 1930s, he finally resettled in the USA, soon recognised a pragmatic American way of thinking, and saw the need for applied science. He made observations of infants in various institutions, applying the methods of experimental psychology using films, tests, and other means. This led to his diagnoses regarding *hospitalism* and *anaclitic depression* (Spitz, 1945; Spitz & Wolf, 1946). Hospitalism is a syndrome that reflects the sum of physical and psychological disorders that develop during the first eighteen months of life; it emerges in infants and young children who have been separated from their mothers through a relatively long treatment in hospitals or through institutionalisation. The experience of being left alone presents a major ordeal as an outcome of which a disorder presents in emotional, psychological, and locomotor development alike. Such children are typically apathetic and impassive, and their resistance to illness is diminished. They might even lose their will to live so entirely that they end up dying (cf. Spitz, 1945, 1983). Anaclitic depression is also a term coined by Spitz (in 1946). It develops as a result of partial deprivation of emotion, where a proper bond between mother and infant had existed previously. This form of depression is the outcome of the child's separation from the mother and disappears as soon as the child returns to her. Spitz's research brought about a change in the theoretical background and practice of the treatment of infants in hospitals.

Psychoanalytic psychosomatics

The line of thinking described above leads us to the field of psychoanalytic psychosomatics. Ferenczi warned us of the psychosomatic consequences of an unsatisfactory early mother–child relationship in 1929 in "The unwelcome child and his death instinct" (Ferenczi, 1980g[1929]). He believed that the symptoms of many of his patients could be interpreted as psychosomatic symptoms that symbolically express an early death instinct. He was in full agreement on this matter with Georg Groddeck. Groddeck also considered early deaths as unconscious suicides. Early psychoanalytic psychosomatics basically developed in connection with the activities of Ferenczi, Lajos Lévy, and Michael Balint. In his study "Psychoanalysis and internal medicine" (M. Balint, 1926), Balint summarised the short history of this field to date as follows:

> Adler was the first to work out the relationship between organic diseases and psychoanalysis. The actual research, however, did not start down the path he had envisaged, but the one seen by Ferenczi. It is interesting that Ferenczi's theoretical report was published at about the same time as that short account of so many years of practical results that was put out by Groddeck, who was working completely independently of him. Somewhat later and under some influence from Groddeck and Ferenczi, Simmel and Deutsch[148] began dealing with this topic (p. 444, translated for this edition)

In 1917, Groddeck thought as follows:

> body and mind are one unit ... they contain an It, a force which lives us while we believe we are living. ... In other words ... I rejected a separation of bodily and mental illnesses, tried to treat the individual patient, the It in him. (Groddeck to Freud, 27 May 1917, Groddeck, 1917, p. 33)]

In 1920, in his book *A pszichoanalízis haladása* (The Progress of Psychoanalysis), Ferenczi devoted a section to Groddeck and the psychoanalysis of organic states, making mention of Groddeck's 1917 booklet:[149] "He claims to have succeeded in demonstrating in numerous cases of purely organic illnesses—inflammations, tumours, and constitutional irregularities—that the disease arose by way of insurance against unconscious 'sensitivities'" (Ferenczi, 1920b, cited in Mészáros, 2009, p. 215).

We can consider what Groddeck said in an interview with writer Dezső Kosztolányi in 1925 as his statement of purpose:

> Disease itself is a secret confession . . . so that we can find shelter from the adversities of life. . . . Every early death is a suicide. . . . If a sick person still goes to see the doctor, he says by this fact that he doesn't want to be sick. This is a pivotal inner contradiction. . . . This is when the battle between patient and doctor begins. . . . [The doctor] clears away all those stumbling blocks towering before the patient's self-healing. (Kosztolányi, 1925, cited in Mészáros, 2009, pp. 216–217)

Ferenczi not only addressed his unconscious motives during his experimentation with automatic writing, but throughout his life he also looked at his own body as the embodiment of his repressed feelings. He considered his own pernicious anaemia as a psychosomatic symptom and noted the following a few months before his death in his *Clinical Diary*:

> Further regression to being dead. . . . In my case the blood-crisis arose when I realised that not only can I not rely on the protection of a 'higher power' but *on the contrary* I shall be trampled underfoot by this indifferent power as soon as I go my own way and not his. (Ferenczi, 1988[1932], p. 257)

In his last letter to his friend Groddeck, Ferenczi shared the pain he was experiencing over the crisis in his relationship with Freud: "The underlying psychological reason for this decline was due, apart from sheer exhaustion, to my disappointment in Freud, about which you also know" (Ferenczi to Groddeck, 20 March 1933, Fortune, 2002, p. 105).

Perhaps it might be said that Ferenczi looked at the body the way others looked at a system of signs, one which talks about unconscious internal conflicts in its own language as a type of messenger, the functioning of which is determined by psychological processes. Ferenczi's friend, the Hungarian writer Sándor Márai, captured Ferenczi's symbolic relationship with the body when he wrote the following at the shock of Ferenczi's death:

Ferenczi's death had a completely primal effect on me: I simply couldn't believe it. When I put down the receiver that brought the news of his death, after a moment of reflection, I called my informant and asked if he had not made a mistake. Later, I thought about it and realised that I was hurt and angry at the death of Ferenczi. I had a childlike idea that he had discovered something, that it didn't apply to him, that he would die when he wanted to. As far as I knew, he hadn't wanted to and . . . he looked down on death and life's primitive structure [the body] . . . he ordered a member of his family, if she happened to find him, dying, not to believe it straight away, but to shake him violently. . . . This is what he thought of the body; it was like a faulty clock that sometimes stops and just needs to be shaken to get it to start ticking again. . . . This is also why I was hurt by his death. Perhaps he simply wasn't shaken properly. (Márai, 1933, cited in Mészáros, 2000a, p. 48, translated for this edition)

Lajos Lévy's psychoanalytic psychosomatic approach and his attitude to the ailing and the ailment are beautifully illustrated in his study "Mire figyeljünk szívbetegek anamnézisében?" (What should we watch for in a cardiac patient's anamnesis?) (Lévy, 1993[1933]). Lévy's patient history shows a number of perspectives that meet the criteria for the first interview in today's dynamic psychotherapy: we must, first and foremost, pay attention to the patient, including every gesture, facial expression, and parapraxis. In his view, "we must get to know the physical and psychological personality of the patient. After all, the physician's task is to cure the patient, not the illness. . . . We need to know from the patient . . . how he views the illness" (Lévy, 1993, cited in Mészáros, 2009, p. 212). Lévy recognised the well-known unconscious relationship of mutual reflectivity in the doctor–patient relationship, which we describe with the expression transference–countertransference, and he drew our attention to the fact that the physician must be capable of making his own unconscious vibrations serve the healing: "the subtle play of the facial expressions that accompany complaints . . . [gives] rise to an unconscious resonance" (p. 213).

A younger and later very famous and important figure of the psychoanalytic generation, Michael Balint, thought of *the doctor, the patient, and the illness* similarly to Lévy. Balint was a student of Ferenczi's, worked with Ferenczi at the psychoanalytic polyclinic in Budapest, and, after Ferenczi's death, directed the institute until he emigrated in 1939. Everything that Lévy had introduced to Hungary through his teachings Balint brought to fulfilment in London. Michael Balint was thirty years of age when he published his study "Pszichoanalízis és belgyógyászat" (Psychoanalysis and internal medicine) (M. Balint, 1926), in which he paid particular attention to the phenomenon called transference in psychoanalytic terminology, which also permeates the dynamic of the doctor–patient relationship in somatic medicine. As he points out, powerful pains experienced in serious cases disappear, for example, when the physician enters the room and this is why patients so frequently request "the visit, which, 'objectively', is so rarely necessary. . . . This art that a good physician feels intuitively is what psychoanalysis uses to attempt to turn the unconscious into the conscious and an intuitive feeling into a learnable science" (M. Balint, 1926, cited in Mészáros, 2009, p. 213).

Ferenczi, who did everything to fashion analysis into an invincible clinical weapon, spoke as early as 1923 about the indispensability for general practitioners of the understanding they gain from psychoanalysis. In that year, he gave a lecture entitled "Psychoanalysis at the service of the practising physician" to a large audience at the Košice Medical Society (in Košice in present-day Slovakia). He said that psychoanalytic knowledge was crucial for family physicians (Ferenczi, 2007[1923]). Balint's efforts, therefore, to introduce the experience of psychoanalysis to general medical practice can be regarded as an early legacy of the Budapest School. Between 1953 and 1955, Balint developed the method of training cum research seminar that later became known as the Balint Method, or Balint Group. The results of this research were published in his 1957 book *The Doctor, the Patient and the Illness* (M. Balint, 1957). In Ferenczi's conceptualisation, any intrapsychic conflicts are manifested in psychosomatic phenomena, be they problems in adult relationships or in early object relations, either postpartum or prenatal. In this case, prenatal means the emotional orientation of the mother and the environment towards the unborn baby. Franz Alexander, who was among those who developed modern psychoanalytic psychosomatics as of the 1930s, made a sharp distinction between conversion symptoms (as physical phenomena with symbolic meaning) and psychosomatic illnesses that are regulated by the vegetative nervous system. At this point, he departed from Ferenczi's position because he contended that manifestations of the vegetative nervous system are not symbolic and that they cannot be interpreted as communicative forms of internal psychological conflicts expressed in physical symptoms. On the contrary, he maintained that they refer to the person's permanent or temporarily recurring emotional tension.

Psychosomatic illnesses can be approached through a process called vector analysis developed by Alexander. The point of it is that three directions of the emotions in the body can be captured: the desire to acquire and the need to retain and to eliminate. The three vectors—reception, retention, and elimination—represent the dynamics of life. The sum of the positive and negative contents of these determines the psychosomatic balance or confusion when there is an imbalance. Vegetative neurosis in this sense means "emotional high blood pressure". It is as if an asthma patient, with his or her breathing difficulties, were always saying: "I cannot love because this would imply the loss of my mother's love" (Grotjahn, 1966, p. 393). Here, therefore, a certain retention effort presents, which is rooted in a void of some sort (Alexander, 1965).

Research on psychosomatic illnesses was the special focus of the Chicago Institute, which Alexander directed for twenty-five years (until 1956). Alexander used every possible forum for this area. In 1939, he established, along with many others, the journal *Psychosomatic Medicine*.

Countertransference[150]

From a historical perspective, the controversy surrounding countertransference exemplifies the numerous basic professional and personal conflicts within the psychoanalytic movement. The thinking on countertransference has undergone a long and complex maturing process from negative opinions and attempts to eliminate it to acceptance and indispensability. Through a series of life experiences that were already expressed in his activities as a young physician, Ferenczi was guided towards an embrace of the feeling of countertransference: his basic attitude that recognised the significance of co-operation between doctor and patient and of authentic communication between them.

In 1919, almost a decade after Freud had determined that the emergence of emotions of countertransference should be avoided in the psychotherapeutic process, it was Ferenczi who stood up for countertransference. Freud first mentioned this phenomenon in his lecture

Franz Alexander and Abraham A. Brill. Archives of the Sándor Ferenczi Society & International Ferenczi Centre, Budapest.

"The future prospects of psychoanalytic therapy" in 1910, emphasising that analysts must overcome any feelings linked to the patient (Freud, 1910d). Freud's position was that psychoanalysis offers intellectual assistance to elevate unconscious events to the level of consciousness through the recognition of the patient's feelings of transference and resistance. As a result, interpretation and reconstruction stood in the focus of therapeutic activity; in order to influence the patient's internal events with her or his own personality as little as possible, the analyst should aim at developing her or his position as a pure observer.

Ferenczi recognised that it was exactly the opposite. Countertransference is an appropriate tool for a special communication between the patent and therapist, one that must be integrated into psychoanalytic work for therapeutic effectiveness (Ferenczi, 1980e [1919]).

It is interesting to examine who embraced these ideas. From this systematic survey, we shall see how soon the dynamic of countertransference became integrated into the perspective of the analysts of the Budapest School. If the Budapest School displays any characteristic features, then this is surely one of them. During their work in Hungary, members of the Budapest School were already applying countertransference, and, wherever they resettled during their emigration, they passed on their knowledge in this area both in their psychotherapeutic and training activities.

Interpersonal communication, authenticity, and trust: the new essential points of the therapeutic process

In the therapeutic process, the key element of the process that brought about change became emotionally re-living the traumatic experience, replacing the former priority of reconstructing memories. In their 1924 book, *The Development of Psycho-Analysis*, Ferenczi and Rank gave voice to this recognition, among other things (Ferenczi & Rank, 1986[1924]).

An experience, however, as is certainly known, contains many subjective elements. This links to the idea of "subjective truth", which Ferenczi recognised in his first scholarly article (Mészáros, 1999a, pp. 397–410). The question of objective–subjective truth, or fact *vs.* psychic reality, brought about a new perspective in the psychoanalytic process. The bidirectional relationship between analyst and patient, which is also experienced emotionally, supersedes early efforts at reconstructing memories and didactic analysis, work focused on interpretation, and the emotionally almost one-way communication formed in the name of neutrality. The central element of this can be grasped in expressions of the patient's transference, to which the analyst reacts by withholding her or his feelings of countertransference, thus remaining neutral emotionally (and, let us add to this, in full intellectual armour). A new atmosphere develops in the analytic situation, at the heart of which lies authentic communication and trust (Ferenczi, 1980g[1928]; Hoffer, 1996). Thus, as Haynal has pointed out, Ferenczi made the quality of the interaction between analyst and analysand one of the important elements of therapeutic effectiveness (Haynal, 1998; Bánfalvi, 1998).

As a result of the nature of his work in the consulting room, within the special psychic space created there, the analyst avoids the re-creation of the hierarchical relations that can be associated with painful experiences for the large majority of patients. This style is very close to Ferenczi's personality and the basic values of his earliest efforts in healing patients. His *Clinical Diary* is the most personal summary of his attitude and of his life's work. We can read it as a type of record of the author's brutally frank self-reflections in the service of healing. Let us read Ferenczi's sarcastic lines about bidirectionality and the most serious weighing of the patient's perspectives and emotions:

> why then should he, the patient, place himself blindly in the power of the doctor? Is it not possible, or even probable, that a doctor who has not been well analysed (and who *is* well analysed?) will not cure me, but instead will act out his own neurosis or psychosis at my expense. (Ferenczi, 1988[1932], pp. 92–93)

In this diary excerpt from May 1932, Ferenczi notes the problem of countertransference and makes a critical comment about an authoritarian attitude cum instructive intention:

> I tend to think that originally Freud really believed in analysis; he followed Breuer with enthusiasm and worked passionately, devotedly, on the curing of neurotics. . . . He must have been first shaken and then disenchanted, however, by certain experiences, rather like Breuer when his patient had a relapse and when the problem of countertransference opened up before him like an abyss. This may well correspond in Freud's case to the discovery that hysterics lie. Since making this discovery Freud no longer loves his patients. (Ferenczi, 1988[1932], p. 93)

Psychoanalysis becomes a system of bidirectional processes in both interpersonal and intersubjective terms. The therapist's authentic communication is a basic requirement. False or mistaken expressions on the therapist's part lead to dissociation; it might even traumatise the patient, throw up a stumbling block in the therapeutic process, and, thus, repeat former pathological experiences from basic relationships (Ferenczi, 1997[1934]). Today, we would say false reflections result in false self-objects. Safety, thus, soon becomes significant not only in its role in the basic atmosphere of therapy, but also as a part of optimal personality development.

Harry Stack Sullivan himself elevated both the sense of safety and the reduction of anxiety that this can achieve as being among the fundamental needs of the individual. Similarly to Ferenczi, Sullivan located the roots of anxiety in the social nature of the human psyche, originating in humiliation within past relationships, and in the sufferings and the shame that one has lived through, which encouraged the individual to make it a priority to prevent these and to achieve safety. Ferenczi, as was discussed earlier in more detail, met Harry Stack Sullivan during his journey through the USA. He was a young psychiatrist and a trained psychoanalyst. Since Sullivan could not use classical analysis to cure patients suffering from schizophrenia, he sought and located a new possibility in the area of interpersonal psychoanalysis (Conci, 2010). The personality or the self is not something that develops internally, he claimed, but is something that takes shape in an interpersonal context through interaction with others.

Therapeutic interaction, the dynamics of transference and countertransference, are so significant because they reveal the unconscious emotional components of the basic relational pattern. We can be sure that the positive or negative emotions or ideas evoked in the therapist through the expressions of a patient's transference—like a print made of a fossil—reflect the dynamic of important ties between the early and the earlier, and this comes alive through the mutual influence of the unconscious processes of the two participants: the patient and the therapist.

Similar elements can be recognised in the self-psychological approach that emerged later, specifically that the individual takes shape through the dynamic of the self-object representation. Theoretical motifs built on the relational model come through clearly in the psychoanalytic theories of Ferenczi, Rank, Sullivan, Balint, and Kohut.

Stations in the history of the development of countertransference theory before the Second World War

As early as 1910, Freud pointed out,

> We have become aware of the 'countertransference' which arises in him [the analyst] as a result of the patient's influence on his unconscious feelings, and we are almost inclined to insist that he shall recognise this countertransference in himself and overcome it. (Freud, 1910d, pp. 144–145)

It was in his 1919 study "On the technique of psychoanalysis" that Ferenczi first considered the opportunities of using countertransference. Countertransference appeared for the first time as a desirable tool for therapy. The task of the therapist is not to exclude emotions and thoughts in countertransference, but to gain control over countertransference. In the late 1910s, Ferenczi made countertransference available to therapeutic processes. He observed that cool, emotionally reserved and rigid behaviour paralyses the patient and limits the deepening of the work of therapy (Ferenczi, 1919).

In their 1924 book *The Development of Psychoanalysis*, Ferenczi and Rank pointed out that the narcissism of the analyst represents a potentially abundant source of a variety of errors, particularly a source for the development, among other things, of a type of narcissistic countertransference which induces the patient to emphasise that which is pleasing to the analyst while he or she suppresses remarks and associations that are disagreeable (Ferenczi & Rank, 1986[1924]). This recognition points to the childhood illness of contemporary psychoanalytic practice: that analysis practised among peers operated with a very limited effect. Who would have allowed herself or himself to reveal negative emotions of transference and countertransference to a peer with whom she or he would need to work in a different context the next day?

In 1926, Helene Deutsch argued that countertransference originated in the interplay of the unconscious processes in the analyst and analysand that develop during analysis (Deutsch, 1926). Deutsch introduced the notions of concordant and complementary countertransference (concordant being identical to the manifestations of the patient's ego, superego, and id) when the "analyst unconsciously identifies himself with the libidinal imago in the unconscious fantasy of the patient" (Hann-Kende, 1993[1933], p. 234).

In 1927, Edward Glover differentiated between positive and negative countertransference as well as resistance in countertransference, that is, instances of countertransference in response to the patient's transference (Glover, 1927).

In 1933, Michael Balint already thought in terms of a dynamic of transference and countertransference in therapy and saw this dynamic as a means to facilitate the internal development of the patient. As he saw it,

> it also becomes clear that the patient has always behaved in the same way; only with other people the picture was distorted through the disturbing effort of the partners' countertransference. Now the partner, the analyst, is passive, the relation is being developed as the patient unconsciously wants it. This interpretation almost regularly evokes violent affects, such as anger, pain, hurt feelings, shame. The analyst should, however, not be led astray; all these affects are only interposed to keep back the development of anxiety. (M. Balint, 1965[1932], p. 155)

Similarly, in "The role of transference and countertransference in psychoanalysis", a study she wrote before she emigrated, Fanny Hann-Kende demonstrated the perspective of the Budapest analysts when she stated: "The point of analytical therapy is to overcome resistance and to bring repressed material to light. In this effort, the analyst is guided by three factors: his theoretical and experiential knowledge, the desexualised libido and *countertransference*" (Hann-Kende, 1993 [1933], p. 238, my italics).

In the very same study, Hann-Kende concluded that

> constantly bringing to light and guiding the dynamic power of countertransference [represent] perhaps the most difficult task in analysis. Countertransference begins within the analyst in his first contact with the patient just as transference does so within the patient vis-à-vis the analyst. p. 235)

In the year of their emigration (1939), in their study "On transference and countertransference", Alice Balint and Michael Balint supported the unity of these two dynamics: "the analytical situation is the result of an interplay between the patient's transference and the analyst's countertransference" (Bálint & Bálint, 1939, p. 228).

These examples stem from the period preceding the emigration of the European analysts, mainly from international conferences; almost all of them appeared in one of the official English- or German-language psychoanalytic publications of the day.

With the exception of Glover and Ferenczi, the authors listed above all left the country in which they had previously worked. After Ferenczi's death (in 1933), a frozen atmosphere not unlike that of a cold war emerged and lasted for a number of decades. This, along with the breaking up of the intellectual context of the Budapest analysts, influenced the process that characterised attitudes to countertransference in the later history of the profession (Mészáros, 1998a).

I should like to emphasise this because it was, interestingly, only after the Second World War, in the late 1940s and early 1950s, that we see the emergence of works on countertransference (Gitelson, 1952; Heimann, 1950; Little, 1951; Racker, 1957; Reich, 1951; Winnicott, 1949). It has been since then that the professional community has considered positive thinking about countertransference in the theory and practice of psychoanalysis—although this was a process that had been set in motion one or two decades earlier.

The early approach to the relationship between training analysis and countertransference: Ferenczi, Vilma Kovács, and Michael Balint

Ferenczi spoke early on about training analysis, which he regarded as important in order to ensure that the analyst can maintain control over her or his own internal processes and the opportunity to experience and work through her or his negative experiences of transfer. All this is in the service of enabling the patient to enjoy the greatest possible internal freedom during therapy.

The question of training analysis was of such keen interest among the Budapest analysts that they discussed it in their early studies and developed a training model—one which was characteristic of Hungarian psychoanalysis at the time (and partly still applies today) and was markedly different from the international standard: that is, during training in Budapest, the first supervisor was the candidate's own training analyst. Michael Balint stated that Ferenczi was the first to declare in 1923 that there is no difference between therapeutic analysis and training analysis (M. Balint, 1948). Issues regarding training analysis were covered by Vilma Kovács in her study "Kiképző analízis és kontroll-analízis" (Training analysis and control analysis) (Kovács, 1993[1933]) and by Michael Balint in "A jellemanalízis és az Újrakezdés" (Character analysis and new beginning) (1993, 1999 [1933]. In this study, Balint observed the following:

> Ferenczi was among those who constantly stressed that ... in therapeutic analysis we must be satisfied every time with the practical results of a relatively deep or superficial healing but that in training analysis, however, we want the individual to become aware, as completely as possible, of the structure of the ego and its prevailing automaticisms, that is of her or his own personality.[151] (M. Balint, 1993, 1999[1933], pp. 9–10, translated for this edition)

This presentation by Balint happened to be given at the same congress in Wiesbaden[152] where Ferenczi gave his last paper, "Confusion of tongues between adults and the child", which, although it caused a storm in its day, is now Ferenczi's most frequently cited work. The earliest experiments on negative countertransference were conducted by Ferenczi, and he made the first *in vivo* experiments with countertransference analysis (Haynal & Falzeder, 1993, p. 615).

The countertransference of which Freud spoke and which many people think is defined in *The Language of Psychoanalysis* as "[t]he whole of the analyst's unconscious reactions to the individual analysand—especially to the analysand's own transference" (Laplanche & Pontalis, 1973, p. 92). If we take a closer look at the definition, it becomes clear that it also covers both the analyst's personal transference reaction *vis-à-vis* the analysand and the analyst's own countertransference reaction to the analysand's expressions of transference. During debates on countertransference, these two components are not clearly separated. The separation of these is most probably among the most difficult tasks, but it might be worth attempting in the hope that it might bring about progress both theoretically and practically. In all likelihood, we agree that the expression of the therapist's own transference in response to his patient belongs much more to the therapist himself than to the therapy of his patient. Naturally, it is not out of the question for the patient to provoke the analyst's transference reaction during therapy. In this case, it must be dealt with very carefully and it is probably the therapist and not the patient who must work on it. However, when the patient's expressions of transference trigger the feeling and thought of the therapist's countertransference, we arrive at an important stage. They both experience the dynamic of a series of intersubjective experiences—for and against—which is characteristic of the basic patterns of relations for the patient.

Allow me to illustrate the simultaneous appearance and separation of the two components through an excerpt from a case. During the third year of his analysis, in the last minute, at the end of our session, B suddenly reached for his pocket and shouted, "Oh my God, I've left my wallet at home!" Then, since the session was practically over anyway, he jumped up from the couch and turned towards me nervously to ask if he could borrow the nearly insignificant sum of 20 forints. My desk was situated behind B—who was standing and waiting—and, unusually, I had left my wallet lying on top of the desk. Both B and the wallet occupied the same visual space. I automatically walked over and took out a 50-forint banknote (now, sadly, little more than a collector's conversation piece!) and handed it over without a word. B thanked me and rushed off. As the door slammed behind him, I came to my senses and was completely surprised at my own reaction. During the next meeting, since B was advanced in his analysis, he brought up the previous meeting. It turned out then that after each session B treated himself to a glass of milk or cocoa and a pastry in the bistro on the ground level of the building. This cost about 20 forints. After this introduction, he animatedly went on to describe his experiences at the end of the last session, especially stressing how good it felt that I had not asked him—as his mother used to—what he needed the money for. He carried on with great excitement, "I could have bought anything I wanted with it. I could even have spent the whole amount on condoms." From the perspective of understanding relational dynamics, I would note that B started analysis in his twenties after his second attempt at suicide—which he was only spared by mere coincidence. He suffered extremely from a cold mother, who expressed her love sparingly, exercised a powerful control over him, and expected him to give an account even of how he spent his pocket money—which was a minimal amount. B attempted to attract his mother's attention in two ways. As a teenager, he would steal small sums of money from home, and each time he made sure he was caught. Later, he would solicit attention with his suicide attempts. Returning to the series of events, the analyst acting out of countertransference on the one hand met B's unconscious desire finally to experience a mother who fulfils his desires without holding him accountable—and the analyst met this unconscious desire. This recognition brought to the surface the deeper dimensions of his earlier painful dissatisfaction and undoubtedly strengthened the emotional load which the relationship between analyst and analysand could bear. This part of the example shows the countertransference component to the patient's transference dynamic—even if this was brought to the surface in the form of acting out or enactment on the part of the analyst. At the same time, we cannot leave unnoticed the fact that the analyst—also without blinking an eye—handed over more than double the sum her analysand had requested. And this is not about the patient, but the analyst—and, more precisely, about the narcissism of the analyst, who was eager to demonstrate that she was a better mother to the patient several times over.

Feelings of countertransference do not only form part of the dynamic between the therapist and the patient, but also components that the patient must be aware of, since it is through them that she or he understands what is happening in others. This is how the patient can notice, recognise, and become aware of what she or he unconsciously elicits in others.

The experience in therapy, the model situation that comes out "here and now", triggers further associations that shed light on basic events and traumatic basic experiences, thus deepening the therapeutic process, assisting the patient in working through the experience, and facilitating his learning to see and react differently, thus ridding himself of his behaviour, which had developed as a form of self-defence but by now had become a barrier. If, therefore, we do not provide feedback on the ways in which the transference relations of the patient have an impact on us, we deprive him of the experiences of himself and their recognition as well as a series of opportunities for correction. At this point, I would argue against Martín Cabré, who claims that "to reveal countertransferential feelings to the analysand is, in fact, an admission of one's own inability to work them through adequately enough" (Martín Cabré, 1998, p. 253). I believe the cautiousness of Martín Cabré stems from the overlap of the analyst's transference–countertransference reactions mentioned above when the transference reaction of the therapist blurs with the countertransference reaction to the patient, or when they are not separated. Perhaps we should rather say that we should consider—after we ourselves have clarified the sources of its existence—when we are encountering countertransference impacts in exactly the same way that we consider our interventions and interpretations: to speak in a way and at a time that will not be likely to offend, frighten away, or silence the patient, but, rather, serve to move the therapeutic process forward.

However, we cannot treat the acting out, or, as Chused and colleagues refer to it, the enactment (Chused, Ellman, Renik, & Rothstein, 1999), of our countertransference in such a predictable way. We do not plan it, and it happens unconsciously. However, it is possible that it is the very appearance of these unconscious reactions that—through our relationship with the patient—indicates something significant to the patient's attachment dynamic in connection with the important characteristics of its operation, which we can integrate into the work of therapy.

Countertransference in the light of object relations and attachment theory

Let us capture a new perspective through which countertransference plays a role in psychoanalytic psychotherapy as a necessary and indispensable psychological process—within the system of clinical experiences and theoretical approaches supported by findings in experimental psychology. In the light of this, the dynamics of transference and countertransference can be interpreted as a special dialogue built on each other and inseparable from each other. This approach fits into the framework of the theory of object relations, links to attachment theories, and makes use of experimental results.

In 1969, Bowlby suggested that internal working models of the self and the other are the prototypes of all other types of relations. These models do not operate on the level of consciousness and remain relatively stable during the life of the individual (Fonagy, Target, & Gergely, 2000). Findings from a number of longitudinal studies bear out the significance of permanence in attachment. Results indicate that there is a correlation of 68–75% in the attachment classification in childhood and adulthood; in other words, this is the level of certainty with which behaviour patterns in infancy correlate with attachment representations in adulthood (Fonagy, 1996, 2001).

This means that within the therapeutic relationship the dynamic of transference–countertransference expresses the individual's method of relational work and offers an insight not only into the experiences which evolved within the relational system, but also into the memories of these experiences. It is, therefore, through these dynamic processes that we have the opportunity to open up the experiences of early injuries and traumas.

If we translate this process to the language of attachment theory, we can say that the therapist should be able to behave in a reflective manner. Unreflective behaviour, such as listening stone-faced, rigidly maintaining one's distance, or offering inappropriate reflections and dishonest responses, brings a manipulative element into the therapeutic process and, thus, throws up roadblocks to the deepening of the working relationship. Moreover, the therapist might end up causing the patient to repeat the unsatisfactory expressions that originate from her or his early parental or care-taker relationships. Furthermore, under such circumstances, the therapist himself ends up becoming the obstacle to the patient's healing process. Therefore, inappropriate communication on the part of the therapist, regardless of the manner in which this is done, might repeat the parent's early inappropriate reflective functioning and, thus, might reproduce pathological communication which stands in contrast to the aims of therapy.

Fonagy and his colleagues draw attention to the role of the reflective and mentalizing function of the therapist—especially in connection with borderline patients: "An on-going understanding and processing of the mental state of both the therapist and the patient must represent an essential element of therapy" (Target, 1998, p. 50). Ferenczi, Michael Balint, Alice Balint, Fanny Hann-Kende, and Therese Benedek were all early forerunners of this intersubjective, reflective therapeutic behaviour.

As the Budapest analysts pointed out in the 1920s and 1930s, analysis, therefore, is not only an attempt at reconstruction and not only presumes the re-living and processing of traumatic events in the past, but also promises a profound learning process and offers a more optimum balance between the real desires and options available to the person. Besides the transformation and understanding of the emotional qualities of the experiences, the experiences gained during analysis also integrate into the personality—as Ferenczi so often noted. Michael Balint expressed this through the concept of a new beginning: "The analyst has to point out that what was once actually rational behaviour is, today, irrational; the patient has grown up since then, today he can bear much more than he could at that time" (M. Balint, 1965[1932], p. 155). In fact, Balint goes on to say, reality looks different as well: at the time, the patient faced overbearing adults who were only able to gratify their unconscious instincts through him; today, he is working with the analyst, who takes care not to engage in any gratification through the patient, and thus "today he can himself determine the amount of excitation which he is capable of bearing" (M. Balint, 1965[1932], p. 155).

At the Chicago institute, Franz Alexander worked on the concept of corrective emotional experience, which he had described and captured and for which he used the experience of transference–countertransference evoked in the analyst; that is, he reacts to the patient's unconscious, and, thus, he encourages her or him to change. As Alexander and French described it,

> [t]he basic therapeutic principle is the same: to re-expose the patient, under more favourable circumstances, to emotional situations which he could not handle in the past. The patient . . . must undergo a corrective emotional experience suitable to repair the traumatic influence of previous experiences. . . . It is important to realise that the mastery of an unresolved conflict in this relationship becomes possible, not only because the transference conflict is less intense than the original one, but also because the analyst assumes an attitude different from that which the parent had assumed toward the child in the original conflict situation. (Alexander & French, 1980, p. 66)

It is not difficult to recognise in this text similar efforts on the parts of Ferenczi and Balint, and to recall Ferenczi's experiments in the 1920s in connection with the active technique to increase the effectiveness of therapy and reduce the time it takes. Working through oppositions, processing traumatic experiences, and integrating experiences undergone during analysis pave the way for possibilities theretofore unavailable.

Ferenczi, Clara M. Thompson, and Winnicott

Clara M. Thompson and Izette de Forest—who both saw Ferenczi for analysis in the final years of his life (Brennan, 2010)—agree that Ferenczi had found honesty in his relationship with his patients especially important in facilitating their recognition of reality and point out that the patients' current situation differs from that of their childhood, in which "the parent's attitude toward the child must be sincere—that insincerity, especially the pretence of infallibility, confuses the child and, in the end, leads him to a false way of life (Thompson, 1988, p. 189).

Winnicott expresses similar ideas in observing that one of the basic points of the maternal function is to reflect the self of the infant (Winnicott, 1967).

Based on experience from the treatment of borderline cases, Fonagy views it as a decisive step when the patient is able to develop her or his self-identity, which is reached through the internal processes of the analyst; that is, the opportunity is provided for the patient to sense the psychic process that he has brought on in the analyst. According to infant research, not even a parent who reflects the feelings of her or his child within the framework of psychic equivalence in an unchanged form is able to calm her or his baby properly, and neither is a parent who avoids responses to the emotional signs of the child. Both reaction types are considered significant in the pathogenesis of the development of borderline disorder (Fonagy, Target, & Gergely, 2000). Here, I wish to refer to Ferenczi's idea regarding countertransference, in which he practically echoes the above ideas as he elaborates on the fact that neither overemphasised empathy on the part of the therapist nor cold, resentful behaviour is appropriate in developing a successful therapeutic process and in achieving appropriate development and change in the patient (Ferenczi, 1980e[1919]).

Therefore, a mode of operation should be found which can withstand tension and which reflects authentically the replication of the expressions of the patient in the other person and, thus, slowly makes the patient realise that she or he needs to look at herself or himself from a different perspective. This cannot be imagined without the use and reflective feedback of the set of experiences of the therapist, that is, without the process of countertransference.

It can, thus, be concluded that during psychoanalytic processes a special interpersonal and intersubjective dialogue develops between patient and therapist. The dialogue, for the reasons mentioned above, raises significant hermeneutical issues. First, as Gadamer puts it, "the [basis] of understanding ... is a composition based on a reproduction with certain ties to an original work" (Gadamer, 1984, cited in B. Gáspár, 1991, p. 24). Second, the language used by the analyst and analysand is not necessarily identical. There might be social and cultural differences as well as those related to specific age, broader era, and mother tongue. The analyst attempts to move in the linguistic universe of the patient and when this language becomes consensual and develops into a shared environment that also reflects the linguistic world of the analyst himself, this can be viewed as a manifestation of their shared work.

Therefore, the process of psychoanalysis is a reflective relationship, a mutual creation by the patient and the therapist, a learning process, and a creative effort. Thus, for the patient, as Balint described it, working through resistances and processing traumatic experiences as well as integrating what has been experienced during analysis leads to a new possibility. As Balint put it, "[f]rom now on, even those functions are exercised, and exercised with pleasure, which up till now were impossible because of the obstructing anxiety" (M. Balint, 1965[1932], p. 158). This is no less than the possibility of a new beginning, as per Balint.

This process began in 1919 when, based on his therapeutic experience, Ferenczi questioned the continued validity of Freud's early ideas (1910) and, thus, opened the way to the development of relational analysis. His colleagues, students, and influential members of the Budapest analytic community knew how important the knowledge was that they had gained—even during the times when countertransference was far from having attained general acceptance within the psychoanalytic movement.

No wonder Therese Benedek encouraged Gedo, whom she supervised at the Chicago Psychoanalytic Institute, in the following manner. When the young colleague in need of assistance turned to her feeling hopelessly stuck with a patient, instead of the ideas and recommendations that he had longed for, he sometimes had to make do with the response "Look at your countertransference" (Mészáros, 2004b).

Lost, Gedo asked how he should look at it, to which Benedek reassuringly repeated, "Just have a look at it" (Gedo, 1996, p. 86). As of the 1940s, Benedek encouraged everyone she trained at the Chicago Psychoanalytic Institute to recognise their feelings of countertransference, while Michael Balint—along with Edward Glover—taught the new generation at the Tavistock Clinic and the British Psychoanalytical Society to be acquainted with and use countertransference phenomena.

Ferenczi's paradigm shift in trauma theory[153]

Ferenczi's new approach to trauma theory marks his crowning achievement. This new view, what we call a paradigm shift today (Mészáros, 2004b), was preceded by a process of approximately a decade, which began in the 1920s and culminated in Ferenczi's "Confusion of tongues between adults and the child" (Ferenczi, 1980k[1933]) and *Clinical Diary* (Ferenczi, 1988[1932]). Ferenczi introduced new perspectives to *how* one thinks about trauma (Bonomi, 2004; Borgogno, 2007b; Dupont, 1998; Frankel, 1998; Mészáros, 2010a; Rachmann, 2000; Vida, 2005). He placed trauma within an interpersonal and intrapsychic sequence of processes and opened a new perspective toward dimensions of object relations.

In the history of psychoanalysis, "Confusion of tongues" represents so much more today than a paper presented at a conference in Wiesbaden in 1932. It soon became emblematic and came to be surrounded by a certain room for play. Ferenczi's ideas poured oil on the emotional embers of the Freud–Ferenczi relationship and blew gale winds in a storm intensified by Jones after Ferenczi's death not long thereafter, one which would surround Ferenczi for decades. Jones' role is well illustrated by the fact that, although Ferenczi's study came out in German in the *Internationale Zeitschrift für Psychoanalyse* in 1933, Jones succeeded in suppressing its publication in English for sixteen years.

En route to the conference, Ferenczi stopped in Vienna and enthusiastically read "Confusion of tongues" to Freud, who reacted with shock. He noted in his own diary in 1932 that "I listened thunderstruck. Ferenczi has totally regressed to the aetiological views I believed in and gave up 35 years ago that the gross sexual traumas of childhood are the regular cause of neuroses" (Freud, 1992, p. 131). However, Ferenczi's approach did not represent a step backward to Freud's first trauma theory; it was much rather a wise and elegant application of empirical findings in an attempt to resolve problematic questions that had arisen from an inflexible trauma theory, which failed to accommodate a great deal of experience. Ferenczi added the theory of the interpersonal relational dynamic between victim and aggressor and their divergent motivations to the intrapsychic approach: the adult's sexualised reaction born of his misreading of the child's need for tenderness put a series of processes into motion that traumatises the child. All of this was complemented by the interpersonal and intersubjective mutual effect; the different ego defence mechanisms of child and adult; and the complexity of the psychological dynamic of the entire traumatic situation. It was all these elements with which Ferenczi went well beyond Freud's earlier seduction theory in 1932 and established the object relations approach to modern trauma theory.

Freud felt that Ferenczi had resuscitated his theory of seduction from several decades before, regardless of the fact that it was Freud who had long ago questioned his patients' stories of childhood or adolescent seduction and regardless of the fact that it was Freud who had used the role of fantasy to account for experiences that were factually unverifiable and, in all certainty, complete fabrications of reality. Now here was his old friend and colleague making the absurd assertion that the traumatic experiences related by patients had in fact taken place. Freud was bitter and disappointed, and, without saying a word, turned his back on Ferenczi and left the room. It was the last time they would see each other—and Ferenczi died within a year.

Freud's theories of trauma as intrapsychic models

We can say that Freud's theories of trauma (1893–1917) are mainly based on intrapsychic models. In the revolutionary first trauma theory, he discovered that at the bottom of the pathogenesis of hysteria there are occurrences of premature sexual experiences/traumas (Freud, 1895d). But soon afterward, Freud became disappointed, and lost his "belief in [his] neurotica" (Freud's letter to Fliess, 21 September 1897, p. 259) concerning the validity of patients' memories related to real sexual events. Finally, he concluded "that these scenes of seduction had never ever taken place, and that they were only fantasies which my patients had made up or which I myself had perhaps forced upon them, I was for some time completely at a loss" (Freud, 1935, p. 37).

In his second trauma theory, Freud arrived at a solution that is a form of compromise: traumas can even be caused by *pathological fantasies*; it is not absolutely necessary for real events to be in the background. The turning point is that reality has been questioned as the basis for events recounted by patients. The traumatic effect of external reality has been replaced by the role of fantasy in the development of traumatic experiences. Continuing his work on the role of fantasy and, as Haynal put it, "in the network of events, desires, and fantasies" (Haynal, 2002, p. 44), Freud arrived at the experience of frustration in the economic model of trauma theory: trauma is caused by lack of satisfaction, independent of whether it was fantasy or reality that contributed to the arousal of desires.

Moreover, Freud also added his concept of the *helpless ego*: one becomes neurotic when one's ego somehow loses its ability to regulate the libido. The individual becomes helpless because she or he *is left alone or is overstimulated* (Freud, 1916–1917). This concept of the lonely self appears in Ferenczi's trauma theory, in Karen Horney's basic anxiety ("an all-pervading feeling of being lonely and helpless in a hostile world" (Horney, 1937, p. 89)), in René Spitz's theory of *hospitalism syndrome*, in Mahler's model of *individualisation–separation*, and in Bowlby's approach to early *separation anxiety*.

Ferenczi's paradigm shift: a combination of the intrapsychic model with interpersonal object relations approaches—some new views

With his concept of trauma, Ferenczi untied the Gordian knot. Freud's main dilemma was whether traumatic events were real or a figment of a person's fantasy. As I see it, Ferenczi's concept consists of the following points:

1. *Trauma is a real event.* It is not fantasy that causes trauma.
2. *Traumatic experience is subjective*: as we shall see, traumatic memories are influenced by effects of intrapsychic and interpersonal origin, which are cleared up during therapy, rounded out by new elements, and incorporated into a new narrative through processing. The analyst accepts the "emotional experiences" related by the patient and does not question their truth content.
3. *The traumatic experience is composed of intrapsychic and interpersonal dynamic elements.* The process shows signs of a system of object relations. The motives of adults and children differ in the sexual seduction situation. The child's need for tenderness is misinterpreted and exploited by the adult; it is also spoilt to create space for his or her own erotic desires. At the same time, this points to the participants' ego defence mechanisms as well as to the relationship that binds them.

4. *The strongest pathogenic factor is the introjection of the aggressor's anxiety and guilt on the part of the child.* Ferenczi writes that the child is paralysed by great anxiety, the source of which is the anxiety and guilt of the perpetrators; this originates from the introjection of the adult's experience in the child. The newly discovered phenomenon is identification with the aggressor. In "Confusion of tongues", Ferenczi was the first to describe the phenomenon of *identification with the aggressor*. In 1936, Anna Freud generalised the use of this term to describe identification with the aggressor within the framework of ego defence mechanisms (A. Freud, 1936). Ferenczi offered a clear description of the functioning of the mechanism when there is no chance to escape: anxiety

   > reaches a certain maximum, it compels them [the victims] to subordinate themselves like automata to the will of the aggressor . . . they identify themselves with the aggressor. . . . Through the identification . . . [the persecutor] disappears as part of the external reality, and becomes intra- instead of extra-psychic. (Ferenczi, 1980k[1933], p. 162)

   Identification with the aggressor brings about a paradoxical situation: it ensures survival, but at the price of perpetuating the traumatic situation, that is, of allowing the possibility of repetition. Taken *ad absurdum*, the aggression becomes acceptable and the aggressor is tamed. Much later, the same principles entered the public consciousness, but with another name, Stockholm Syndrome (1973).

5. Ferenczi first described the *defence mechanisms* that come into play during traumatisation, which differ for victim and aggressor: (a) the victim experiences dissociation and identification with the aggressor's intentions; guilt and anxiety are taken in through introjection; (b) on the part of the aggressor, there is bagatellisation/minimisation, projection, and denial. Ferenczi seized upon a defence mechanism that goes beyond the protection that develops in situations of erotic seduction; in it, we find one of the characteristic ego defence mechanisms of a survival strategy for a variety of aggressions, one that can be applied generally.

6. *Dread and desire/fear and satisfaction: the realisation of the pleasure principle in trauma.* As absurd as it might appear, the endurance

of trauma also provides an answer to the question of why it is worthwhile for the victim to carry on the trauma and to withstand this condition. Ferenczi wrote that the intrapsychic process might even develop along the lines of the pleasure principle during traumatisation: "in the traumatic trance the child succeeds in maintaining the previous situation of tenderness" (Ferenczi 1980k[1933], p. 162). I call this new compromise the dread and desire phenomenon. The greatest payoff that this process guarantees is that the person loved need not be given up on. There is a huge price to be paid by the victim: the door is left open for repetition.

7. *Post-trauma condition.* In Ferenczi's often-mentioned final lecture, "Confusion of tongues", he called attention to the presence or lack of a trusted person in the post-trauma condition. Is there somewhere for the child in trouble to turn or not? The role of the trusted person is of key importance in terms of the later fate of the traumatised individual—and this holds true not only for children, but also for the person suffering trauma in a general sense. Perhaps I succeed in negotiating the trap of overgeneralisation when I state that the interpersonal outcome of trauma is determined in the post-trauma situation. With a bit of simplification, we might say that the presence or lack of the trusted person decides the extent to which the traumatic experience affects the person and influences his or her fate in the long run. In general, lasting change in the eventual fate of the personality is not necessarily brought about even if there is a chance to share the events with others after the trauma. Here again, we see the extraordinary importance of the social situation, the role of publicness, solidarity, and the emotional and intellectual aid of a trusted person or people, all of which provide an opportunity to process the trauma. It is at this time that anxiety, guilt, feelings of shame, and the experience of being both helpless and defenceless rapidly decrease. In the presence of a trusted other, trauma sufferers do not remain without help or alone, and they are not isolated. The traumatic event does not become a secret and then a taboo, and the process of transgenerational trauma is not launched. Talking to the trusted person and sharing the traumatic experience represents the first step in working through the trauma. The absence of such a person has relevance for both PTSD and

transgenerational traumatisation, and, indeed, for resilience in the context of attachment theory.

If somebody were to point out that all these new approaches could not possibly fit into a single paper, he might well be right. However, Ferenczi's last lecture did plant the seeds for further research in the field of resilience.

Ferenczi's "wise baby" syndrome as a precursor to resilience

I believe it was Ferenczi who first called attention to the resilient child phenomenon. Using the metaphor of the "wise baby", he described the traumatised child who can grow up, who will suddenly be mature, more mature than either that child's peers or even the adults who have traumatised her or him. According to Ferenczi, there is

> a surprising rise of new faculties after a trauma, like a miracle that occurs upon the wave of a magic wand. . . . One is justified—as opposed to the familiar regression—to speak of a *traumatic progression*, of a *precocious maturity*. . . . The trauma can bring a part of the person to maturity not only emotionally, but also intellectually. (Ferenczi, 1980k[1933], pp. 164–165)

One can look at traumatic progression as a key word in the development of resilience—a new phrase in psychoanalytic theory—that means that intellectually as well as emotionally a child can suddenly grow up under the pressure of traumatic experience. This is what Ferenczi metaphorically called the "wise baby" syndrome.

Later, the term resilience appeared—very sporadically—in the literature from the late 1940s and early 1950s, but we find it with increasing frequency from the 1960s on (Bowlby, 1969, 1973, 1980). Systematic studies and research on attributes of resilience and resilient children came out after the late 1980s. It was found that resilient children cope remarkably well in traumatic situations without showing signs of psychic damage (Antonovsky, 1987; Apfel & Simon, 1996; Dugan & Coles, 1989; Fonagy, Steele, Steele, Higgitt, & Target, 1994; Rolf, Masten, Cichetti, Neuchterlein, & Weintraub, 1990; Varvin, 2009; Werner, 1990).

Ferenczi's concept of trauma led to new approaches that would later emerge in the complex system of modern trauma theory and therapy.

Psychoanalytic institutions and training programmes

As it evolves, every scholarly field reaches a point when shared thinking, accumulated experience, and established training programmes represent a recognisable value for those involved in the field. As a result of the innovative work of the Hungarian analysts, a number of institutional systems and training structures developed in Europe, the USA, and Australia:

1. The development and formation of the International Association signified this in the psychoanalytic movement. In 1910, with Freud's assent, Ferenczi proposed the establishment of the IPA at a meeting of psychoanalysts in Nuremberg. The recommendations he prepared were approved with some changes, and the Association has been in operation since 30 March 1910.
2. Ferenczi founded the Hungarian Psychoanalytical Society in 1913.
3. As was mentioned in previous chapters, the introduction of psychoanalysis in medical training is also associated with Ferenczi (1919). However short-lived the Department of Psychoanalysis and the associated clinic were among the traditional departments and clinics within the medical school in Budapest, it demonstrated that it was possible in practice and that psychoanalysis had become an acknowledged branch of medicine. For Sándor Radó, who supported Ferenczi's appointment and had close contact with Ferenczi at the time, this would serve as a preliminary experience when he established the second such department at his own initiative by then—in New York.
4. After he had emigrated from Budapest, Radó took with him the experiences he had gained as the former secretary of the Hungarian Society, which proved to be useful in Berlin when he established the first training model. It was through Radó's mediation that the Berlin training model was introduced at the New York Psychoanalytic Institute.
5. In the early 1930s (1932), the number one favourite of the Berlin training system, Franz Alexander, founded the Chicago Institute for Psychoanalysis, naturally also based on the Berlin Model. After this, he remained its director for twenty-five years, and, with his institutional background, he played a role not only in

psychoanalytic training, but also in the formation of the psychoanalytic approach to psychosomatics and the management of systematic research. Alexander aided a number of colleagues in their flight from Berlin and brought them to his institute. Among them were Karen Horney, Helen Ross, and Therese Benedek (Pollock, 1977). It is impossible to include every single colleague who once underwent training with analysts of the Budapest School, but I do wish to mention Karl Menninger, who was Alexander's analysand. Later, this influenced the clinic's operation and the development of its atmosphere and perspective. In particular, I am thinking of its openness to research associated with another analyst trained in Hungary, David Rapaport. Rapaport would have an enormous impact on research on cognitive psychology and perception studies from a psychoanalytic perspective between the 1940s and the 1960s as well as the diagnostic application of tests that spread all over the USA in the practice of clinical psychologists working at psychiatric clinics.

6. It was Radó who established the psychoanalytic clinic for training and research at Columbia University in New York in 1945. The Columbia University Centre for Psychoanalytic Training and Research has been in operation since then and is still one of the most significant training institutes in the USA.

7. Another analyst from Budapest, Clara Lázár Gerő, established the Melbourne Institute for Psychoanalysis in 1941 after her arrival in Australia. She was the first training analyst in that country. It was through her that psychoanalytic training was launched within an institutionalised framework in the southern hemisphere.

8. The Hungarian analysts not only established institutions and laid down the foundations for training programmes in Europe, the USA, and Australia, but they also actively participated in leading psychoanalytic societies as elected presidents. This role is an honour and acknowledgement for both the professional and personal qualities of the person involved. Of the erstwhile Hungarian analysts, Lóránd Sándor (1947–1948), Robert Bak (1957–1959), and Endre Pető (1975–1977) were each elected president of the New York Psychoanalytical Association, while Michael Balint (1968–1970) served his peers in Britain as president of the British Psychoanalytical Association.

Analysts belonging to the intellectual community of the Budapest School effectively shaped professional opinion and influenced newer generations as leaders of institutions, training and research programmes, and psychoanalytic communities.

Epilogue

The erstwhile Budapest analysts and the youth who had emigrated from Hungary and became analysts later carried with them the initiatives of the Budapest School, which had a seminal influence on the theoretical and therapeutic development of modern psychoanalysis. The first wave of emigration in 1919–1920 kept them in Europe, while the anti-Semitic laws in Hungary during the second wave of emigration swept most of them overseas away from a Europe in the ever more powerful grip of Nazism—and thus they shared in the fate of the analytic diaspora from Berlin and Vienna.

The Emergency Committee on Relief and Immigration set up by the US analysts was conceived out of an exceptional sense of solidarity. In league with the International Psychoanalytical Association, this civil society organisation of modest scale but high professional competence fought against domestic and international political forces, pushed personal and professional rivalries into the background, and contributed in an extraordinarily effective way to saving the European psychoanalysts. They aided with every possible means both in the survival of their peers in trouble and in these peers' professional and social integration into their new country; they therefore transplanted the spirit of European psychoanalysis to a continent, thus creating enormous possibilities for the development of the discipline. The American Emergency Committee and the London-based leadership of the psychoanalytic movement played a key role in this solidarity, which remains exceptional in intellectual history. An American colleague characterised the relationship he and other American analysts shared with the members of the émigré generation as follows: They became our teachers and our friends, who had a great effect on our lives. Europe's loss represented an enormous gain for us.

Europe's loss was indeed America's gain. Psychoanalysis, intellectual history, and we ourselves still gained an important experience—there are moments and periods in which loyalty and solidarity transcend the conflicts of personal rivalries. Without this experience not only modern psychoanalysis, but all of us, would be that much poorer.

NOTES

1. After the Menninger Clinic moved in 2004, it donated its documents to the Kansas State Historical Society.
2. Chapter One is an updated version of the afterword to *Ferenczi Sándor: A pszichoanalízis felé* (Sándor Ferenczi: Towards Psychoanalysis) (Mészáros, 1999a).
3. "I wish to remind you of the typical 'dream of the wise baby' described by me several years ago in which a newly born child or an infant begins to talk, in fact teaches wisdom to the entire family" (Ferenczi, 1980k [1933], p. 165). Ferenczi describes himself as follows: "I am fairly generally regarded as a restless spirit, or, as someone recently said to me at Oxford, the *enfant terrible* of psychoanalysis" (Ferenczi, 1980i[1931], pp. 126–127).
4. "In my case the blood-crisis arose when I realised that not only can I not rely on the protection of a 'higher power', but *on the contrary* I shall be trampled underfoot by this indifferent power as soon as I go my own way and not his. . . . A certain strength of my psychological makeup seems to persist, so that instead of falling ill psychically I can only destroy—or be destroyed—in my organic depths" (Ferenczi, 1988[1932], pp. 212–213).
5. The family name appears in both versions in a variety of documents.

6. *Spiritism* was the term used for the version of this belief system in continental Europe and Latin America, while it was called *spiritualism* in the English-speaking world.
7. *Thalassa: A Theory of Genitality* was first published in German as *Versuch einer Genitaltheorie* (Internationale Psychoanalytische Bibliothek. Vol. XV, Internationaler Psychoanlytischer Verlag, Leipzig and Vienna, 1924). It appeared in Hungary in 1929 (Pantheon, Budapest). After having been translated into English ("Thalassa: theory of genitality", *Psychoanalytic Quarterly*, 1933, 2: 361–403; 1934, 3: 1–29, 200–222; 1936, 5: 249–260), the book was then published with the same title in 1938 by The Psychoanalytic Quarterly in Albany, New York, and in 1989 by Karnac. A new Hungarian edition was published in 1997 by Filum in Budapest.
8. It was only after a great deal of difficult experience that a rule was set down that analysing close relatives, friends, and close colleagues was contraindicated. The first generation of analysts learnt from each other's personal analysis. Freud analysed his daughter, Anna. Ferenczi went to Freud for analysis, and a number of colleagues saw Ferenczi. For further information, see the Budapest psychoanalytic family tree in this book. For a more detailed list of Ferenczi's analysands, see Brennan (2011).
9. These included *Orvosi Hetilap* (Medical Weekly), *Pester Medizinisch-Chirurgische Presse* (Budapest Medical and Surgical Journal), *Jövendő* (Future), *Az Újság* (The News), *Politikai Hetiszemle* (Political Review), *Politikai Hetilap* (Political Weekly), *Jó Egészség* (Good Health), *Budapesti Orvosi Újság* (Budapest Medical News), and *A Nő és a Társadalom* (Woman and Society).
10. This is *Igazságügyi Orvosi Tanács* in Hungarian.
11. *Honvédorvos* was "the gazette for the scientific and social interests of the institution for army physicians", which was published as a supplement to *Gyógyászat* between 1888 and 1914 with Sándor Szénásy as its first editor. Ferenczi began working there in 1902. Also called *Honvédorvos*, an independent publication was launched in 1929 as the journal of the Learned Society of Army Physicians (*Honvédorvosok Tudományos Egyesülete*), which folded in 1944 with the sixteenth volume and resumed publication in 1948 with the same title and new numbering.
12. For further details, see the Hungarian-language study by Lívia Nemes (1994).
13. *Lélekelemzés. Értekezések a pszichoanalízis köréből* (Psychoanalysis) was published in 1910 with a foreword by Freud. *Lelki problémák a pszicho-*

analízis megvilágitásában (Psychic Problems in the Light of Psychoanalysis) became available in 1912.
14. As the standard English translation is not entirely accurate here, the original has been translated anew.
15. This is *Budapesti Királyi Orvosegyesület* in Hungarian.
16. Ferenczi joined the Society in 1900. It had forty-six members in 1903. (For further details, see Magyar & Mészáros, 1999, pp. 413–414.)
17. For more on contemporary psychiatry in Hungary, see Emese Lafferton. "A magántébolydától az egyetemi klinikáig. A magyar pszichiátria történetének vázlata európai kontextusban, 1850–1908" [From the private mental institution to the university clinic: a brief history of Hungarian psychiatry in the European context, 1850–1908] at http://zeus.phil-inst.hu/recepcio/htm/3/303_beslo.htm.
18. Sándor Bródy (1863–1924) was an influential Hungarian writer, dramatist, and journalist.
19. Ignotus (born Hugó Veigelsberg) (1869–1949) was a liberal critic, essayist, and journalist, one of the founders of the literary journal *Nyugat* (West), and a leading figure in the literary scene. His journal welcomed publications tied to psychoanalysis. He was one of the founders of the Hungarian Psychoanalytical Society. Ignotus fled to the United States in 1938 due to Hungary's anti-Semitic laws. He was granted the prestigious Arts and Letters Award for Literature by the American Academy of Arts and Letters in 1944. In 1948, terminally ill, he returned to Hungary. (For more on his life and emigration, see Frank (2009).)
20 Róbert Berény (1887–1953) was a painter and graphic artist who had been influenced by Fauvism in Paris. He was a member of the Eight (*Nyolcak*), an *avant-garde* movement of Hungarian painters, active mostly in Budapest from 1909 to 1918.
21. The Budapest School was not a school in the strict sense of the word, but it displayed certain features that emerged as a common denominator in the intellectual orientation of its members. This will be covered in detail in later chapters.
22. Paul Möbius (1853–1907) was a German neurologist and phrenologist. He focused on the pathological aspects of famous people. He wrote books on Goethe (*Über das Pathologische bei Goethe*, 1898) and Schopenhauer (*Über Schopenhauer*, 1899). He had a strong impact on medical science in his day, and his works were also published in Hungarian: for example, *Az idegesség és az idegbetegségek gyógyítása* (Curing Nervousness and Neurological Diseases). Ferenczi reviewed his books in *Gyógyászat* and cited his publications in numerous writings.

23. The official name of this institution was the *Erzsébet Szeretetotthon Kórház* (Erzsébet Nursing Home). Later known as Korányi Hospital and now as Szent Erzsébet Hospital, it is located at No 7 Alsó erdősor Street in Budapest's 7th district. It was founded in 1856 and consisted of several building complexes at Dohány Street, Rózsák Square, and Péterfy Sándor Street. Ferenczi worked at the neurology and psychiatry ward of the hospital as of 1900 and lived on the hospital grounds between 1901 and 1902.
24. This translates as the Scientific Humanitarian Committee.
25. This is *Általános Munkás-betegsegélyező Pénztár* in Hungarian.
26. At thirty-eight, Ferenczi fell in love with Elma Pálos, the daughter of his companion and later wife, Gizella Pálos. It was during analysis, prompted by the suicide of a young man who had fallen in love with Elma, that Ferenczi became enamoured of her and they were engaged. Ferenczi turned to Freud for help with carrying on her analysis. (For further details, see Berman (2004).) Gizella would have given her blessing to the love of the two people whom she loved the most, but Freud forced Ferenczi to put an end to it (Harmat, 1994; Haynal, 1995). As Ferenczi wrote to his friend Groddeck in 1921,

    Freud's prompted me to fight this love tooth and nail—literally to push the girl away from me. . . . The trouble with this is my eroticism refuses to be satisfied by barren explanations. I, my 'It', isn't interested in analytical interpretations, but wants something real, a young wife, a child! (Fortune, 2002, pp. 9, 11)

27. The original Hungarian title is "A neurózisok Freud tanának világításában és a pszichoanalízis", in which the word *világítás* clearly connotes a light being shone.
28. Cf. findings from the Reception and Creativity Research Programme at the Institute of Philosophy of the Hungarian Academy of Sciences, published in several edited volumes, including Békés (2004).
29. The Eight was a group of Hungarian artists who were followers of Fauvism, a Modern school of painting that included Henri Matisse and Georges Braque.
30. For further reference, the original Hungarian titles of these studies are "Schopenhauernak Goethéhez írt levele, pszichoanalicite nézve" (Ferenczi, 2000a[1912]), "Egy versmondó betegről" (Hollós, 1990[1914]), and "Nemzeti géniusz és pszichoanalízis" (Hollós, 1929). To date, these have not been translated into English.
31. The English translation here differs from that published in Ferenczi (1950).

32. Mihály Polányi (Michael Polanyi) (1891–1976) was a noted scholar whose impressive career as a physician, a professor of physical chemistry, and, finally, a professor of social studies took him from Hungary to Germany and on to Britain. One of his sons, John Charles Polanyi, would go on to win the Nobel Prize in Chemistry.
33. Edit Gyömrői (1896–1987) was born Edit (Gelb) Gyömrői. She married several times, changing her name with each marriage to Rényi, Glück, Újvári, and, finally, Edith Gyömrői-Ludowyk.
34. The original Hungarian ditty went as follows: "Eresz alatt fészkel az ösztön / Gátlásomat Ferenczinél / Hófehérre fürösztöm" (Mészáros, 2010b, p. 72).
35. For further reference, these books were published in Hungarian as *Lélekelemzés. Értekezések a pszichoanalízis köréből* (1910); *Lelki problémák a pszichoanalízis megvilágításában* (1912); and *Ideges tünetek keletkezése és eltűnése és egyéb értekezések a pszichoanalízis köréből* (1914).
36. This book was published in Hungarian as *Az álomról* in 1915, translated by Ferenczi (Budapest: Dick Manó, 1915, 1919; Hatágú Síp, 1991).
37. The interview was published in the literary journal *Esztendő* (Year).
38. This was the enthusiastic observation Freud shared with Karl Abraham in a letter he wrote on 27 August 1918 (Falzeder, 2002, p. 382).
39. The German abbreviation *o.ö. Professor* stands for *ordentlicher öffentlicher Professor*, that is *rendes nyilvános egyetemi tanár* in Hungarian. This was an academic rank that amounted to *professor ordinaries*, or full professor.
40. Using papers given by Abraham, Ferenczi, and Ernst Simmel (1882–1947) as a springboard, *Világ* highlighted the psychoanalytic treatment of war neuroses; it also stressed that the conference had been attended by officials from the Prussian and Austro-Hungarian imperial war ministries as well as from Hungary's own ministry of homeland defence—the majority of whom were officers with medical training (Anon, 1918b, p. 12).
41. Antal Freund of Tószeg (1880–1920) was a chemist and one of the proprietors of a brewery (*Kőbányai Polgári Serfőző*) in the Kőbánya section of Budapest, still known for its beermaking. He consistently used the "of Tószeg" (*tószegi*) element of his name, a reminder of the title of nobility granted by the Emperor to his grandfather for his achievements in business and industry. Antal Freund's various links to the psychoanalytic movement included family ties. One of his sisters, Kata Freund, was married to Lajos Lévy. After Antal Freund had undergone surgery for sarcoma of the testes, his psychological condition took a turn for the worse and he saw Freud for psychoanalysis. It was during

analysis that the idea came to Freund to back the psychoanalytic movement financially and to aid the international association in setting up its own publishing house for books and periodicals, thus making it independent of the Viennese publisher, Hugo Heller.

42. Letter from Antal Freund's son, Dr Antal Tószeghi, to Dr Mariann Dobossy, dated 28 February 1988 (Sándor Ferenczi Society, Budapest).
43. Studies on the life of Géza Révész are available in Hungarian by Éva Gábor (1991) and Csaba Pléh (2009).
44. Hungarian National Archives, No. 172417/1919.
45. Hungarian National Archives, No. 83981/1919.
46. Zur Psychoanalyse der Kriegsneurosen. Diskussion auf dem V. Internationalen Psychoanalytischen Kongreß in Budapest, 28 und 29 September 1918. Beiträge von Freud, Ferenczi, Abraham, Simmel, Jones. In: *Internationale Psychoanalytische Bibliothek Nr. 1*. Leipzig und Wien: Internationaler Psychoanalytischer Verlag, 1919.
47. Lawrence Kolb: Interview with Sándor Lóránd, 1963. Manuscript (The Library of Congress).
48. The dual monarchy of Austria-Hungary was dissolved on 31 October 1918, and the White Terror was launched in August 1919.
49. The collapse of Austria-Hungary altered the map of Europe, with the many former countries of the realm gaining their independence. This not only had economic consequences, but also transformed everyday communication and people's way of life. For example, postal service slowed, and passports and border checks were introduced, rendering a completely free journey between Budapest and Vienna rather difficult.
50. See the basic book on the emigration of Hungarian intellectuals by Tibor Frank (2009).
51. See Christfried Tögel's biographical study in Hungarian, which provides a glimpse into the history of psychoanalysis in the Soviet Union through the life of Jenő Varga (Tögel, 2000).
52. Questionnaire completed on Sándor Lóránd's joining the Educational Committee, 30 September 1932 (The Archives & Special Collections of the A. A. Brill Library, The New York Psychoanalytic Society and Institute).
53. Ferenczi met A. A. Brill (1874–1948) in 1909, when Freud held lectures at Clark University.
54. Hárnik underwent treatment at the National Institute for Psychiatry and Neurology in Budapest during the 1950s (Gábor Paneth, personal communication).

55. This is discussed in detail in Chapter Eight.
56. George Devereux (1908–1985) only encountered psychoanalysis after the Second World War. See biographical studies by Benjamin Kilborne (2008[1988]) and Michael Gill (1967).
57. These were *Imago, Zeitschrift für Psychoanalyse*, and the *International Journal of Psychoanalysis*.
58. The word *tjurunga* comes from Arrernte, an indigenous language spoken in Central Australia. It denotes sacred or taboo items that are to be kept secret. These are oval-shaped ritual objects made of stone or wood that range in length from 5 cm to 3 m. According to folk belief, after ancestors are dreamt of and walk the earth, they turned into *tjurungas* and then unborn children swarm out of them and into the women. The *tjurunga* symbolises the eternity of ancestors and the link between the dream and the mythological dream time.
59. One key publication in Hungarian is "Irodalom és pszichoanalízis" (Literature and psychoanalysis) (*Helikon Világirodalmi Figyelő* (1990, pp. 2–3). More specifically to the topic at hand, I would recommend studies (also in Hungarian) by Antal Bókay, György Kassai, and István Kapás. See also Bókay & Erős, 1998; Vajda, 2005; Valachi, 2005.
60. Both studies and the Karinthy–Ferenczi debate were published in a special issue of the Hungarian-language journal *Helikon* (1990), entitled "Irodalom és pszichoanalízis" (Literature and psychoanalysis). Karinthy's and Ferenczi's articles were never translated into English. For further reference, the titles in Hungarian are "A Macbeth-jóslat lélektana és erkölcstana" and "Altató vagy ébresztő tudomány", respectively; *Helikon*, 2–3: 331–340.
61. Having been published in Hungarian as *Feleségem története* and made available to readers of German as *Die Geschichte meiner Frau*, Füst's novel has yet to be translated into English.
62. *Helikon* (1990), 2–3: 322–330.
63. Mihály József Eisler was a physician, psychoanalyst, and art critic for the daily *Pester Lloyd*. For a biography and selection of his writing from 1908 to 1913 (in Hungarian), see Bognár, 2002.
64. From the wealth of literature on Attila József, there are quite a few articles and books that cover the ties between the poet, psychoanalysis, and the psychoanalysts. These include the following Hungarian-language publications: Bókay, 1980; Bókay, Jádi, & Stark, 1982; Valachi, 2005; and a special issue of *Thalassa* (2005, 2–3) entitled "József Attila—hatások és párhuzamok" (Attila József: Influences and parallels).

65. This news is covered in the *Zeitschrift* (1928, *14*: 252). Cf. see the Note in the Hungarian edition of the Freud–Ferenczi correspondence, Vol. III (2), Ferenczi to Freud, 8 February 1928, p. 186.
66. Issued a licence by the Ministry of Public Welfare, the "Hungarian Psychoanalytical Society opened its Polyclinic for Neurology and Mood Disorders. Head physician: Dr Sándor Ferenczi; Deputy: Dr Mihály Bálint [Michael Balint]; Staff physicians: Dr Imre Hermann, Dr István Hollós, Dr Zsigmond Pfeifer, and Dr László Révész. Exclusively treating those certified as low-income outpatients" (*Gyógyászat*, 28 June 1931, *71*(26): III).
67. These were published in Hungarian as *A gyermekszoba pszichológiája* (A. Bálint 1990[1931]) and *A pszichoanalízis mint módszer* (Hermann, 1933), respectively.
68. Activity report for the Hungarian Psychoanalytical Society (1932–1934) (Archives of the British Psychoanalytical Society, G07/B5/F01/095X).
69. This edited volume was published in Hungarian. For further reference, the title of the book itself is *Lélekelemzési tanulmányok*. The titles of the studies mentioned here are "Jellemanalízis és újrakezdés" by Mihály Bálint, "A tudattalan és az ösztönöknek-örvény elmélete" by Imre Hermann, "A szeretet fejlődése és a valóságérzék" by Alice Bálint, "Kiképző analízis és kontroll-analízis" by Vilma Kovács, and "Mire figyeljünk szívbetegek anamnézisében?" by Lajos Lévy.
70. From among his writer friends, Ignotus, Sándor Márai, Dezső Kosztolányi, and Frigyes Karinthy all wrote remembrances, as did his many psychoanalyst friends, former students, and peers, including Freud, Max Eitingon, Paul Federn, Ernst Simmel, Eduard Hitschmann, Ernest Jones, Mihály Bálint, István Hollós, Imre Hermann, Sándor Radó, and Sándor Lóránd.
71. Less than a year later, on 13 March 1938, one day after the Anschluss, the Vienna Psychoanalytic Society was dissolved by its members. Anna Freud, her father, and a few family members managed to escape to London. The rest were also forced to flee. Paul Federn left Vienna the same year and resettled in New York, Eduardo Weiss built a new life for himself working at the Menninger Clinic in Topeka, Kansas, and Otto Fenichel emigrated to Los Angeles. Theodor Reik, who had already fled Berlin for Vienna, found a new home in New York. Karl Landauer, however, died in the Bergen-Belsen concentration camp in Germany. From among the Hungarian analysts listed, the Bálints migrated to Great Britain in early 1939.
72. The American Psychoanalytic Association was formed in May 1911 in Washington, D.C. Putnam (1846–1918) served as its first president, and

its first secretary was Ernest Jones. As of 1932, it operated as a federation with its first member associations in Chicago, New York, and the Washington–Baltimore region and with Boston (1933) and Topeka, Kansas (1938) as slightly later additions. While the Emergency Committee was active and for some time thereafter, the abbreviation for the American Psychoanalytic Association was actually APA but has been changed more recently to APsaA.

73. Published in 1987 and based on a complex analysis of primary sources, *American Refugee Policy and European Jewry, 1933–1945* by Richard Breitman and Alan M. Kraut represents one of the most comprehensive studies of the USA's refugee policy. Both professors of history in the USA, the authors aimed to uncover the causes of the tension between humanitarian principles and national interests in the formation and implementation of this policy. Another indispensable source on the subject is a book by Laura Fermi (1907–1977). Published in 1968, *Illustrious Immigrants* is the first major treatment of Europe's intellectual emigration between 1930 and 1941.

74. This was the view of forty-one per cent of those who responded to a survey conducted in March 1938 (Breitman & Kraut, 1987, p. 88).

75. The Public Charge Clause was named for its concern with an immigrant being "likely to become a public charge".

76. Having been appointed Secretary of State by Roosevelt in 1933, Hull represented the USA's foreign policy for the next twelve years. He was awarded the Nobel Peace Prize in 1945.

77. US diplomat George S. Messersmith spent thirty-two years in the Foreign Service. Between 1930 and 1934, he served as the consul general in Berlin. In 1934, he received the title of minister and returned to Washington.

78. The University in Exile rescued 167 Jewish scholars and their family members from Central Europe.

79. For a detailed treatment of the lives of the Hungarian scholars and artists who immigrated to Berlin, Vienna, and New York between the two world wars, see Frank (1999, 2002, 2009).

80. Kubie later became the president of the American Psychosomatic Society, secretary general of the APsaA, and a member of the New York Academy of Medicine. Generally held to be an outstanding teacher, he taught at Columbia, Yale, and Johns Hopkins, among other universities. He was principally concerned with problems of research and technique associated with psychoanalysis, as well as with psychopathological and psychosomatic issues. His key publications include a discussion of matters of technique in psychoanalysis (Kubie, 1937–1938) and a history

of the Austen Riggs Psychiatric Centre in Stockbridge, Massachusetts (Kubie, 1960).

81. After his university years, Lewin worked in Adolf Meyer's department at the Henry Phipps Psychiatric Clinic and then in the Department of Neuropathology of the New York State Psychiatric Institute (on Ward's Island in New York City at the time). He worked with Charles P. Dunlop, whose wonderful scepticism had a great effect on him. His peers and friends called him "the Renaissance cosmopolite with tongue in cheek" (Kubie, 1973, p. 1). He was on the staff of the New York Psychoanalytic Institute from the very beginning. His wide-ranging interests came to the fore in the field of psychoanalysis. His publications explored child psychiatry (Lewin, 1949) as well as theoretical questions (Lewin, 1954, 1961). In writing Lewin's obituary, Kubie felt that he must not forget to mention the tireless devotion Lewin had put into his work as a member of the Emergency Committee to rescue their colleagues in Europe.

82. Helene Deutsch was the president of the Boston Psychoanalytic Society between 1939 and 1941 (Gifford, 1983). She published significant findings in psychoses and borderline syndrome as well as in a psychoanalytic approach to female sexuality (Deutsch, 1991).

83. See Kubie's memorandum of 13 March 1938.

84. John Cooper Wiley was the USA's consul general in Vienna in 1938.

85. Hugh R. Wilson (1885–1946) was the American ambassador to Germany between 1938 and 1939.

86. Archives of the British Psychoanalytical Society, Refugee File.

87. Marie Bonaparte (1882–1962) was a princess of Greece and Denmark, a French psychoanalyst, and an analysand of Freud's intermittently between 1925 and 1938. She was a committed patron of the psychoanalytic movement and a devotee of Freud's. At his recommendation, she joined the Paris analysts and launched the formation of the Société Psychoanalytique de Paris. She played a key role in the rescue of part of Freud's family and in the translation and publication of Freud's work in France. She sponsored Róheim's research in Australia, New Guinea, and Somalia. She also wrote numerous studies in psychoanalysis, the most famous being a psychobiography of Edgar Allan Poe in 1933 (Loewenstein, 1963).

88. US State Department cable, 19 March 1938 (Archives of the British Psychoanalytical Society, Refugee File).

89. Ross McC. Chapmann, letter from the President of the American Psychiatric Association to Secretary of State Cordell Hull, 25 March 1938 (Archives of the British Psycho-Analytical Society, Refugee File).

90. Telegram from the Bellevue Psychiatric Hospital, New York City, to Secretary of State Cordell Hull, 23 March 1938 (Archives of the British Psychoanalytical Society, Refugee File).
91. Donations could be sent to Dr Bertram D. Lewis, 25 Fifth Avenue, New York, with a note about the purpose for which it was intended.
92. The organisers took care to ensure that donations made to the fund were tax-deductible.
93. The Emergency Committee Bulletin of Information, 19 March 1938 (The Archives & Special Collections of the A. A. Brill Library, The New York Psychoanalytic Society and Institute).
94. The Archives & Special Collections of the A. A. Brill Library, The New York Psychoanalytic Society and Institute.
95. The Nansen passport was developed by Fridtjof Nansen (1861–1930), a Norwegian arctic explorer and Nobel Peace Prize-winning politician. He intended it for—primarily Eastern European—refugees who had become stateless. The Nansen passport enabled the bearer to prove her or his identity, to resettle, and to find employment. By 1942, fifty-two countries had recognised it. It was by analogy that the now stateless analysts who were granted membership-at-large were referring to this exemption as "Nansen membership" among themselves. Thus, any of the refugee analysts—irrespective of whether his or her university degree was in medicine or not—could have become a "Nansen member" and, therefore, a member of the IPA if their American colleagues had accepted it.
96. Fromm underwent personal analysis in Berlin with Hanns Sachs. In 1929 in Frankfurt, he founded the Frankfurt Psychoanalytic Institute in conjunction with Karl Landauer, his wife, Frieda Fromm-Reichmann, and others. It was in operation until 1933, when Hitler seized power in Germany. In the early 1930s, Fromm took part in the neo-Marxist social critique of the Frankfurt School. In 1934, he and his wife escaped fascism and immigrated to New York. The New York Psychoanalytic Society accepted him as one of their own, but he soon left. After he split with Karen Horney's group, he co-founded the William Alanson White Institute in New York with Harry Stack Sullivan and Frieda Fromm-Reichmann in 1943. Between 1950 and 1974, he lived in Mexico, where he established a psychoanalytic institute in 1963. Afterwards, he returned to Europe, settled in Switzerland, and spent the rest of his life in Locarno (Funk, 2000). In contrast to Freud's instinct theory, Fromm saw the human motivation system and the development of the human psyche as stemming from non-social relations. The question of the

"social character" is central to his psychoanalytic thinking. Fromm was influenced by Ferenczi's approach and in 1958 wrote a piece in *The Saturday Review* on the rumour spread by Jones of Ferenczi being mentally ill. In it, he blasted it as a Stalinist-type rewriting of history, which he saw as an impermissible instrument of rivalry. He had gathered the views of family members, colleagues, and students who knew Ferenczi well, and all of them spoke with one mind against Jones, who had painted Ferenczi as a paranoid lunatic (Bonomi, 1998, p. 203). Fromm's piece was the bravest and most open demonstration of support for Ferenczi at the time). Among his many important books are *Escape from Freedom* (1941), *The Sane Society* (1955), and *The Art of Loving* (1956). See also Erős, 1991, 2004.

97. Letter from Erich Fromm to Ernest Jones, 25 March 1936 (Archives of the British Psycho-Analytical Society, GO7/BF/F04/07d)8

98. Naturally, members of the committee—and others, at least publicly—were unaware that the national origins quota had never been filled.

99. Report of the Emergency Committee on Relief and Immigration, 22 November 1938 (The Archives & Special Collections of the A. A. Brill Library, The New York Psychoanalytic Society and Institute).

100. Report of the Emergency Committee on Relief and Immigration, 22 November 1938 (The Archives & Special Collections of the A. A. Brill Library, The New York Psychoanalytic Society and Institute).

101. Colorado, Connecticut, Idaho, Indiana, Kentucky, Maryland, Massachusetts, Mississippi, Nevada, New Jersey, New York, Ohio, Utah, and Virginia.

102. See the complete membership list for the Vienna Psychoanalytic Society from its founding to its dissolution (1906–1938) with the destinations of the émigré analysts indicated (Mühlleitner & Reichmayr, 1995).

103. Letter from Eduardo Weiss to Ernest Jones, 29 March 1939 (Archives of the British Psycho-Analytical Society, G01/BB/F0R/Refugee File).

104. Between 1938 and 1941, Hungary's Parliament passed a total of three anti-Semitic laws.

105. This is the original letter (without corrections) from István Hollós to Lawrence S. Kubie, 9 January 1939 (Archives of the British Psychoanalytical Society G07/BJ/F01).

106. I trust that it is no more than a confluence of unexpected and unhappy coincidences that Riccardo Steiner published this letter from Hollós in a book in 2000 (Steiner, 2000), having apparently forgotten that both this letter and the rest of the correspondence, replete with documentation and commentary, had already been in print in a publication—and a

language—to which he would have had access: *The International Forum of Psychoanalysis* (The Tragic Success of European Psychoanalysis: 'The Budapest School', Mészáros 1998a). In 1998, after one year of research in the USA, I returned to the archives in London to check materials examined earlier as a starting point to my study in order to connect them to the strands found across the sea and, thus, round out the documents in Britain. Towards that end, I sent a letter on 28 July 1998, requesting permission to publish the sources relevant to Hungary with a list of those sources attached. In yet another in a series of coincidences, the addressee was Riccardo Steiner, who was authorised by the British Psychoanalytical Society to grant permission in such cases. In this case, however, no response was ever forthcoming. The next mysterious event involved the publication two years later of the very same documents listed in the attachment in a book by Steiner entitled *It is a New Kind of Diaspora*—to no small surprise and amazement to me. My favourite lines from Steiner's book would be: "Consider the vicissitudes of the Hungarian analysts, for instance: is there *something* [emphasis added] in London that would help us to understand what happened to them? ... Indeed, the Archives of the British Psycho-Analytical Society contain a certain amount of correspondence that, although fragmented, enables us to piece together the various episodes of this part of the 'story'" (Steiner, 2000, p. 114). This book contains references primarily to documents from my own research, many of which can be found in Steiner's book in excerpts or in their entirety (pp. 114–143).

107. Letter from Géza Róheim to John Rickman, 29 May 1938 (Archives of the British Psycho-Analytical Society, CRB/A0/05).
108. Letter from Géza Róheim to Ernest Jones, 28 May 1933 (Archives of the British Psychoanalytical Society, CRB/A0/03).
109. Letter from an unknown sender to Ernest Jones, 14 January 1939 (Archives of the British Psychoanalytical Society, 13R).
110. In brief, the conflict was as follows: after Ferenczi's death, Jones spread his view that Ferenczi had become "paranoid" in his final years and that "pathological reactions had developed" in him which naturally appeared in his later work. His first open point of attack was Ferenczi's "Confusion of tongues between adults and the child" (Ferenczi, 1980k [1933]), the paper he gave at the Wiesbaden congress in 1932 which led to Freud's split with Ferenczi. Owing to his influence and power position, Jones succeeded in shaping how Ferenczi was viewed internationally. As becomes clear from Freud's correspondence with Jones (Paskauskas, 1993), Freud also made mention of his hostile feelings

toward Ferenczi (Freud to Jones, 12 September 1932, Paskauskas, 1993). Still, it was Jones whose role—and therefore whose responsibility—was significant in both Ferenczi and his work becoming taboo in conservative and official psychoanalytic circles from the mid-1930s to the late 1970s. In his own gentle manner, Balint did everything to reinforce Ferenczi's position and refute that of Jones—but without success. In his biography of Freud, Jones had even included his own denunciations of Ferenczi (Jones, 1957). Balint tread cautiously with Jones, though he always made it clear that Ferenczi was far from mad. He even declared this before the British Psychoanalytical Society in 1948 when he read his paper on Ferenczi (Balint, 1949b). Here, he attempted to paint a realistic, complex, and demythologised picture of him. Then, from time to time, Balint made efforts to change Jones' position in their personal correspondence, without any success. He wished to avoid levelling open criticism against Jones because of the latter's advanced age and ill health, but from first to last he asked Jones to rid the manuscript for his Freud biography of his deprecating and improbable claims about Ferenczi. In the end, however, after Jones would not redact what he had said about Ferenczi's alleged mental illness, Balint changed his method of fighting. For more on his efforts, see Mészáros (2003). For more on this topic, see overviews by Judith Dupont (Dupont, 1988b), Haynal, (1988), Carlo Bonomi (Bonomi, 1998), and Peter and Axel Hoffer (Hoffer & Hoffer, 1998).

111. There was only one patient of Alice Balint's on whom we have any information. This patient discussed Alice Balint's work based on her own experience. What follows is an excerpt on the Balints' emigration taken from my interview with the patient.
112. Many, including Hajdu herself, spelled her first name in a number of different ways: Lilly, Lilli, and Lili. I use the Lilly version unless a quote obliges me to use another.
113. Letter from Dr Lilly Hajdu Gimes addressed "Dear Sir", 27 January 1939 (Archives of the British Psychoanalytical Society G07/B5/F01/16).
114. Lilly Hajdu's training analyst was Vilma Kovács. She made no mention of this in her curriculum vitae.
115. On the lives of Lilly Hajdu's family, see Regula Schiess's book written with the co-operation of both Juca Gimes-Magos and her husband Gábor Magos: Schiess (1999).
116. List of analysts wishing to go to Australia (Archives of the British Psychoanalytical Society, CRB/A0/05); G03/BJ/09G).
117. Letter from Ernest Jones to Lawrence S. Kubie, 27 April 1938 (Archives of the British Psychoanalytical Society, G07/BJ/ F01/29).

118. Before resettling in Berlin, Edit Gyömrői had been deported from Romania due to her communist activism. She and her husband, László (Glück) Tölgy, moved to Berlin in 1923. For more on her biography, see Schröter (1995) and Borgos (2006). An authentic source on the Berlin years is Edith Gyömrői-Ludowyk: "Emlékezés Otto Fenichelre és a Német Pszichoanalitikus Egyesületre" [Otto Fenichel and the German Psychoanalytic Society: A remembrance]. *Thalassa*, 2005, *16*(2–3): 195–202.
119. Letter from Edith Gyömrői-Újvári to Ernest Jones, 11 February 1939 (Archives of the British Psychoanalytical Society, G07/BJ/F01/20x); cf. Steiner (2000, p. 188).
120. The "U" in Gyömrői's name on the certificate indicates the name of her husband, László Újvári (Archives of the Sándor Ferenczi Society).
121. Letter from István Schönberger to Ernest Jones, 26 January 1939 (Archives of the British Psychoanalytical Society G07/BJ/F01/12).
122. Letter from István Schönberger to Ernest Jones, 4 February 1939 (Archives of the British Psycho-Analytical Society G07/BJ/F01/13).
123. It was published with a different title: "A dream of Descartes: reflections on the unconscious determinants of the sciences" (Schönberger, 1939).
124. Letter from Hollós to Kubie, 19 January 1939 (Archives of the British Psychoanalytical Society G07/BJ/F01).
125. Cable received 29 April 1941, from Dr Pfeifer of the Hungarian Psychoanalytic Society (Payne Whitney/Cornell Archives, New York Academy of Medicine, Box 13, p. 48).
126. Adolf (Wolf) Fisch changed his name to Andras József after 1945.
127. Summary of Individual Services Rendered by the Emergency Committee (1938–1948) (Payne Whitney/Cornell Archives, New York Academy of Medicine, Box 13, p. 48).
128. For Bak's biography and a list of publications, see Mészáros 1999b.
129. Bak's nephew, Giulio (Gyula) Szegő, was a wealthy and influential businessman.
130. Summary of Individual Services Rendered by the Emergency Committee (1938–1948) (Payne Whitney/Cornell Archives, New York Academy of Medicine, Box 13, pp. 10, 13, 14, 20, 32, 39, and 48).
131. Owing to professional conflicts, Sandor Rado split with the New York Psychoanalytic Institute and Society, which, being the most conservative American professional community, had difficulty tolerating his departure from Freudian instinct theory. Rado's "adaptation theory" had left open the possibility for processes tied to physiology and the

psychology of learning. Cf. Rado, 1969. This is an edited volume of papers by Rado on this subject.

132. Hanna Peto's account contradicted the presumption represented by Lívia Nemes that Erzsébet Kardos had died after stepping on a landmine (Nemes, 1985). In the Hungarian Society's report prepared in 1946 at the request of *The International Journal of Psychoanalysis*, Imre Hermann confirmed Hanna Peto's account. Hermann described how Kardos had been killed by "terrorists" shortly before the country's liberation from German occupation (Hermann, 1946). In all likelihood, the word "terrorists" here refers to members of Hungary's fascist Arrow Cross party.

133. With communist ideology having prevailed, psychoanalysis became persecuted as the "personal psychology of imperialism". While the Hungarian Psychoanalytic Society had managed to preserve its legal continuity even under German occupation, the organisation dissolved itself at a general meeting held on 8 February 1949 (Mészáros, 2012).

134. Dr Samuel Atkin was the president of the New York Psychoanalytic Institute.

135. Letter from Bettina Warburg to Samuel Atkin, 24 September 1940 (The Archives & Special Collections of the A. A. Brill Library, The New York Psychoanalytic Society and Institute).

136. Tibor Ágoston's biography, no date, after June 1941.

137. Dr Samuel Feigin worked with the Psychiatric Advisory Board.

138. Letter from Bettina Warburg to Samuel Atkin, 24 January 1941 (The Archives & Special Collections of the A. A. Brill Library, The New York Psychoanalytic Society and Institute).

139. Letter from Fanny von Hann-Kende to Adolf Stern, 10 October 1938 (The Archives & Special Collections of the A. A. Brill Library, The New York Psychoanalytic Society and Institute). Dr Adolf Stern chaired the Educational Committee of the New York Psychoanalytic Society.

140. Instructors were members of the New York Psychoanalytic Institute staff who carried out training analysis and supervised clinical cases. (Letter from Otto Isakower to Fanny Hann-Kende, 27 January 1948, The Archives & Special Collections of the A. A. Brill Library, The New York Psychoanalytic Society and Institute.)

141. There is not a single document that reveals the identity of Feldman's training analyst, though he makes mention of psychoanalytic training in his CV. (S. S. Feldman, Curriculum vitae, 12 March 1949, The Archives & Special Collections of the A. A. Brill Library, The New York Psychoanalytic Society and Institute.)

142. Summary of Individual Services Rendered by the Emergency Committee (1938–1948) (Payne Whitney/Cornell Archives, New York Academy of Medicine, Box 13, p. 48).
143. Letter from Lawrence S. Kubie to George Gero, 27 September 1938 (The Archives & Special Collections of the A. A. Brill Library, The New York Psychoanalytic Society and Institute).
144. Summary of Individual Services Rendered by the Emergency Committee (1938–1948) (Payne Whitney/Cornell Archives, New York Academy of Medicine, Box 13, p. 48).
145. The names are written here as they appear on the document.
146. In my own research, I have reported that the Emergency Committee was in contact with approximately 150 psychoanalysts as well as their family members (Mészáros, 1998a, 2012). A recent publication by Nellie Thompson draws on Bettina Warburg's final report on the work of the Committee in communicating with a total of 254 individuals—both psychoanalysts and others; specifically:

> The four groups were persons in the US assisted financially (51); persons outside the US assisted financially (14); persons in the US in contact with the committee (134); and persons who requested affidavits (55). These individuals included not only analysts, but also candidates, medical students, psychologists, social workers, teachers, lay analysts, family members of analysts, and nonanalyst physicians, (Thompson, 2012, p. 22)

147. Various journals have devoted special issues to the Ferenczi legacy, for example, Ferenczi et la psychanalyse contemporaine (TI, TII). *Le-Coq-Héron*, Nos. 154 and 155, 1999; Sándor Ferenczi: Psychoanalysis and the confusion of tongues. *International Forum of Psychoanalysis*, 1998, 7(4); Why Ferenczi today? *International Forum of Psychoanalysis*, 2004, 13(1–2); Themenschwerpunkt: Sándor Ferenczi. *Integrative Therapie, 29.* Jg. Heft 3/4, Jungermann Verlag, 2003; *Psychoanalytic Perspectives*, 2010 7(1). Research on Ferenczi has also produced a number of significant volumes both in Hungary and abroad, including Aron & Harris, 1993; Berman, 2004; Bokanowsky, 1997; Bokanowsky, Kelley-Laine, & Pragier, 1995; Bonomi, 2001, 2004; Borgogno, 1999, 2004, 2007b; Dupont, 1988a; Erős, 2004; Fortune, 2002; Gero-Brabant, 1993; Harmat, 1994; Haynal, 1988, 2002; Kahtuni & Sanches, 2009; Mészáros, 1999a, 2000a, 2008; Pfizner, 2005; Rachman, 1997; Rudnytsky, 1996, 2002; Sabourin, 1985, 2011; Székács-Weisz & Keve, 2012.
148. Ernst Simmel was a member of the Berlin Psychoanalytic Society in Berlin; Felix Deutsch belonged to that society's counterpart in Vienna.

Both fled Nazism and immigrated to the USA. Simmel was on friendly terms with Ferenczi. See his memorial speech on Ferenczi's death (Simmel, 2000[1933]).

149. Dr Georg Groddeck: *Die psychische Bedingtheit und psychoanalytische Behandlung organischer Leiden*. Verlag von S. Hirzel, Berlin, 1917.
150. Parts of this section are drawn from a previous study by the author: "Psychoanalysis is a two-way street" (Mészáros, 2004b).
151. This quote is cited from the original study "A jellemanalízis és az Újrakezdés" (Character analysis and new beginning) (Balint, 1999 [1933], pp. 9–10), which is longer than the English-language version and contains more parts that pertain to Ferenczi.
152. The 12th International Psychoanalytical Association Congress in September 1932.
153. This section relies on earlier publications by the author, especially Mészáros 2010a.

REFERENCES

Alexander, F. (1923). The castration complex in the formation of character. *International Journal of Psychoanalysis*, 4: 11–42.
Alexander, F. (1960). *The Western Mind in Transition: An Eyewitness Story*. New York: Random House.
Alexander, F. (1965). *Psychosomatic Medicine: Its Principle and Application*. New York: W. W. Norton.
Alexander, F., & French, T. M. (1980). The principle of corrective emotional experience. In: *Psychoanalytic Therapy, Principles and Application* (pp. 66–70). Lincoln, NE: University of Nebraska Press.
Almásy, E. et al. (1993)[1933]. *Lélekelemzési tanulmányok. Dolgozatok a pszichoanalízis főbb kérdéseiről* [Psychonalytic Studies: Papers on the Key Questions in Psychoanalysis]. Budapest: Somló Béla Könyvkiadó [reprinted Budapest: Párbeszéd Kiadó, T-Twins Kiadó].
Anderson, A. R. (1958). Lewis B. Hill, M.D.—1894–1958. *Bulletin of the American Psychoanalytic Association*, 14: 740–742.
Anon (1901). Könyvismertetés [Book review]: S. Freud: Über den Traum. *Orvosi Hetilap* [Medical Weekly], 10 February 1901, (45)6: 92.
Anon (1918a). Hiradás az 5. nemzetközi pszichoanalitikus kongresszusról [News of the Fifth International Psychoanalytical Congress]. *Gyógyászat* [Therapy], 58(20): 231.

Anon (1918b). Hiradás az 5. nemzetközi pszichoanalitikus kongresszusról [News of the Fifth International Psychoanalytical Congress]. *Világ* [World], 29 September 1918.

Anon (1952). F. von Hann-Kende, psychoanalyst. *New York Times*, 15 April 1952.

Antonovsky, A. (1987). *Unraveling the Mystery of Health: How People Manage Stress and Stay Well*. San Francisco, CA: Jossey-Bass.

Apfel, R. J., & Simon, B. (1996). Introduction. In: R. Apfel & B. Simon (Eds.), *Minefields in their Hearts: The Mental Health of Children in War and Communal Violence* (pp. 1–17). New Haven, CT: Yale University Press.

Aron, L., & Harris, A. (Eds.) (1993). *The Legacy of Sándor Ferenczi*. Hillsdale, NJ: Analytic Press.

B. Gáspár, J. (1991). Nyelvzavar és fordítás a mélylélektani gondolkodás történetében [Confusion of tongues and translation in the history of thinking on depth psychology]. *Thalassa*, 2: 19–29.

Bak, R. C. (1934). A skizofrénia inzulinkezelése [Insulin treatment for schizophrenia]. *Gyógyászat* [Therapy], 74: 105–107.

Bak, R. C. (1938). József Attila betegsége [Attila József's illness]. *Szép Szó* [Beautiful Word], 21: 105–115.

Bak, R. C. (1939). Regression of ego-orientation and libido in schizophrenia. *International Journal of Psychoanalysis*, 20: 64–71.

Bak, R. C. (1971). Object-relationships in schizophrenia and perversion. *International Journal of Psychoanalysis*, 52: 235–242.

Bak, R. C. (1973). Being in love and object loss. *International Journal of Psychoanalysis*, 54: 1–8.

Balázs, B. (1982)[1920]. *Napló* [Diary], *Volume 2 (1914–1922)*. Budapest: Magvető.

Bálint, A. (1928). Magyar néphit [Hungarian folk belief]. *Századunk* [Our Century], 3: 181–183.

Bálint, A. (1949)[1939]. Love for the mother and mother love. *International Journal of Psychoanalysis*, 30: 251–259.

Bálint, A. (1953). *The Psycho-Analysis of the Nursery: The Early Years of Life*. London: Routledge & Kegan Paul, 1953. Originally published 1931 as: *A gyermekszoba pszichológiája* (Előszó [Preface]: Ferenczi Sándor). Budapest: Pantheon [reprinted Előszó [Preface]: I. Székács-Schönberger, Budapest: Kossuth 1990].

Bálint, A. (1993)[1933]. A szeretet fejlődése és a valóságérzék [The development of love and a sense of reality]. In: *Lélekelemzési tanulmányok. Dolgozatok a pszichoanalízis főbb kérdéseiről* [Psychonalytic Studies: Papers on the Key Questions in Psychoanalysis] (pp. 30–40). Budapest:

Somló Béla Könyvkiadó [reprinted Budapest: Párbeszéd Kiadó, T-Twins Kiadó].
Bálint, A., & Bálint, M. (1939). On transference and counter-transference. *International Journal of Psychoanalysis, 20*: 223–230.
Bálint, M. (1926). Psychoanalysis és belgyógyászat [Psychoanalysis and internal medicine]. *Gyógyászat* [Therapy], *66*(19): 439–445.
Bálint, M. (1936). The final goal of psycho-analytic treatment. *International Journal of Psychoanalysis, 17*: 206–216.
Balint, M. (1948). On the psycho-analytic training system. *International Journal of Psychoanalysis, 29*: 163–173.
Balint, M. (1949a). Early developmental states of the ego: primary object love. *International Journal of Psychoanalysis, 30*: 265–273.
Balint, M. (1949b). Sándor Ferenczi, Obituary 1933. *International Journal of Psychoanalysis, 30*: 215–219.
Balint, M. (1957). *The Doctor, His Patient and the Illness*. London: Pitman Medical.
Balint, M. (1965)[1932]. Character analysis and new beginning. In: *Primary Love and Psycho-analytic Technique* (pp. 151–164). London: Tavistock.
Balint, M. (1992)[1968]. *The Basic Fault: Therapeutic Aspects of Regression*. Evanston, IL: Northwestern University Press.
Bálint, M. (1993)[1933]. A jellemanalízis és az Újrakezdés [Character analysis and new beginning]. In: *Lélekelemzési tanulmányok. Dolgozatok a pszichoanalízis főbb kérdéseiről* [Psychonalytic Studies: Papers on the Key Questions in Psychoanalysis]. Budapest: Somló Béla Konyvkiadó [reprinted Budapest: Párbeszéd Kiadó, T-Twins Kiadó] (pp. 65–79). Reprinted in: *Elsődleges szeretet és pszichoanalitikus technika* [Primary Love and Psychoanalytic Technique] *II*. Budapest: Animula, 1999.
Bálint, M. (2000)[1933]. Ferenczi Sándor, mint orvos [Sándor Ferenczi as a physician]. In: J. Mészáros (Ed.), *In Memoriam Ferenczi Sándor* (pp. 148–154). Budapest: Jószöveg Műhely. English translation: Dr. Sándor Ferenczi as psycho-analyst. *Indian Journal of Psychology* (1934), *20*: 312–215.
Bánfalvi, A. (1998). *A szabadság arcai a pszichoanalízisben* [The Faces of Freedom in Psychoanalysis]. Budapest: Osiris.
Barteimer, L. H. (1974). Lawrence S. Kubie (1896–1973). *American Journal of Psychiatry, 131*: 5.
Békés, V. (Ed.) (2004). *A kreativitás mintázatai* [Patterns of Creativity]. Budapest: Áron Kiadó.
Benedek, T. (1949). The psychosomatic implications of the primary unit: mother–child. *American Journal of Orthopsychiatry, 19*(4): 642–654.

Berman, E. (2004). Sándor, Gizella, Elma. *International Journal of Psychoanalysis, 85*: 489–520.
Bognár, Z. (2002). *Michael Joseph Eisler. Eine Werkauswahl*. Pilicsaba, Hungary: Katholische Péter-Pázmány Universität, Philosophische Fakultät.
Bokanowsky, T. (1997). *Sándor Ferenczi*. Paris: Presses Universitaires de France.
Bokanowsky, T., Kelley-Lainé, K., & Pragier, G. (1995). *Sándor Ferenczi. Monographies de la Revue française de psychanalyse*. Paris: Presses Universitaires de France.
Bókay, A. (1980). Pszichoanalízis, freudizmus marxizmus, József Attila világképében [Psychoanalysis, Freudianism, and Marxism in Attila József's worldview]. *Literatura, 2*: 248–266.
Bókay, A., & Erős, F. (1998). *Pszichoanalízis és irodalomtudomány* [Psychoanalysis and Literary Studies]. Budapest: Film Kiadó.
Bókay, A., Jádi, F., & Stark, A. (1982). *"Köztetek lettem én bolond . . ."* ["It was among you people that I went mad"]. Budapest: Magvető.
Bonomi, C. (1998). Jones's allegation of Ferenczi's mental deterioration: a reassessment. *International Forum of Psychoanalysis, 7*: 201–206.
Bonomi, C. (Ed.) (2001). *La catastrofe e i suoi simboli: il contributo di Sándor Ferenczi alla teoria psicoanalitica del trauma*. Turin: UTET Libreria.
Bonomi, C. (2004). Trauma and the symbolic function of the mind. *International Forum of Psychoanalysis, 13*: 45–50.
Borgogno, F. (1999). *Psicoanalisi come percorso*. Turin: Bollati Boringhieri.
Borgogno, F. (Ed.) (2004). Perché Ferenczi oggi? In: *Ferenczi oggi*. Turin: Bollati Boringhieri.
Borgogno, F. (2007a). Ferenczi and Winnicott: searching for a "missing link" (of the soul). *The American Journal of Psychoanalysis, 67*(3): 221–234.
Borgogno, F. (2007b). A contribution by Ferenczi to child psychoanalysis: the trauma and the traumatic – are they thinkable? In: *Psychoanalysis as a Journey* (pp. 171–186). London: Open Gate Press.
Borgos, A. (2006). *Edit Gyömrői (also Edit Gelb, Rényi, Glück, Újvári and Ludowyk)*. Vienna: Psychoanalytic Document Database (www.padd.at).
Bowlby, J. (1969). *Attachment and Loss. Volume 1: Attachment*. New York: Basic Books.
Bowlby, J. (1973). *Attachment and Loss. Volume 2: Separation*. New York: Basic Books.
Bowlby, J. (1980). *Attachment and Loss. Volume 3: Loss*. New York: Basic Books.
Brabant, E., Falzeder, E., & Giampieri-Deutsch P. (Eds.) (1993). *The Correspondence of Sigmund Freud and Sándor Ferenczi, Volume 1,*

1908–1914, P. Hoffer (Trans.). Cambridge, MA: Harvard University Press.

Brabant, E., Falzeder, E., & Giampieri-Deutsch (Eds.) (1996). *The Correspondence of Sigmund Freud and Sándor Ferenczi, Volume 2, 1914–1919*, P. Hoffer (Trans.). Cambridge, MA: Harvard University Press.

Brabant, E., Falzeder, E., & Giampieri-Deutsch P. (Eds.) (2000). *The Correspondence of Sigmund Freud and Sándor Ferenczi, Volume 3, 1920–1933*, P. Hoffer (Trans.). Cambridge, MA: Harvard University Press.

Braham, R. L. (1988). *A magyar holocaust* [The Hungarian Holocaust], *Volume 1*. Budapest: Gondolat; Wilmington, DE: Blackburn International.

Brecht, K., Volker, F., Hermanns, L. M., Kaminer, I. J., & Juelich, D. H. (Eds.) (1985). *"Here Life Goes on in a Most Peculiar Way . . ." Psychoanalysis Before and After 1933*. London: Goethe-Institut.

Breitman, R., & Kraut, A. M. (1987). *American Refugee Policy and European Jewry, 1933–1945*. Bloomington, IN: Indiana University Press.

Brennan, B. W. (2010). Ferenczi's forgotten messenger: the life and work of Izette de Forest. *American Imago*, 66(4): 427–455.

Brennan, B. W. (2011). Decoding Ferenczi's Clinical Diary. Paper presented at the Ferenczi Center at The New School, 2 December.

Bulletin (1938). Bulletin of the American Psychoanalytic Association, 1: 53–72.

Chused, J. F., Ellman, S. J., Renik, O., & Rothstein, A. (1999). Four aspects of the enactment concept: definitions, therapeutic effects, dangers, history. *Journal of Clinical Psychoanalysis*, 8: 9–61.

Conci, M. (2010). *Sullivan Revisited – Life and Work. Harry Stack Sullivan's Relevance for Contemporary Psychiatry, Psychotherapy and Psychoanalysis*. Trento: Tangram Edizioni Scientifiche.

Deutsch, H. (1926). Okkulte Vorgänge während der Psychoanalyse. *Imago*, 12: 418–433.

Deutsch, H. (1991). *Psychoanalysis of the Sexual Function of Women*, P. Roazen (Ed.). London: Karnac.

Dugan, T. F., & Coles, R. (Eds.) (1989). *The Child in Our Time: Studies in the Development of Resiliency*. New York: Brunner/Mazel.

Dupont, J. (1988a). Introduction. In: S. Ferenczi: *The Clinical Diary*. Cambridge, MA: Harvard University Press.

Dupont, J. (1988b). Ferenczi's "madness". *Contemporary Psychoanalysis*, 24: 250–261.

Dupont, J. (1997–1998). Alice Balint. Oeuvres complètes. *Le Coq-Héron*, 1–2: 147 & 153.

Dupont, J. (1998). The concept of trauma according to Ferenczi and its effects on subsequent psychoanalytical research. *International Forum of Psychoanalysis,* 7: 235–240.
Dupont, J. (Ed.) (2002–2003). The life and work of Michael Balint. First, Second and Third Special Issues, *American Journal of Psychoanalysis,* 62(1 & 4), 63(3).
Emergency Committee on Relief and Immigration (1938). Report to the Council on Professional Training and to the General Session of the American Psychoanalytic Association in Chicago, June 2–3, 1938. *Bulletin of the American Psychoanalytic Association,* 1: 53–72.
Erős, F. (1991). A történelem sztálinista újraírása [Stalinist rewriting of history]. *Thalassa,* 1: 92–97.
Erős, F. (Ed.) (2000). *Ferenczi Sándor.* Budapest: Új Mandátum.
Erős, F. (2004). *Kultuszok a pszichoanalízis történetében* [Cults in the History of Psychoanalysis]. Budapest: Jószöveg Műhely.
Erős, F. (2007). Lélekgyógyászat a háború szolgálatában. Freud, Ferenczi és a "háborús neurózisok" [Psychology in the service of the war: Freud, Ferenczi, and "war neuroses"]. In: F. Erős, *Trauma és történelem* [Trauma and History] (pp. 103–120). Budapest: Jószöveg Műhely.
Erős, F., Kapás, I., Kiss, G., & Giampieri Spanghero, P. (1987). Ferenczi Sándor és a Budapesti Egyetem [Sándor Ferenczi and the Budapest University], *Pszichológia,* 7(4): 584–592.
Falzeder, E. (Ed.) (2002). *The Complete Correspondence of Sigmund Freud and Karl Abraham 1907–1925.* London: Karnac.
Faulkner, H. J., & Pruitt, V. D. (Eds.) (1988). *The Selected Correspondence of Karl A. Menninger, 1919–1945.* Columbia, MI: University of Missouri Press.
Ferenczi, S. (1910). A hipnózis és a szuggesztió pszichoanalízise [The psycho-analysis of hypnosis and suggestion]. *Gyógyászat* [Therapy], 50(46): 776.
Ferenczi, S. (1919). Az orvosképzés reformja [Reforming medical training]. *Gyógyászat* [Therapy], 59(8): 120–121.
Ferenczi, S. (1920a)[1919]. Open letter. *International Journal of Psychoanalysis,* 1: 1–2.
Ferenczi, S. (1920b). Organikus állapotok pszichoanalízise [The psychoanalysis of organic conditions]. In: S. Ferenczi (Ed.), *Pszichoanalízis haladása.* Budapest: Dick Manó.
Ferenczi, S. (1921)[1918]. Symposium on Psychoanalysis and the War Neurosis Held at the Fifth International Psycho-Analytical Congress Budapest, September 1918. *International Psycho-Analytical Library,* 2: 5–21.

Ferenczi, S. (1980a). On the organisation of the psycho-analytic movement. In: M. Balint (Ed.), *Final Contributions to the Problems and Methods of Psycho-Analysis* (pp. 299–307). London: Maresfield Reprints.

Ferenczi, S. (1980b)[1908]. Actual and psycho-neuroses in the light of Freud's investigations and psycho-analysis. In: *Further Contributions to the Theory and Technique of Psychoanalysis* (pp. 30–55). London: Hogarth, 1959 [reprinted London: Karnac, 1980].

Ferenczi, S. (1980c)[1913]. A lecture for judges and barristers. In: J. Rickman (Ed.), *Further Contributions to the Theory and Technique of Psycho-Analysis* (pp. 424–434). London: Hogarth Press.

Ferenczi, S. (1980d)[1916–1917]. Two types of war neuroses. In: J. Rickman (Ed.), *Further Contributions to the Theory and Technique of Psycho-Analysis* (pp. 124–141). London: Hogarth, 1959 [reprinted London: Karnac, 1980].

Ferenczi, S. (1980e)[1919]. On the technique of psycho-analysis. In: M. Balint (Ed.), *Further Contributions to the Theory and Technique of Psycho-Analysis* (pp. 177–189). London: Maresfield Reprints.

Ferenczi, S. (1980f)[1928]. The adaptation of the family to the child. In: M. Balint (Ed.), *Final Contributions to the Problems and Methods of Psycho-Analysis* (pp. 61–76). London: Maresfield Reprints.

Ferenczi, S. (1980g)[1928]. The elasticity of psycho-analytic technique. In: M. Balint (Ed.), *Final Contributions to the Problems and Methods of Psycho-Analysis* (pp. 87–101). London: Maresfield Reprints.

Ferenczi, S. (1980h)[1929]. The unwelcome child and his death instinct. In: M. Balint (Ed.), *Final Contributions to the Problems and Methods of Psycho-Analysis* (pp. 102–107). London: Maresfield Reprints.

Ferenczi, S. (1980i)[1931]. Child analysis in the analysis of adults. In: M. Balint (Ed.), *Final Contributions to the Problems and Methods of Psycho-Analysis* (pp. 126–142). London: Maresfield Reprints.

Ferenczi, S. (1980j)[1908]. Psychoanalysis and education In: M. Balint (Ed.), *Final Contributions to the Problems and Methods of Psycho-Analysis* (pp. 280–290). London: Maresfield Reprints.

Ferenczi, S. (1980k)[1933]. Confusion of tongues between adults and the child. In: M. Balint (Ed.), *Final Contributions to the Problems and Methods of Psycho-Analysis* (pp. 156–167). London: Maresfield Reprints.

Ferenczi, S. (1982)[1914]. A pszichoanalízisről s annak jogi és társadalmi jelentőségéről [On psychoanalysis and its judicial and sociological significance: a lecture for judges and barristers]. In: A. Linczényi (Ed.), *Lelki problémák a pszichoanalízis tükrében. Válogatás Ferenczi Sándor tanulmányaiból* [Psychological Problems in the Light of Psychoanalysis: A

Selection of Studies by Sándor Ferenczi] (pp. 158–174). Budapest: Magvető.

Ferenczi, S. (1988)[1932]. *The Clinical Diary*, J. Dupont (Ed.). Cambridge, MA: Harvard University Press.

Ferenczi, S. (1989)[1924]. *Thalassa: A Theory of Genitality.* London: Karnac.

Ferenczi, S. (1993)[1917]. My friendship with Miksa Schächter. *British Journal of Psychotherapy*, 9(4): 430–433.

Ferenczi, S. (1997)[1934]. A trauma a pszichoanalízisben [Trauma in psychoanalysis]. In: *Technikai írások* [Papers on Technique] (pp. 113–121). Budapest: Animula.

Ferenczi S. (1999a)[1899]. Spiritizmus [Spiritism]. In: J. Mészáros (Ed.), *Ferenczi Sándor: A pszichoanalízis felé. Fiatalkori írások 1897–1908.* [Towards Psychoanalysis: Early Papers 1897–1908] (pp. 27–30). Budapest: Osiris.

Ferenczi, S. (1999b)[1899]. Spiritism, G. Sagi (Trans.) *Bulletin*, 36: 44–50.

Ferenczi, S. (1999c)[1900]. Öntudat, fejlődés (Consciousness, development]. In: J. Mészáros (Ed.), *Ferenczi Sándor: A pszichoanalízis felé. Fiatalkori írások 1897–1908.* [Towards Psychoanalysis: Early Papers 1897–1908] (pp. 45–48). Budapest: Osiris.

Ferenczi, S. (1999d)[1900]. Über den physiologischen Schwachsinn des Weibes. In: J. Mészáros (Ed.), *Ferenczi Sándor: A pszichoanalízis felé. Fiatalkori írások 1897–1908.* [Towards Psychoanalysis: Early Papers 1897–1908] (pp. 54–57). Budapest: Osiris.

Ferenczi, S. (1999e)[1900]. Két téves kórisme [Two errors in diagnosis]. In: J. Mészáros (Ed.), *Ferenczi Sándor: A pszichoanalízis felé. Fiatalkori írások 1897–1908* [Towards Psychoanalysis: Early Papers 1897–1908] (pp. 63–65). Budapest: Osiris. English edition: Two errors in diagnosis. In: J. Borossa (Ed.), *Selected Writings* (pp. 9–12). London: Penguin.

Ferenczi, S. (1999f)[1901]. A szerelem a tudományban [Love within science]. In: J. Mészáros (Ed.), *Ferenczi Sándor: A pszichoanalízis felé. Fiatalkori írások 1897–1908.* [Towards Psychoanalysis: Early Papers 1897–1908] (pp. 76–79) Budapest: Osiris. English edition: Love within science. In: J. Borossa (Ed.), *Selected Writings* (pp. 13–18). London: Penguin.

Ferenczi, S. (1999g)[1901]. Apoplexiás roham sikeres gyógykezelése [A successful therapy for apoplectic stroke]. In: J. Mészáros (Ed.), *Ferenczi Sándor: A pszichoanalízis felé. Fiatalkori írások 1897–1908.* [Towards Psychoanalysis: Early Papers 1897–1908]. (pp. 93–96). Budapest: Osiris.

Ferenczi, S. (1999h)[1902]. Homosexualitas feminina. In: J. Mészáros (Ed.), *Ferenczi Sándor: A pszichoanalízis felé. Fiatalkori írások 1897–1908.*

[Towards Psychoanalysis: Early Papers 1897–1908] (pp. 112–115). Budapest: Osiris. English edition: Feminine homosexuality. In: J. Borossa (Ed.), *Selected Writings* (pp 19–22). London: Penguin.

Ferenczi, S. (1999i)[1902]. Beichten eines praktischen Arztes. In: J. Mészáros (Ed.), *Ferenczi Sándor: A pszichoanalízis felé. Fiatalkori írások 1897–1908.* [Toward Psychoanalysis. Early Papers 1897–1908] (p. 118). Budapest: Osiris.

Ferenczi, S. (1999j)[1902]. Book review: Sante de Sanctis: Die Träume, medizinisch-psychologische Untersuchungen. In: J. Mészáros (Ed.), *Ferenczi Sándor: A pszichoanalízis felé. Fiatalkori írások 1897–1908.* [Towards Psychoanalysis: Early Papers 1897–1908] (p. 134). Budapest: Osiris.

Ferenczi, S. (1999k)[1903]. Amiről hallgat a krónika [Where memory sleeps]. In: J. Mészáros (Ed.), *Ferenczi Sándor: A pszichoanalízis felé. Fiatalkori írások 1897–1908.* [Towards Psychoanalysis: Early Papers 1897–1908] (pp. 175–179). Budapest: Osiris.

Ferenczi, S. (1999l)[1904]. A villamosság mint gyógyszer [Electricity as therapy]. In: J. Mészáros (Ed.), *Ferenczi Sándor: A pszichoanalízis felé. Fiatalkori írósok 1897–1908.* [Towards Psychoanalysis: Early Papers 1897–1908] (pp. 197–199). Budapest: Osiris.

Ferenczi, S. (1999m)[1906]. Szexuális átmeneti fokozatokról [On sexual transitionary stages]. In: J. Mészáros (Ed.), *Ferenczi Sándor: A pszichoanalízis felé. Fiatalkori írások 1897–1908.* [Towards Psychoanalysis: Early Papers 1897–1908] (pp. 255–263). Budapest: Osiris.

Ferenczi, S. (1999n)[1906]. Gyógyítás hipnotikus szuggesztióval [Treatment with hypnotic suggestion]. In: J. Mészáros (Ed.), *Ferenczi Sándor: A pszichoanalízis felé. Fiatalkori írások 1897–1908.* [Towards Psychoanalysis: Early Papers 1897–1908] (pp. 264–267). Budapest: Osiris.

Ferenczi, S. (1999o)[1922]. Psychoanalysis and social policy. In: J. Borossa (Ed.) *Selected Writings* (pp. 210–213). London: Penguin.

Ferenczi, S. (2000a)[1912]. Schopenhauernak Goethéhez írt levele, pszichoanalitice nézve (A "kedvtelési" és a "valósági" elv jelképes ábrázolása az Oedipus-mithosban). [Symbolical representation of the pleasure and reality principles in the Oedipus myth]. In: F. Erős (Ed.), *Ferenczi Sándor* (pp. 52–58). Budapest: Új Mandátum.

Ferenczi, S. (2000b)[1927]. [Interview with Sándor Ferenczi] Figyelmezetés az amerikai élet veszélyeire [Warns of danger in American life]. *The New York Times*, June 1927. In: J. Mészáros (Ed.), *In Memoriam Ferenczi Sándor* [In memoriam Sándor Ferenczi] (pp. 195–196). Budapest: Jószöveg Műhely.

Ferenczi, S. (2007)[1923]. A pszichoanalízis a gyakorló orvos szolgálatában [Psychoanalysis in the service of the practising physician]. *Thalassa*, *18*(1): 107–117.
Ferenczi, S., & Rank, O. (1986)[1924]. *The Development of Psycho-Analysis*. Madison, CT: International Universities Press.
Fermi, L. (1968). *Illustrious Immigrants. The Intellectual Migration from Europe*. Chicago, IL: University of Chicago Press.
Fonagy, P. (1996). The significance of the development of metacognitive control over mental representations in parenting and infant development. *Journal of Clinical Psychoanalysis*, *5*: 67–86.
Fonagy, P. (2001). *Attachment Theory and Psychoanalysis*. New York: Other Press.
Fonagy, P., Steele, M., Steele, H., Higgitt, A., & Target, M. (1994). The Emanuel Miller Memorial lecture 1992. The theory and practice of resilience. *Journal of Child Psychology and Psychiatry*, *35*(2): 231–257.
Fonagy, P., Target, M., & Gergely, G. (2000). Attachment and borderline personality disorder: a theory and some evidence. *Borderline Personality Disorder Special Issue of the Psychiatric Clinics of North America*, *23*(1): 103–122.
Fortune, C. (Ed.) (2002). *The Sándor Ferenczi–George Groddeck Letters 1921–1933*. London: Open Gate Press.
Frank, T. (1999). Station Berlin. Ungarische Wissenschaftler und Künstler in Deutschland 1919–1933, *IMIS-Beiträge*, *10*: 7–38.
Frank, T. (2002). Polányi Mihály Berlinben [Mihály Polányi in Berlin]. *Polanyiana*, *1–2*: 117–133.
Frank, T. (2009). *Double Exile: Migrations of Jewish-Hungarian Professionals through Germany to the United States, 1919–1945*. Bern: Peter Lang, European Academic.
Frankel, J. B. (1998). Ferenczi's trauma theory. *American Journal of Psychoanalysis*, *58*(1): 41–61.
French, T. M. (1941). Bausteine zur Psychoanalyse. (The Fundamentals of Psychoanalysis.) Four Volumes. By Sándor Ferenczi. Vols. I and II published by Internationaler Psychoanalytischer Verlag. Vols. III and IV published by Verlag Hans Huber, Berne.
Freud, A. (1936). *The Ego and the Mechanisms of Defence*. London: Hogarth Press.
Freud, S. (1895d). *Studies on Hysteria*. S.E., 2. London: Hogarth.
Freud, S. (1897). Letter 69. Extracts from the Fliess Papers. S.E., *1*: 259–260. London: Hogarth.
Freud, S. (1900a). *The Interpretation of Dreams*. S.E., 4–5. London: Hogarth.
Freud, S. (1901a). On dreams. S.E., *5*: 629–686. London: Hogarth.

Freud, S. (1910)[1909]. Bevezető [Introduction]. In: S. Ferenczi, *Lélekelemzés* [Psychoanalysis]. Budapest: Szilágyi Béla könyvkereskedése.
Freud, S. (1910b). Preface to Sándor Ferenczi's Psycho-Analysis: Essays in the Field of Psycho-analysis. *S.E.*, 9: 252. London: Hogarth.
Freud, S. (1910d). The future prospects of psycho-analytic therapy. *S.E.*, 11: 139–152. London: Hogarth.
Freud, S. (1914d). On the history of the psychoanalytic movement. *S.E.*, 14: 3–66. London: Hogarth.
Freud, S. (1916–1917). *Introductory Lectures on Psycho-Analysis. S.E.*, 15–16. London: Hogarth.
Freud, S. (1917a). A difficulty in the path of psycho-analysis. *S.E.*, 17: 135–144. London: Hogarth.
Freud, S. (1919j). On the teaching of psycho-analysis in universities. *S.E.*, 17: 169–174. London: Hogarth.
Freud, S. (1935). *An Autobiographical Study*, J. Strachey (Ed. & Trans.). New York: W. W. Norton.
Freud, S. (1992). *The Diary of Sigmund Freud 1929–1939: A Record of the Final Decade*, M. Molnar (Ed. and Trans.). London: The Freud Museum.
Funk, R. (2000). Erich Fromm's role in the foundation of the IFPS. *International Forum of Psychoanalysis*, 9: 187–197.
Gábor, É. (1991). Révész Géza (1978–1955). In: G. Kiss (Ed.), *Tanulmányok a magyar pszichoanalízis történetéből* [Studies from the History of Hungarian Psychoanalysis] (pp. 24–36). Budapest: Akadémiai Kiadó.
Gedo, J. (1996). O, Patria Mia. In: P. L. Rudnytsky, A. Bókay, & P. Giampieri-Deutsch (Eds.), *Ferenczi's Turn in Psychoanalysis* (pp. 77–88). New York: New York University Press.
Gergely, G., & Watson, J. S. (1996). The social biofeedback theory of parental affect-mirroring. *International Journal of Psychoanalysis*, 77: 1181–1212.
Gero, G. (1936). The construction of depression. *International Journal of Psychoanalysis*, 17: 423–461.
Gero, G. (1953). Defenses in symptom formation. *Journal of the American Psychoanalytic Association*, 1: 87–103.
Gero, G. (1962). Sadism, masochism, and aggression: their role in symptom-formation. *Psychoanalytic Quarterly*, 31: 31–42.
Gero-Brabant, E. (1993). *Ferenczi et l'école hongroise de psychanalyse*. Paris: L'Harmattan.
Gifford, S. (1983). Helene Deutsch (1884–1982). *Psychoanalytic Quarterly*, 52: 427–431.
Gill, M. M. (1967). In memoriam David Rapaport. In: M. M. Gill (Ed.), *The Collected Papers of David Rapaport* (pp. 3–7). New York: Basic Books.

Gitelson, M. (1952). The emotional response of the analyst in the psychoanalytic situation. *International Journal of Psychoanalysis*, 33: 1–10.
Glover, E. (1927). Lectures on technique in psycho-analysis. *International Journal of Psychoanalysis*, 8: 504–520.
Glover, E. (1940). Letter to Kubie, L. *Bulletin of the American Psychoanalytic Association*, 3: 16–65.
Groddeck, G. (1917). Letter from Georg Groddeck to Sigmund Freud, May 27, 1917. *International Psycho-Analytical Library*, 105: 31–36.
Grosskurth, P. (1986). *Melanie Klein. Her World and her Work*. Northvale, NJ: Jason Aronson.
Grotjahn, M. (1966). Franz Alexander. In: F. Alexander, S. Eisenstein, & M. Grotjahn (Eds.), *Psychoanalytic Pinoneers* (pp. 384–398). New York: Basic Books.
Hajdu, L. (1993)[1933]. Adatok a skizofrénia analíziséhez [Data for analysis of schizophrenia]. In: *Lélekelemzési tanulmányok* [Psychoanalytic Studies] (pp. 155–167). Budapest: Párbeszéd Kiadó, T-Twins Kiadó.
Hann-Kende, F. (1993)[1933]. Az áttétel és viszontáttétel szerepéhez a pszichoanalízisben [The role of transference and countertransference in psychoanalysis]. In: *Lélekelemzési tanulmányok* [Psychoanalytic Studies] (pp. 229–234). Budapest: Párbeszéd Kiadó, T-Twins Kiadó.
Harmat, P. (1994). *Freud, Ferenczi és a magyarországi pszichoanalízis* [Freud, Ferenczi, and Hungarian psychoanalysis]. Budapest: Bethlen Gábor Könyvkiadó.
Hárs, G. P. (2004). A Ferenczi–Groddeck–Füst Milán háromszög [The Ferenczi–Groddeck–Milán Füst triangle]. *Thalassa*, 2: 45–84.
Haynal, A. (1988). *The Technique at Issue. Controversies in Psychoanalysis from Freud and Ferenczi to Michael Balint*. London: Karnac.
Haynal, A. (1995). Ferenczi helye a pszichoanalitikus eszmetörténetben [Ferenczi's place in the intellectual history of psychoanalysis]. In: D. Lukács (Ed.), *Irányzatok és kutatások a mai magyar pszichoanalízisben* [Trends and Studies in Contemporary Hungarian Psychoanalysis] (pp. 19–28). Budapest: Animula.
Haynal, A. (1998). La contra-transferencia y Ferenczi. *Revisita de Psicoanálisis de la Asociación Psicoanalítica de Madrid*, 28: 57–72.
Haynal, A. (2002). *Disappearing and Reviving. Sándor Ferenczi*. London: Karnac.
Haynal, A., & Falzeder, E. (1993). Empathy, psychoanalytic practice in the 1920s, and Ferenczi's Clinical Diary. *Journal of The American Academy of Psychoanalysis*, 2(4): 605–621.

Haynal, A., & Mészáros, J. (2004). Psychoanalyse in Budapest von 1928–1929. In: L. Lehrman Weiner (Ed.), *Sigmund Freud durch Lehrmans Linse* (pp. 107–116). Gießen: Psychosocial-Verlag.
Heimann, P. (1950). On countertransference. *International Journal of Psycho-Analysis, 31*: 81–84.
Hermann, I. (1933). *A pszichoanalízis mint módszer* [Psychoanalysis as Method]. Budapest: Novák R. és tsa.
Hermann, I. (1946). Members and candidates lost in the war. *International Journal of Psychoanalysis, 27*: 90–92.
Hidas, G., & Mészáros, J. (1988). Fin de siècle, occultism, psychoanalysis. In: *Seventh European Cheiron Conference* (pp. 300–306). Budapest: Hungarian Psychological Association.
Hill, L. B. (1955). *Psychotherapeutic Intervention in Schizophrenia*. Chicago, IL: University of Chicago Press.
Hoffer, A. (1996). Asymmetry and mutuality in the analytic relationship: contemporary lessons from the Freud–Ferenczi dialogue. In: P. L. Rudnytsky, A. Bókay, & P. Giampieri-Deutsch (Eds.), *Ferenczi's Turn in Psychoanalysis* (pp. 107–119). New York: New York University Press.
Hoffer, P. T., & Hoffer, A. (1998). Ferenczi's fatal illness in historical context. *International Journal of Psychoanalysis, 47*: 1257–1268.
Hollós, I. (1929). Nemzeti géniusz és pszichoanalízis [Psychoanalysis and the spirit of a nation]. *Nyugat* [West], *22*(1): 195–200.
Hollós, I. (1990a)[1914]. Egy versmondó betegről [On a patient who recites poems]. *Nyugat* [West], *7*(5): 333–344 [reprinted *Helikon, 36*(2–3): 297–309.).
Hollós, I. (1990b)[1927]. *Búcsúm a sárga háztól*. [My Farewell to the Yellow House]. Budapest: Cserépfalvi.
Horney, K. (1937). *The Neurotic Personality of Our Time*. New York: W. W. Norton.
Ignotus, H. (2000)[1933]. Búcsúztató [Farewell]. In: J. Mészáros J. (Ed.), *In Memoriam Ferenczi Sándor* [In memoriam Sándor Ferenczi] (pp. 37–41). Budapest: Jószöveg Műhely.
Jacobs, T. J. (1983). Dreams and responsibilities: notes on the making of an institute. *Annual of Psychoanalysis, 11*: 29–49.
Jeffrey, W. D. (1989). After the Anschluss. The Emergency Committee on Relief and Immigration of the American Psychoanalytic Association. *American Psychoanalyst, 23*(2): 19–37.
Jones, E. (1955). *The Life and Work of Sigmund Freud. Volume 2. Years of Maturity 1901–1919*. New York: Basic Books.
Jones, E. (1957). *The Life and Work of Sigmund Freud. Volume 3. The Last Phase 1919–1939*. London: Hogarth Press.

Jószef, A. (1990). *Szabad-ötletek jegyzéke két ülésben* [List of Free Ideas in Two Sittings]. Budapest: Atlantisz.

Kahtuni, H. C., & Sanches, G. P. (2009). *Dicionário do Pensamento de Sándor Ferenczi*. Rio de Janeiro: Elsevier.

Kapronczay, K., & Kiss, G. (1986). Adatok Ferenczi Sándor egyetemi tanári működésével kapcsolatban [Data on Sándor Ferenczi's professorship]. *Magyar Pszichológiai Szemle* [Hungarian Psychological Review], 2: 111–118.

Kapusi, K. (2000). A gyermek Ferenczi Sándor és családjának miskolci története [The Miskolc story of young Sándor Ferenczi and his family]. *Levéltári évkönyv* [Archives Annual], *10*, Miskolc: 67–86.

Kassai, G. (1990). A Nyugat és a pszichoanalízis [*Nyugat* (West) and psychoanalysis]. *Helikon Világirodalmi Figyelő* [Helikon Literary Observer], 2–3: 171–182.

Kende, Z. (1974). *A Galilei kör megalakulása* [The Formation of the Galileo Circle]. Budapest: Akademiai Kiado.

Kilborne, B. (2008)[1988]. In memoriam George Devereux. *Thalassa*, 19(1): 7–22.

King, P., & Steiner, R. (Eds.) (1991). *The Freud–Klein Controversies 1941–45*. London: Tavistock.

Knight, R. P. (1961). David Rapaport 1911–1960, *Psychoanalytic Quarterly*, 30: 262–264.

Kolb, L. (1963). Interview with Sándor Lóránd. Manuscript. The Library of Congress.

Kosztolányi, D. (2000)[1918]. Orvosi konzílium [Medical consultation]. In: J. Mészáros (Ed.), *In Memoriam Ferenczi Sándor* [In memoriam Sándor Ferenczi] (pp. 189–193). Budapest: Jószöveg Műhely.

Kosztolányi, D. (2000)[1933]. Ferenczi Sándor. In: J. Mészáros (Ed.), *In Memoriam Ferenczi Sándor* [In memoriam Sándor Ferenczi] (pp. 53–56). Budapest: Jószöveg Műhely.

Kosztolányi, D. (2001)[1931]. A freudizmus az irodalomban (Nyilatkozat) [Freudianism in literature: A declaration]. *Literatura*, 9: 167–171 [reprinted *Thalassa*, 1: 125–126].

Kovács, M. (1994). The radical right and the Hungarian professions: the case of doctors and lawyers, 1918–1945. In: C. McClelland, S. Merl, & H. Siegrist (Eds.), *Professionen im modernen Osteuropa*. Berlin: Duncker & Humblot.

Kovács, V. (1993)[1933]. Kiképző analízis és kontroll analízis [Training analysis and control analysis]. In: *Lélekelemzési tanulmányok* [Psychoanalytic Studies] (pp. 240–248). Budapest: Párbeszéd Kiadó, T-Twins Kiadó.

Kubie, L. S. (1937–1938). Emergency Committee on Relief and Immigration. *Bulletin of the American Psychoanalyic Association, 1*: 65–68.
Kubie, L. S. (1960). *The Riggs Story: The Development of the Austen Riggs Center for the Study and Treatment of the Neuroses*. New York: Paul B. Hoebner.
Kubie, L. S. (1973). Bertram D. Lewin (1896–1971): the Renaissance cosmopolite with tongue in cheek. *Psychoanalytic Study of the Child, 28*: 1–16.
Kurzweil, E. (1992). Psychoanalytic science: from Oedipus to culture. *Psychoanalytic Review, 79*(3): 341–360.
Laplanche, J., & Pontalis, J. B. (1973). *The Language of Psycho-Analysis*, D. Nicholson-Smith (Trans.). London: Hogarth Press and the Institute of Psycho-Analysis.
Lévy, L. (1918). Editorial: Szerkesztőségi vezércikk. *Gyógyászat* [Therapy], *41*: 13 October.
Lévy, L. (1993)[1933]. Mire figyeljünk szívbetegek anamnézisében? [What should we watch for in a cardiac patient's anamnesis?] In: *Lélekelemzési tanulmányok* [Psychoanalytic Studies] (pp. 297–311). Budapest: Párbeszéd Kiadó, T-Twins Kiadó.
Lévy, L. (2004)[1919]. [Lévy Lajos vezércikke] [Editorial by Lajos Lévy]. *Thalassa, 15*(2): 131–132.
Lewin, B. D. (1949). Child psychiatry in the 1980s: three little homicidal monomaniacs. *Psychoanalytic Study of the Child, 4*: 489–493.
Lewin, B. D. (1954). Sleep, narcissistic neurosis and the analytic situation. *Psychoanalytic Quarterly, 23*: 487–510.
Lewin, B. D. (1961). Reflexions on depression. *Psychoanalytic Study of the Child, 28*: 1–16.
Little, M. (1951). Counter-transference and the patient's response to it. *International Journal of Psychoanalysis, 32*: 32–40.
Loewenstein, R. M. (1963). Marie Bonaparte (1882–1962). *Bulletin of the American Psychoanalytic Association, 19*: 861–863.
Lorin, C. (1983). *Le jeune Ferenczi. Premiers écrits 1899–1906*. Paris: Aubier-Montaigne.
Losonczi, Á. (2005). *Sorsba fordult történelem* [History Turned Fate]. Budapest: Holnap Kiadó.
Magyar, L., & Mészáros, J. (1999). Szakkifejezések és névmagyarázatok jegyzéke [Glossary]. In: J. Mészáros (Ed.), *Ferenczi Sándor: A pszichoanalízis felé. Fiatalkori írások 1897–1908*. [Towards Psychoanalysis: Early Papers 1897–1908] (pp. 411–436). Budapest: Osiris.
Márai, S. (2000)[1933]. Élők és holtak [The quick and the dead]. In: J. Mészáros (Ed.), *In Memoriam Ferenczi Sándor* [In memoriam Sándor Ferenczi] (pp. 47–50). Budapest: Jószöveg Műhely.

Martín Cabré, L. J. (1998). Ferenczi's contribution to the concept of countertransference. *International Forum of Psychoanalysis*, 7: 247–255.

May, U. (2000). Therese Benedek (1892–1977). Freudsche Psychoanalyse im Leipzig der zwanziger Jahre. In: H. Bernhardt & R. Lockot (Eds.), *Mit ohne Freud. Zur Geschichte der Psychoanalyse in Ostdeutschland* (pp. 51–91). Gießen: Psychosozial-Verlag.

McGuire, W. (Ed.) (1994). *The Freud/Jung Letters: The Correspondence Between Sigmund Freud and C. G. Jung* (abridged edn). Princeton, NJ: Princeton University Press.

Mészáros, J. (1993a). Comment on Ferenczi and Schächter. *British Journal of Psychotherapy*, 9(4): 434–435.

Mészáros, J. (1993b). Ferenczi's preanalytic period embedded in the cultural streams of the fin de siècle. In: L. Aron & A. Harris (Eds.), *The Legacy of Sándor Ferenczi* (pp. 41–52). Hillsdale, NJ: Analytic Press.

Mészáros, J. (1996). Interjú Hanna Petovel [Interview with Hanna Peto]. Manuscript.

Mészáros, J. (1997). Interjú Székács Istvánnal [Interview with István Székács]. Manuscript.

Mészáros, J. (1998a). The tragic success of European psychoanalysis: "The Budapest School". *International Forum of Psychoanalysis*, 7: 207–214.

Mészáros, J. (1998b). Entretien avec un patient d'Alice Balint au cours des années trente (Interrogé par Judit Mészáros). *Le Coq-Héron*, 153: 101–115.

Mészáros, J. (Ed.) (1999a). *Ferenczi Sándor: A pszichoanalízis felé. Fiatalkori írások 1897–1908* [Towards Psychoanalysis: Early Papers 1897–1908]. Budapest: Osiris.

Mészáros, J. (1999b). Világpolgárnak született . . . (Portré Bak Róbertről) [Born to be a world citizen: a portrait of Robert Bak]. *Thalassa*, 2–3: 157–170.

Mészáros, J. (Ed.) (2000a). *In Memoriam Ferenczi Sándor* [In memoriam Sándor Ferenczi]. Budapest: Jószöveg Műhely.

Mészáros, J. (2000b). Interjú Herbert Schlesingerrel [Interview with Herbert Schlesinger]. Manuscript.

Mészáros, J. (2002). Ferenczi's trauma theory: solving a dilemma: intra- and interpersonal dynamics of the traumatization process. In: S. Varvin & T. Štajner-Popović (Eds.), *Upheaval: Psychoanalytical Perspectives on Trauma* (pp. 195–205). Belgrade: International Aid Network.

Mészáros, J. (2003). Could Balint have done more for Ferenczi? *American Journal of Psychoanalysis*, 63(3): 239–255.

Mészáros, J. (2004a). 'Budapest School' a School? Yes and No. In: J. Szekacs-Weisz & I. Ward (Eds.), *Lost Childhood and the Language of Exile* (pp. 112–133). London: Freud Museum.

Mészáros, J. (2004b). Psychoanalysis is a two-way street. *International Forum of Psychoanalysis*, 13: 105–113.

Mészáros, J. (2008). "Az Önök Bizottsága" Ferenczi Sándor, a budapesti iskola és a pszichoanalitikus emigráció. ["Your Committee": Sándor Ferenczi, the Budapest School and the psychoanalytic emigration]. Budapest: Akadémiai Kiadó.

Mészáros, J. (2009). Contribution of Hungarian psychoanalysts to psychoanalytic psychosomatics. *American Journal of Psychoanalysis*, 69(3): 207–220.

Mészáros, J. (2010a). Building blocks toward contemporary trauma theory: Ferenczi's paradigm shift. *American Journal of Psychoanalysis*, 70: 328–340.

Mészáros, J. (2010b). Sándor Ferenczi and the Budapest School of psychoanalysis. *Psychoanalytic Perspectives*, 7(1): 69–89.

Mészáros, J. (2012). Effect of dictatorial regimes on the psychoanalytic movement in Hungary before and after World War II. In: J. Damousi & M. B. Plotkin (Eds.), *Psychoanalysis and Politics. History of Psychoanalysis under Conditions of Restricted Political Freedom* (pp. 79–108). New York: Oxford University Press.

Molnar, M. (Ed.) (1992). *The Diary of Sigmund Freud 1929–1939*. London: The Freud Museum.

Mühlleitner, E., & Reichmayr, J. (1995). The exodus of psychoanalysts from Vienna. In: F. Stadler & P. Weibel (Eds.), *The Cultural Exodus from Austria* (pp. 98–121). Vienna: Springer.

Nemes, L. (1985). The fate of the Hungarian psychoanalysts during the time of fascism. In: K. Brecht, V. Friedrich, L. M. Hermanns, I. J. Kaminer, & D. H. Juelich (Eds.), *"Here Life Goes On in a Most Peculiar Way . . .": Psychoanalysts Before and After 1933* (pp. 92–95). London: Goethe-Institut.

Nemes, L. (1994). Adalékok a Ferenczi–Freud viszonyhoz: egy lehetséges interpretáció [Contributions to the Ferenczi-Freud relationship: a possible interpretation]. In: *Alkotó és alkotás. Pszichoanalitikus esszék* [Creator and Creation: Psychoanalytic Essays] (pp. 144–158). Budapest: T-Twins.

Németh, A. (2000). *József Attila pszichiátriai betegségei* [Attila József's Psychiatric Diseases]. Budapest: Filum Kiadó.

Ornstein, P. H. (2002). Michael Balint then and now: a contemporary appraisal. *American Journal of Psychoanalysis*, 62: 25–35.

Palló, G. (2004). *Zsenialitás és korszellem* [Genius and a Spirit of the Age]. Budapest: Áron Kiadó.

Pareja, J. (1986). Oral history. Interview with Dr. George Gero. Archives and Special Collections of the A. A Brill Library. The New York Psychoanalytic Institute. Manuscript.

Paskauskas, R. A. (Ed.) (1993). *The Complete Correspondence of Sigmund Freud and Ernest Jones 1908–1939*. Cambridge, MA: Belknap Press of Harvard University Press.

Peto, A. (1958). The demonic mother image in the Jewish religion. *Psychoanalytic Study of the Child, 5*: 280–287.

Peto, A. (1959). Body image and archaic thinking. *International Journal of Psychoanalysis, 40*: 223–231.

Peto, A. (1961). The fragmentizing function of the ego in the transference neurosis. *International Journal of Psychoanalysis, 42*: 238–245.

Peto, A. (1963). The fragmentizing function of the ego in the analytic session. *International Journal of Psychoanalysis, 44*: 334–338.

Peto, A. (1975). On crowd violence: the role of archaic superego and body image. *International Review of Psycho-Analysis, 2*: 449–466.

Pfitzner, R. (2005). *Kalandozásaim Ferenczi nyomában* [My Adventures in Search of Ferenczi]. Budapest: Animula.

Pléh, C. (2008). *History of the Mind*. Budapest: Akademiai Kiado.

Pléh, C. (2009). Révész Géza – A sors feszültségei levelezése és székfoglalója tükrében [Géza Révész – Tensions of fate in the light of his correspondence and inaugural speech]. *Thalassa, 20*(4): 75–100.

Pollock, G. H. (1977). The Chicago Institute for Psychoanalysis: from 1932 to the present. *Annual of Psychoanalysis, 5*: 3–22.

Rachman, A. W. (1997). *Sándor Ferenczi: The Psychotherapist of Tenderness and Passion*. Northvale, NJ: Jason Aronson.

Rachman, A. W. (2000). Ferenczi's "confusion of tongues" theory and the analysis of the incest trauma. *Psychoanalytic Social Work, 7*: 27–53.

Racker, H. (1957). The meanings and uses of countertransference. *Psychoanalytic Quarterly, 26*: 303–356.

Rado, S. (1969). *Adaptional Psychodynamics: Motivation and Control*, J. Jameson & H. Klein (Eds.). New York: Science House.

Ránki, V. (1999). *Magyarok – Zsidók – Nacionalizmus. A befogadás és a kirekesztés politikája* [Hungarians, Jews, and Nationalism: The Politics of Acceptance and Exclusion]. Budapest: Új Mandátum Könyvkiadó.

Rapaport, D. (1939). *Az asszociáció fogalom-története Bacontól Kantig*. [A History of the Concept of Association from Bacon to Kant]. Budapest: Pázmány Péter Tudományegyetem Lélektani Intézete.

Rapaport, D. (1950)[1942]. *Emotion and Memory* (2nd edn). Baltimore, MD: William & Wilkins. New York: International University Press.
Rapaport, D. (1951). *Organization and Pathology of Thought.* New York: Columbia University Press.
Rapaport, D., Schafer, R., & Gill, M. M. (1945–1946). *Diagnostic Psychological Testing.* Chicago, IL: Year Book Publishers.
Rathkolb, O. (1995). The exodus of jurisprudence. In: F. Stadler & P. Weibel (Eds.), *The Cultural Exodus from Austria* (pp. 160–172). Vienna: Springer.
Reich, A. (1951). On counter-transference. *International Journal of Psychoanalysis, 32*: 25–31.
Roazen, P. (1985). *Helene Deutsch: A Psychoanalist's Life.* New York: New American Library.
Roazen, P. (2001). *Ferenczi (1873–1933),* E. Szendi (Ed.). Film for Hungarian Television.
Roazen, P. (2005). Sandor Rado. Vienna: Psychoanalytic Document Database (www.padd.at).
Roazen, P., & Swerdloff, B. (1995). *Heresy:* Sandor Rado *and the Psychoanalytic Movement.* Northvale, NJ: Jason Aronson.
Róbert-Kelen, L. (1933). Révész Géza dr. amsterdami egyetemi professzor [Dr. Géza Révész, professor at the University of Amsterdam]. *Literatura, 8*(3): 117–119.
Róheim, G. (1918). Psychoanalysis és ethnologia II. A symbolumok tartalma és a libido fejlődéstörténete [Psychoanalysis and ethnology II: The content of symbols and the development of the libido]. *Ethnographia, 29*: 206–245.
Róheim, G. (1992)[1932]. *A csurunga népe* [The People of the Tjurunga]. Budapest: Leblang Könyvkiadé [reprinted Budapest: Párbeszéd Kiadó].
Rolf, J., Masten, A. S., Cichetti, D., Neuchterlein, K. H., & Weintraub, S. (Eds.) (1990). *Risk and Protective Factors in the Development of Psychopathology.* New York: Cambridge University Press.
Rudnytsky, P. L. (1996). Introduction. In: P. L. Rudnytsky, A. Bókay, & P. Giampieri-Deutsch (Eds.), *Ferenczi's Turn in Psychoanalysis* (pp. 1–22). New York: New York University Press.
Rudnytsky, P. L. (2002). *Reading Psychoanalysis: Freud, Rank, Ferenczi, Groddeck.* Ithaca, NY: Cornell University Press.
Sabourin, P. (1985). *Ferenczi. Paladin et grand vizir secret.* Paris: Editions Universitaires.
Sabourin, P. (2011). *Sándor Ferenczi. Un pionnier de la clinique.* Paris: Campagne Première.

Schächter, M. (1909). Szerkesztőségi vezércikk [Editorial]. *Gyógyászat* [Therapy], *49*: 22.
Schiess, R. (1999). *Wie das Leben nach dem Fieber*. Gießen: Psychosozial-Verlag.
Schönberger, S. (1939). A dream of Descartes: reflections on the unconscious determinants of the sciences. *International Journal of Psychoanalysis*, *20*: 43–57.
Schröter, M. (1995). Edith Gyömrői (1896–1987). Eine biographische Skizze. *Luzifer-Amor. Zeitschrift zur Geschichte der Psychoanalyse*, 8 Jg., H. *16*(3): 102–115.
Schröter, M. (2011). Ein Memorandum Freuds für Budapest (Marz 1919). "Soll die Psychoanalyse an den Universitäten gelehrt werden?" Bemerkungen zum Entstehungskontext und Abdruck des verschollenen Originals. In: A. Berger, F. Henningsen, L. M. Hermanns, & J. C. Togay (Eds.), *Der psychoanalytische Aufbruch. Budapest–Berlin 1918–1920* (pp. 85–114). Frankfurt: Brandes & Apsel.
Silver, A.-L. (1996). Ferenczi's early impact on Washington, D.C. In: P. L. Rudnytsky, A. Bókay, & P. Giampieri-Deutsch (Eds.), *Ferenczi's Turn in Psychoanalysis* (pp. 89–106). New York: New York University Press.
Simmel, E. (2000)[1933]. Ferenczi Sándor emlékbeszéd [Sándor Ferenczi memorial speech]. In: J. Mészáros (Ed.), *In Memoriam Ferenczi Sándor* [In memoriam Sándor Ferenczi] (pp. 80–96). Budapest: Jószöveg Műhely.
Spitz, R. A. (1945). Hospitalism: an inquiry into the genesis of psychiatric conditions in early childhood. *Psychoanalytic Study of the Child*, *1*: 53–74.
Spitz, R. A. (1983). *Dialogues from Infancy: Selected Papers*, R. N. Emde (Ed.). New York: International Universities Press.
Spitz, R. A., & Wolf, K. M. (1946). Anaclitic depression – an inquiry into the genesis of psychiatric conditions in childhood. *Psychoanalytic Study of the Child*, *2*: 313–342.
Stark, A., & Bókay, A. (1980). "Köztetek lettem bolond". Bak Róbert József Attila patográfiájának újraértelmezése ["It was among you people that I went mad": Reinterpreting Robert Bak's pathography of Attila József]. In: M. Szabolcsi & E. Erdődy (Eds.), *József Attila útjain. Tanulmányok* [On the Paths of Attila József: Studies]. Budapest: Kossuth.
Steiner, R. (2000). *"It is a New Kind of Diaspora": Explorations in the Sociopolitical and Cultural Context of Psychoanalysis*. London: Karnac.
Steiner, R. (2005). Einige Bemerkungen über die theoretischen und klinischen Entwicklungen in der Psychoanalyse nach Auflösung der Wiener

Psychoanalytischen Vereinigung. In: Wiener Psychoanalytische Vereinigung (Ed.), *Trauma der Psychoanalyse? Die Vertreibung der Psychoanalyse aus Wien 1938 und die Folgen* (pp. 119–143). Vienna: Mille Tre Verlag.

Stewart, W. A. (1975). Robert C. Bak, M.D. 1908–1974. *Psychoanalytic Quarterly*, 44(4): 638–639.

Swerdloff, B. (2002). An interview with Michael Balint. *American Journal of Psychoanalysis*, 62(4): 383–413.

Székács, I. (1981–1982). Hári Pál professzor: egy orvostudományi iskola a numerus clausus idején [Professor Pál Hári: A faculty of medicine in the *numerus clausus* period]. In: *Évkönyv* [Annual] (Ed. S. Scheiber). Budapest: Magyar Izraeliták Országos Képviselete.

Székács-Schönberger, I. (2007). *Egy zsidó polgár gyermekkora analitikus háttérrel* [A Middle-Class Jewish Childhood Through the Lens of a Psychoanalyst]. Budapest: Múlt és Jövő.

Szekacs-Weisz, J., & Keve, T. (Eds.) (2012). *Ferenczi and His World: Rekindling the Spirit of the Budapest School*. London: Karnac.

Takács, M. (2002). Előszó Hollós István nyelvelméleti kéziratához [Foreword to István Hollós's manuscript on language theory]. *Thalassa*, 13(1–2): 66–76.

Target, M. (1998). A kötődés reprezentációja súlyos személyiségzavarban szenvedő betegeknél [Representation of attachment in patients suffering from serious personality disorder]. *Thalassa*, 9(1): 44–55.

Thompson, C. M. (1988). Sándor Ferenczi, 1873–1933. *Contemporary Psychoanalysis*, 24: 182–195.

Thompson, N. L. (2012). The transformation of psychoanalysis in America: émigré analysts and the New York Psychoanalytic Society and Institute, 1935–1961. *Journal of the American Psychoanalytic Association*, 60: 9–44.

Tögel, C. (2000). *Varga Jenő, a pszichoanalízis, a Tanácsköztársaság és a sztálinizmus* [Jenő Varga, psychoanalysis, the Soviet Republic, and Stalinism], A. Gromon (Trans.). *Thalassa*, 11(2–3): 207–219.

Vajda, B. (2005). *Sigmund Freud és a XX. század eleji magyar irodalom* [Sigmund Freud and Early 20th-Century Hungarian Literature]. Pozsony (Bratislava): AB-Art Könyvkiadó.

Valachi, A. (2005). "Bolondot játszottak velem..." József Attila és az elmebetegség stigmája. ["They made a fool of me": Attila József and the stigma of mental disease]. *Új Forrás* [New Source] 37(6): 30–45; revised version: In: A. Valachi: *"Irgalom, édesanyám..." A lélekelemző József Attila nyomában* ["Mercy, mother": In Search of the Psychoanalytic Attila József] (pp. 413–434). Budapest: Háttér Kiadó.

Varvin, S. (2009). Trauma e resilienza [Trauma and resilience]. Trauma e psicoanalisi [Trauma and Psychoanalysis]. *Rivista di Psicoanalisi applicata "Frenis Zero", (12) 6.*

Verebélyi, K. (1990). *Róheim Géza.* Budapest: Akademiai Kiado.

Verebélyi, K. (2005). *Géza Róheim.* Vienna: Psychoanalytic Document Database (www.padd.at).

Vida, J. E. (2005). Treating the "wise baby". *The American Journal of Psychoanalysis, 65:* 3–12.

Werner, E. E. (1990). Protective factors and individual resilience. In: S. J. Meisels & M. Shonkoff (Eds.), *Handbook of Early Intervention* (pp. 97–116). New York: Cambridge University Press.

Winnicott, D. W. (1949). Hate in the countertransference. *International Journal of Psychoanalysis, 30:* 69–74.

Winnicott, D. W. (1967). Mirror-role of the mother and family in child development. In: P. Lomas (Ed.), *The Predicament of the Family: A Psycho-Analytical Symposium* (pp. 26–33). London: Hogarth.

Winnicott, D. W. (1971). *Playing and Reality.* London: Tavistock.

Zsoldos, S. (1996). Ferenczi Sándor, a *Jövendő* munkatársa [Sándor Ferenczi, *Jövendő* (Year) contributor]. *Thalassa,* 2: 137–140.

INDEX

Abraham, K., xxiii, 36, 41, 63, 65, 68–69, 102, 107, 225–226
aggression/aggressor, 20, 87, 187, 210, 213
Ágoston, T., 166–168, 181, 236
Agoston, T., 61, 168, 179, 181
alcohol, 19–20
  anti-, 13
Alexander, F., xiv, xxvii, 60–61, 65, 67, 70, 102, 105–108, 119, 129–130, 174, 181, 193–195, 207, 216–217
Almásy, E., 72, 83, 86, 102, 148
Amar, R., 158–159
America/USA
  Census of 1910, 91
  consuls, 92, 94–100, 111, 116–118, 178, 229–230 *see also*: Consular Bureau
  foreign policy, xxvi, 89, 110, 229
  government, 89–90, 92–94, 97, 114
  immigration policy, xiv–xv, xxvi, 58, 89, 95, 97, 127, 178
  Labour Department, 94, 96–97, 117, 178
  Secretary of Labour, 92–93
  Secretary of State, 93–94, 111–112, 229–231
    Deputy, 111
    Under-, 94, 97
  State Department, 90–92, 94–97, 99, 111, 114, 116–117, 178, 230
  unemployment, 93, 95, 97–98
American Psychoanalytic Association (APsaA), xv, xxvi, 89, 105, 108–110, 113, 115, 120, 124, 128, 173–174, 228–229
Anderson, A. R., 109
Anon, 16, 39, 169, 225
anti-Semitism, xxiii, 52, 56–58, 90, 97–98, 107, 135
  law, 133–134, 166, 172, 219, 223, 232

INDEX

Antonovsky, A., 215
anxiety, 34, 42, 111, 124, 127, 162, 188, 198, 200, 209, 212–214
    attacks, 174
    separation, 212
    states of, 17, 41
Apfel, R. J., 215
Aron, L., 237
Aster Revolution, 51, 54
Atkin, S., 166–168, 236
attachment, 2, 205, 233
    theory, 205–206, 215
Austria/Austrian, xv, 36, 49, 57, 62, 87–88, 92, 99–101, 110–111, 116, 118, 124–126, 164, 169 *see also*: Jews/Jewish
    Anschluss, xv, xxii, xxvi, 88–89, 99–101, 105, 107, 110, 115–116, 124, 127, 133, 135, 138, 142, 165, 228
    -Hungary, xix, 51, 59, 226
    Labour Service, 163

B. Gáspár, J., 208
Bak, R. C., 20, 61, 80, 103, 155, 158–165, 169, 179, 181, 184, 217, 235
Balazs, B., 58–59, 66
Bálint, A., 60, 70, 72, 86, 102, 143, 181, 200, 228
Balint, A., xiv, xxii, 32, 60, 66–67, 73–74, 77–78, 83, 85, 88, 142–146, 148, 152–153, 155, 157, 162, 184–186, 200, 206, 234
Bálint, M., 60, 70, 72, 86, 102, 143, 181, 200, 228
Balint, M., xiv, xxii, xxvii, 12–13, 32, 60, 66–67, 73–74, 78, 83, 88, 142–146, 148, 153, 155, 157, 165, 184–190, 192–193, 198, 200–202, 206–207, 209, 217, 228, 234, 238
Bánfalvi, A., 197
Bartemeier, L. H., 106
Bartók, B., 25, 59
Batizfalvy sanatorium, 45, 53

Békés, V., 224
Benedek, T., xxvii, 60–61, 67–70, 73, 102, 163, 181, 184, 186, 206, 209, 217
Berény, R., 14, 25, 27, 223
Berlin
    Institute, 63–64, 69, 106–108
    model, 64, 119, 125, 216
    Psychoanalytic Institute, 68, 107, 119, 177
    Psychoanalytic Society, 65, 177, 237
Berman, E., 224, 237
Bognár, Z., 227
Bokanowsky, T., 237
Bókay, A., 163, 227
Bókay, J., 47
Bolshevism, 56, 90–91
Bonaparte, M., 75, 111, 230
Bonomi, C., 210, 232, 234, 237
borderline
    cases, 109, 208
    condition, 161–162
    patients, 122, 206
    personality disorder, 80, 208
    syndrome, 230
Borgogno, F., 188, 210, 237
Borgos, A., 67, 235
Boston Psychoanalytic Society, 105, 107, 230
Bowlby, J., 205, 212, 215
Brabant, E., 21–22, 31, 41, 48, 55–57, 63, 65, 82–83, 85, 87, 129
Braham, R. L., 56
Brecht, K., 150
Breitman, R., 90–93, 96–98, 100–101, 118, 229
Brennan, B. W., 207, 222
Brill, A. A., 64, 119, 129, 195, 226
    Library, 114, 168, 226, 231–232, 236–237
British Psychoanalytical Society (BPS), xxvi–xxvii, 32, 66, 112, 114, 135–136, 139, 148, 154, 157, 174, 209, 228, 230–235

INDEX 263

Bródy, S., 14, 102, 223
Budapest Royal Medical Society, 13, 22, 24, 54
Budapest School, xiii–xv, xix–xxiv, xxvii, 1–3, 7, 14, 20, 23, 32–33, 36, 71, 73–75, 77, 87, 125, 153, 155, 183, 185–186, 193, 196, 217–219, 223, 233
Budapest University, 68, 169, 184, 189
Bulletin, 124

Carr, W. J., 97–98
case study
  B, 203–204
Chicago Institute for Psychoanalysis, 95, 108, 130, 181, 194, 207, 209, 216
Chicago Psychoanalytic Society, 105
Chused, J. F., 205
Cichetti, D., 215
Coles, R., 215
communism/communists, 29, 56, 66, 148–149, 180, 235–236
communities, xxvi, 29, 76, 85, 123–124, 149, 184, 218
  analytic, xv, 82, 209
  populated, xv, 124
  professional, 110, 113, 119, 163, 179, 201, 235
  psychoanalytic, xxvii, 3, 42, 75, 87, 119, 124–126, 146, 148–149, 152, 180, 218
concentration camp(s), 97, 100, 116, 118, 148, 228
Conci, M., 198
conscious(ness), 5, 7, 9, 13, 16–17, 24, 193, 195, 205, 213 *see also*: self, unconscious(ness)
  human, 4–5
  mind, 73
  semi-, 4–6, 24
Consular Bureau, 97, 101, 114
countertransference, 8, 72, 86, 153, 169, 185–186, 192, 194, 196–205, 207–209 *see also*: transference

Csáth, G., xix, 78
Cziner, A., 48, 102 *see also*: Hermann, A.

Daniels, G., 105, 110
Darwin, C., 4–5, 18, 28
de Forest, I., 102, 207
depression, 19, 65, 127, 146, 179
  see also: Great Depression
  anaclitic, 189
Deri, S., 61, 159, 181
Deutsch, F., 107, 237
Deutsch, H., 103, 105–107, 169, 190, 199, 230
Devereux, G., 60, 67, 70, 181, 227
Dobó, G., 60, 67, 70
dream(s), 4, 15–16, 24, 28, 34, 55, 63, 76, 34, 221, 227
  interpretation of, xx, 4, 16, 28, 31, 45 *see also*: Freud, S.
  theory, 15, 28
Dubovitz, M., 102–103, 158–159
Dugan, T. F., 215
Dukes, G., 102, 158–159, 180
Dupont, J., 185, 210, 234, 237

ego, 6, 20, 28, 42, 73, 162, 166, 173, 199, 202, 212
  alter, 77
  defence mechanism, 88, 211–213
  ideal, 20
  super, 20, 36, 77, 199
Eisler, M. J., 80, 83, 102, 227
Eitingon, M., 41, 63, 83, 228
Ellman, S. J., 205
Emergency Committee on Relief and Immigration, xv, xxi–xxii, xxvi, 89, 95, 101, 105–106, 110–113, 115–118, 120–122, 124, 127, 157–160, 163–164, 166, 168–170, 172, 176, 178–180, 184, 219–220, 229–232, 235, 237
Erős, F., 22, 31, 40–41, 45, 227, 232, 237
experimental psychology, 47–49, 173, 177, 189, 205

264   INDEX

experimentation, 1, 4–7, 9–10, 13, 15, 17, 21, 34, 41, 47, 71, 82, 189, 191, 202, 205, 207

Falzeder, E., 21–22, 31, 36, 41, 48, 55–57, 63, 65, 82–83, 85, 87, 129, 202, 225
fantasy, 108, 199, 211–212
Farkashazi, M., 102, 158–159
fascism/fascists, 80, 92, 99, 184, 189, 231, 236
Faulkner, H. J., 174–175
Federn, P., 74, 88, 103, 130, 228
Feigin, S., 167, 236
Feldman, S., 61, 78, 166, 169–170, 179, 181, 236
Fenichel, O., 65–68, 88, 103, 150, 177, 228, 235
Ferenczi, G., 72, 76, 78, 224
Ferenczi, S. (*passim*) *see also*:
    International Ferenczi Centre, Sándor Ferenczi Society
    Budapest Psychoanalytic Family Tree, 102–103, 222
    cited works, 1, 4–12, 15–21, 24, 29, 34, 42, 44–45, 54–55, 70–71, 79, 84–85, 162, 186–187, 190–191, 196–199, 208, 210, 213, 215–216, 221, 224, 233
    Clinical Diary, 2, 7, 21, 84, 185–186, 191, 197, 210
    enfant terrible, 1–2, 8, 187, 221
    "wise baby", 1–2, 215, 221
Fermi, L., 98, 229
Fisch, A., 103, 159, 235
folk
    belief, 75, 77, 227
    customs, 75, 77
    -lore, 75–76
    song, 33
Fonagy, P., 205–206, 208, 215
Ford, H., 90, 107
Fortune, C., 84, 191, 224, 237
Frank, T., 51, 56, 59, 62, 145, 223, 226, 229

Frankel, J. B., 210
Frankfurter, F., 92, 94
free association, xix, 13, 16, 80
French, T. M., 105–106, 108, 110, 207
Freud, A., xxvii, 13, 66, 87–88, 100, 107, 127–128, 213, 228
Freud, S. (*passim*)
    cited works, xxiii, 4, 16, 23, 26, 28, 34, 36, 39, 44, 72, 99, 195, 199, 210–212
    Interpretation of Dreams, 4, 15–16, 21, 34, 177
    Prize, 67, 75
Freund, A., xxiii, 32–33, 43–44, 49, 54, 78, 83, 102, 225–226
Freund, K., 78, 103, 159, 225 *see also*: Lévy, K.
Fromm, E., 79, 120–121, 178, 188, 231–232
Funk, R., 121, 231
Füst, M., 78, 103, 227

Gábor, E., 226
Galileo Circle, 26–27, 31–32, 43, 68, 147
Gedo, J., 209
General Workers' Sick-Benefits Society, 19
Gergely, G., 186, 205, 208
German/Germany *see*: Gestapo, Hitler, A., Jews/Jewish, Nazi(s)/Nazism, Third Reich, Weimar Republic
German Psychoanalytic Society, 69, 121
Gerő, G., 60, 67, 70, 102, 148, 150, 176–179, 184
Gero, G., 61, 176, 179, 181, 237
Gerő, V., 153
Gero-Brabant, E., 237
Gestapo, 100, 150
Giampieri-Deutsch P., 21–22, 31, 41, 48, 55–57, 63, 65, 82–83, 85, 87, 129
Giampieri Spanghero, P., 40, 45

Gifford, S., 230
Gill, M. M., 172–173, 227
Gimes, M., 32, 102, 147, 149, 158–159, 180
Gitelson, M., 201
Glover, E., 66, 106, 128, 130, 200–201, 209
Göring, H., 97, 100, 118
Great Depression, 91, 93
Groddeck, G., 78, 84, 102, 190–191, 224, 238
Grosskurth, P., 73
Grotjahn, M., 194
Gyógyászat (Therapy), 8–12, 14, 24, 26–27, 39, 41, 83, 222–223, 228
Gyömrői, E., xix, 32, 60, 66–67, 70, 78, 80, 103, 149–151, 153, 157, 162, 181, 225, 235 see also: Rényi, E.
Gyömrői-Ludowyk, E., 60, 225, 235
Gyömrői-Újvári, E., 61, 148, 157, 225, 235

Haeckel, E., 4–6, 42
Hajdu, L., 12, 32, 75, 147–148, 234
Hajdu Gimes, L., 72, 146, 148–149, 158–159, 180, 234
Hann-Kende, F. (von), 61, 86, 102–103, 155, 166, 168–169, 179, 181, 184, 199–200, 206, 236
Harmat, P., 13, 40, 48, 88, 224, 237
Hárnik, J., 32, 60, 62, 65, 68, 70, 226
Harris, A., 237
Hárs, G. P., 78
Hartmann, H., 68, 107, 179
Haynal, A., 5, 71, 185, 197, 202, 212, 224, 234, 237
Heimann, P., 201
Hermann, A., 48, 72, 79, 148, 159
Hermann, I., 32, 48, 64, 72–73, 78–79, 83, 85–86, 88, 103, 148, 153, 157–159, 162, 228, 236
Hermanns, L. M., 150
Hidas, G., 5

Higgitt, A., 215
Hill, L. B., 105, 109–110
Hitler, A., xxvi, 66–67, 69, 87, 93, 118, 135, 177–178, 231
Germany, 93, 135
laws, 98
Hoffer, A., 197, 234
Hoffer, P. T., 234
Hoffer, W., 107
Hollós, I., 103, 136–138, 146, 148, 151, 153, 157–159, 162, 168, 180, 224, 228, 232, 235
Holocaust, xxvi, 92, 95, 180
Honvédorvos (Army Doctor), 11, 222
Hoover, H., 91, 93–94, 98
Horney, K., 129–131, 212, 217, 231
Horthy, M. (Admiral), 51, 56
Hull, C., 94, 111–112, 229–231
Hungarian Academy of Sciences, 41, 224
Hungarian Psychoanalytical Society, xxv, 12, 14, 32, 53–54, 65, 68–70, 82, 134, 143, 147, 151–152, 162, 165–166, 169–170, 216, 223, 228
Huszadik Század (Twentieth Century), 26, 31
hypnosis, 4, 16–17, 172
hysteria, 4, 16–17, 29, 34, 42, 197, 211

id, 77, 199
Ignotus, H., xix, 14–15, 26–28, 30, 32, 34, 59, 69–70, 80, 86, 102, 223, 228 see also: Veigelsberg, H.
Imago, 68, 87, 227
Immigration Act (1924), 95
intelligentsia, xxii–xxiii, 14, 24–25, 27, 33, 98, 107
International Ferenczi Centre, xiii, 35, 40, 44, 72, 74, 79, 143, 171, 195
International Journal of Psychoanalysis, The, 87, 183, 227, 236

International Psychoanalytical
    Association (IPA), xix, xxv,
    xxvi, 12, 26, 32, 43, 54–55, 100,
    110, 113–114, 120, 128–129, 134,
    163, 178, 216, 219, 231
    Congress, 152, 238

Jacobs, T. J., 119
Jacobson, E., 66–67, 150, 179
Jadi, F., 227
Jászi, O., 31, 56
Jeffrey, W. D., 105, 115
Jendrassik, E., 44–45
Jews/Jewish, xv, 53, 56–57, 59, 87,
    90–93, 97–100, 107–108, 115,
    118, 133–134, 149, 164–165, 170,
    174 see also: anti-Semitism,
    Holocaust
    American, 90–92, 97–98
    Austrian, 101, 116, 118
    Czech, 101
    European, 97–98, 101, 164, 174,
        229
    faith, 57
    German, 93, 96–97, 101
    Hungarian, 57, 59, 134
    Labour Service, 163
    law (anti-), 133–135
    persecution of, 57, 62, 97, 116, 118
    students, xv, 52–53, 56–57, 133,
        229
    victims, 62, 92
Johns Hopkins University, 106, 109,
    229
Johnson–Reed Immigration Act,
    90–91
Jones, E., xiv, xxvi–xxvii, 32, 36, 47,
    54–55, 65–66, 102, 108, 114, 116,
    119–122, 126–130, 134–135, 139,
    141–142, 148–157, 174–175, 200,
    210, 226, 228–229, 232–235
Joszef, A., xix, 25, 80–81, 103, 143,
    162, 170, 227
Jövendő (Future), 14, 222
Juelich, D. H., 150
Jung, C. G., 13, 21, 107

Kahtuni, H. C., 237
Kaminer, I. J., 150
Kapas, I., 40, 45
Kapos, V., 102–103, 151, 155, 158,
    160
Kapronczay, K., 40, 54
Kapusi, K., 3
Kardos, E., 102, 148, 151, 153,
    157–158, 160, 164–165, 180, 236
    see also: Peto, E.
Karinthy, F., 27, 78, 102, 147,
    227–228
Kármán, T., 48, 58
Kassai, G., 27, 227
Kaufman, M. R., 105, 108, 110
Kelley-Lainé, K., 237
Kende, Z., 32
Kernstok, K., 25, 59
Keve, T., 237
Kilborne, B., 227
King, P., 66
Kiss, G., 40, 45, 54
Klein, M., xxvii, 60, 62, 65–67, 70,
    73–74, 102, 127–128, 184, 187
Knight, R. P., 171
Kohut, H., 188, 198
Kolb, L., 226
Kosztolányi, D., xxii, 25, 27, 35, 71,
    77–78, 147, 191, 228
Kovács, F., 72
Kovács, M., 53
Kovács, V., 64, 72, 78, 83, 86, 102,
    141, 146, 152–153, 162, 169, 184,
    201–202, 228, 234
Kraut, A. M., 90–93, 96–98,
    100–101, 118, 229
Kubie, L. S., xv, 105–107, 109–110,
    112–119, 121–122, 128, 130–131,
    133–138, 146, 149–150, 157, 178,
    180, 229–230, 232, 234–235, 237
Kurzweil, E., 117, 131

Landauer, C., 88
Landauer, K., 228, 231
Lantos, B., 60, 69, 103, 150
Laplanche, J., 202

Lázár-Gerő, K., 61, 72, 86, 102, 144, 148, 153, 156–157, 165, 181, 184, 217
Lazar-Geroe, C., 61, 102, 144, 148, 150, 165
Lévy, K., 78, 103, 151, 158–159
  see also: Freund, K.
Lévy, L., 12–15, 32, 44, 72, 78, 86, 103, 190, 192, 225, 228
Lewin, B. D., xv, 105–106, 113, 115, 230
Lewin, K., 177
Lewin Fund, 113
libido, 6, 42, 73, 163, 200, 212
  see also: sexual hunger
Little, M., 201
Loewenstein, R. M., 230
Lóránd, S., 51, 60–62, 64, 70, 103, 181, 217, 226, 228
Lorin, C., 16
Losonczi, A., 134

Magyar, L., 223
Mahler, M., xxvii, 60–61, 67, 70, 73, 181, 184, 188, 212
Major, I., 158–159
Manó, D., 32–33
Márai, S., xix, xxii, 25, 27, 59, 191–192, 228
Martín Cabré, L. J., 204
Masten, A. S., 215
May, U., 69
McGuire, W., 21
memory, 7–8, 13, 73, 107, 196, 206, 211–212
Menninger, K., 172, 174–176, 217
  Clinic, xxvi, 130, 170, 172–174, 176, 221, 228
Messersmith, G. S., 97–98, 101, 118, 229
Mészáros, J., xiii–xv, xvii–xx, 5–6, 9, 11, 15, 54, 57, 71, 83, 86, 105, 133–134, 141, 144–145, 152, 162–163, 165–166, 169, 173–174, 176, 186, 191–193, 196, 201, 209–210, 221, 223, 225, 233–238

Meyer, M. A., 105, 109
Möbius, P., 16, 20–21, 223
Molnar, M., 87, 99–100
mother
  –child relationship, xxvii, 21, 68, 73, 76, 155, 186, 188–190
  good enough, 188
Mühlleitner, E., 232
Murray, H. A., 105, 107

narcissism, 28, 42, 73–74, 83, 85, 187–188, 199, 204
National Institute for Psychiatry and Neurology, 14, 75, 148, 226
National Medical Board, 47
National Refugee Service, 158–159, 167
Nazi(s)/Nazism, xiv–xv, xxi, xxvi, 92–93, 97–100, 115–116, 118, 145–146, 150, 156, 219, 238
  see also: German/Germany, Hitler, A., Third Reich, 91, 94, 98, 145
Nemes, L., 222, 236
Németh, A., 162–163
Neuchterlein, K. H., 215
Neumann, J., xix, xxv
New School for Social Research, The, 77, 81–82, 98
New York Psychoanalytic Society and Institute, xxvi, 64, 105–106, 108–109, 114, 119, 129, 142, 160, 164, 166–169, 173, 178, 181, 216–217, 226, 230–232, 235–237
New York Times, The, 82, 93
numerus clausus, xv, 56–58, 133–134, 164
  Act, 52
Nuremberg Laws, 99, 134
Nyolcak (the Eight), 25, 27, 223–224
Nyugat (West), xix, 14, 25–28, 33, 77–78, 223

object, 20, 42, 73, 162, 186
  cultic, 76
  external, 73

love, 73–74, 186–187
relations, 73–74, 155, 161,
    186–189, 193, 205, 210–212
ritual, 227
self-, 198
objective/objectivity, 5, 193, 196
Ormos, M., 158, 160
Ornstein, P. H., 188–189
Orvosi Hetilap (Medical Weekly),
    10, 16, 222

Palló, G., 58
Pálos, E., 102–103, 224
Pareja, J., 177, 179
Paskauskas, R. A., 47, 55, 65,
    233–234
Perkins, F., 92–95, 97, 101
Perl-Balla, L., 158, 160
Peto, A., 61, 102, 159–160, 164, 166,
    181
Pető, E., 148, 153, 155, 157–160, 162,
    164–166, 169, 184, 217
Peto, E., 160 *see also*: Kardos, E.
Pető, H., 164, 166
Peto, H., 165, 236
Pfeifer, Z., 12, 32, 83, 102–103,
    151–153, 157–159, 161, 180, 228,
    235
Pfitzner, R., 6
Pléh, C., 67, 173, 226
Polányi, K., 31, 147
Polányi, M., 31–32, 58, 147–148,
    225
Polanyi, M., 145, 225
Pollock, G. H., 69, 217
Pontalis, J. B., 202
post traumatic stress disorder
    (PTSD), 34, 214
Pragier, G., 237
Pruitt, V. D., 174–175
Public Charge
    Bond, 96–97
    Clause, 91, 93, 95–96, 229

Rachman, A. W., 210, 237
Racker, H., 201

Radó, S., xiv, xxvii, 14–15, 27, 32,
    45, 47, 54, 60, 62–65, 67–68, 70,
    82, 102, 177, 216–217, 228
Rado, S., 61, 105–106, 108, 110, 119,
    130–131, 164, 169, 179, 181, 185,
    235–236
Rajka, T., 103, 155, 172
Rank, O., 68, 196, 198–199
Ránki, V., 133
Rapaport, D., xxvii, 61, 103, 166,
    170–176, 179, 181, 184, 217
Rapaport, S., 80, 170
Rathkolb, O., 99
Reich, A., 66, 150, 179, 201
Reich, T., 88
Reich, W., 66, 68, 79, 107, 150, 177
Reichmayr, J., 232
Reik, T., 107, 228
Renik, O., 205
Rényi, E., 32, 225 *see also*:
    Gyömrői, E.
repression, 7, 9, 16, 20–21, 29, 31,
    36, 73, 130, 138, 187, 191, 200
Révész, G., 32, 47–49, 226
Révész, L., 103, 158–159, 180, 228
Rickman, J., 103, 138–140, 142–143,
    233
Roazen, P., 47, 63, 68, 107, 183, 185
Róbert-Kelen, L., 49
Róheim, G., 32–33, 61, 75–77, 80,
    102–103, 138–142, 148, 152, 157,
    161, 166, 181, 230, 233
Róheim, I., 72, 76, 138
Rókus Hospital, 9, 12, 17
Rolf, J., 215
Roosevelt, F. D., 90, 92–95, 100–101,
    111, 229
    administration, xv, 101
Rothstein, A., 205
Rotter-Kertész, L., 72, 86, 88, 103,
    148, 158–159
Rubin Farber, Z., 158, 160
Rudnytsky, P. L., 237

Sabourin, P., 237
Sachs, H., 66–67, 102, 231

Sanches, G. P., 237
Sándor Ferenczi Society, 35, 40, 44,
    72, 74, 79, 143, 149, 161, 171,
    195, 226, 235
Schächter, M., 9–12, 36
Schafer, R., 173
Schiess, R., 234
schizophrenia, 109, 146–147,
    160–161, 163, 176, 198
Schlesinger, H. J., 173–176
Schönberger, S., 148, 159, 235
Schröter, M., 44, 235
self, 20, 24, 198, 205, 208, 212
    see also: object
    -confidence, 17
    -conscious(ness), 5
    -development, 88
    -discipline, 55
    -healing, 191
    love, 20, 28
    observation, 15
    -reflection, 1–2, 7–8, 24, 144, 197
sexual, 200, 210
    desires, 22
    deviance, 24
    disorders, 4, 18
    drive, 6
    energy, 6
    events, 211
    experience, 211
    hunger, 42 see also: libido
    intercourse, 18
    matters, 11
    pathogenesis, 16, 24
    practices, 76
    problems, xx
    prying, 82
    psycho-, 65
    seduction, 212
    stage, 19
    theory, 31
    trauma, 210–211
sexuality, 31
    female, 86, 230
    homo-, 18–19, 62
    trans-, 18

Silver, A.-L., 81
Simmel, E., 190, 225–226, 228,
    237–238
Simon, B., 215
social sciences, xxv, 26, 106
    Free University, 26–27, 31
    Society for the, 26, 31
Soviet
    Republic of Hungary, 45, 47–48,
        51, 53–54, 56, 58, 62–63, 65,
        169
    Russia, 51, 63
    Union, 178, 226
spiritism, 4–5, 9–10, 222
Spitz, R. A., xxvii, 32, 60–61, 67, 70,
    73, 102, 148, 181, 184–185, 189,
    212
Stark, A., 163, 227
Steele, H., 215
Steele, M., 215
Stein, F., 13, 16, 21–22
Steiner, R., 66, 128, 139, 232–233,
    235
Stern, A., 169, 236
Stewart, W. A., 161
subjective, 212
    inter-, 197, 203, 206, 208, 211
    truth, 5–6, 196
Sullivan, H. S., 81, 130, 188, 198,
    231
Swerdloff, B., 47, 63, 142, 145–146,
    185
symbol(-ism), xx, 6, 28, 42, 69,
    86–87, 122, 190–191, 193,
    227
Századunk (Our Century), 77, 80
Székács, I., 56
Székács-Schönberger, I., 59, 72, 83,
    103, 138, 148, 151–155, 157,
    158–159, 162, 165, 169, 180, 184,
    235
Szekacs-Weisz, J., 237
Szép Szó (Beautiful Word), 77, 80
Szilágyi, G., 32, 103
Szilárd, L., xxv, 58
Szuts, J., 158–159

Takács, M., 14, 28
Target, M., 205–206, 208, 215
Tavistock Clinic, 145–146, 209
Teller, E., xix, xxv, 58
Thematic Apperception Test (TAT), 107
Third Reich, 95, 97–99, 118
Thompson, C. M., 81, 103, 130, 188, 207–208
Thompson, N. L., 105, 160, 237
tjurunga, 76, 227
Tögel, C., 63, 226
Tölgy, L., 66, 235
transference, 7, 72, 83, 85, 169, 192–193, 195–196, 198–202, 204–205, 207 see also: countertransference
trauma/traumatic, xiv, xvi, 34, 57, 84, 155, 198, 206–207, 210–215 see also: post traumatic stress disorder, sexual, war
experience(s), 9, 34, 73, 196, 204, 207, 209, 211–212, 214–215
neurosis, 17, 19, 41–42
theory, 6, 71, 108, 186, 210–212, 215

unconscious(ness), 4–7, 15, 21–22, 33, 72, 74, 122, 190–193, 195, 198–200, 202–202, 204–205, 207 see also conscious(ness)
conflicts, 22, 191
desire, 203–204
phenomena, 24
process(es), 28, 198–199

Vajda, B., 227
Valachi, A., 163, 227
Varga, J., 32, 60, 62, 70, 226
Varvin, S., 215
Veigelsberg, H., 27, 223 see also: Ignotus, H.
Verebélyi, K., 76
Vida, J. E., 210
Vienna Psychoanalytic Society, 63, 99, 189, 228, 232

Világ (World), 41, 78, 225
Volker, F., 150

war, xvii, 3, 28–29, 32, 34–36, 39, 41, 43, 49, 51, 63, 69, 92, 118, 128, 148, 164, 169, 174
Cold, 201
First World, xiv, xxiii, 14, 28, 32, 48, 51, 62, 67, 90, 107, 109, 229
neuroses, xxiii, 12, 34, 39, 41, 43, 225
Refugee Board, 95
Second World, xiii, xxiv, 148, 199, 201, 227, 229
trauma, 34, 41
Warburg, B., xv, 106, 113, 115, 166–168, 237
Washington Baltimore Psychoanalytic Society, 105, 109, 121
Watson, J. S., 186
Weimar Republic, 62, 68, 156
Weintraub, S., 215
Weiss, E., 88, 130, 228, 232
Werner, E. E., 215
White Anglo-Saxon Protestant (WASP), 90–91
White Terror, 51, 53, 56–58, 62, 226
Wiley, J. C., 111, 118, 230
Wilson, H. R., 111, 230
Winn, R., 151, 154–156
Winnicott, D. W., 188, 201, 207–208
Wolf, K. M., 189
world
artistic, 14
literary, 14, 27, 80
view, 4, 15, 80

"Yellow House" see: National Institute for Psychiatry and Neurology

Zeitschrift für Psychoanalyse, 68, 87, 210, 227
Zsoldos, S., 14